NEWENT

© Published by Newent Local History Society
Arron, Ross Road, Newent, Glos, GL18 1BE

I.S.B.N. 0-9544648-0-X

All rights reserved. No part of this publication may be reproduced, stored in a retrieval system, or transmitted, in any form or by any means, electronic, mechanical, photocopying, recording or otherwise, without the permission of the publishers.

To be consistent with the times imperial units have been retained where appropriate and metric units only used where necessary.

Credits for illustrations have been included where known and where they are not the individual author's.

Printed by Print Logic Ltd,
Netherwood Road, Rotherwas Industrial Estate,
Hereford HR2 6JU

Foreword

Newent is an ancient town, having existed for over 1,000 years, and it would be difficult to write a comprehensive history spanning such a length of time. This volume does not attempt to cover every aspect, but to give the reader a broad insight into its fascinating past.

Individual authors have researched and written about their own specialist subjects and in their own way. This makes every chapter unique in itself and we hope they gel together to form an informative and interesting historical work.

We have drawn considerably on previous publications and mixed this with much original research. We are grateful to many people for the loan of documents and photographs and to those who have given us their memories.

Newent Public Library has assembled several box files of interesting material which is available for further research

We must also thank the organizations that have given financial grants to enable the book to be published :-
> Newent Onion Fair Committee
> Newent Town Council
> Forest of Dean District Council
> Heritage Lottery Fund

Newent Local History Society was formed in 1984 after an inaugural meeting in the Market House promoted by local historian David Bick. The membership fee in the first year was £1 and numbers reached 68. In the early days meetings were held at the Community Centre in Ross Road, then later transferred to the Library. David Bick became the first chairman and then President of the Society. Dr Kenneth Tomlinson was the first President in 1987 followed by David Bick and then Joe Hillaby. Other officials have included chairman J R Hartley (1992-1998), Secretaries Tony Russell (1986), Derek Bridle (1987-1999) and Kathleen Setters (2001-2003), and Treasurers Peter Street (1984-1986) and Derek Pearce (from 1986) The present committee comprises :- Chairman Frances Penney, Secretary Jenny Grassom, Treasurer Derek Pearce, plus Margaret Phillips, Dot Pealing and Brenda Passant.

> We hope you enjoy reading our book.
> Newent Local History Society
> May 2003

Contents

		Author	Page No
1.	Early History	Don Sherratt	1
2.	Buildings	Derek Pearce	16
3.	Newent in the 18th and 19th Centuries	Frances Penney	40
4.	Population and Occupations	Frances Penney	52
5.	People	Derek Pearce	55
6.	War prior to the 20th Century	Eric Warde	86
7.	Newent in the Hockaday Abstracts	Eric Warde	92
8.	Doctors	Dr Kenneth Tomlinson	103
9.	Law and Order Transportees Policing	Dr Kenneth Tomlinson Eric Warde	106
10.	Services	Derek Pearce	111
11.	Education	Kathleen Setters & Len Millar	126
12.	The Relief of the Poor	Frances Penney	137
13.	Industries	David Bick	153
14.	Glassmaking and Pottery	Don Sherratt	171
15.	Religion	D A Pearce	184
16.	From the Church Records	Frances Penney	205
17.	Transport	David Bick	217
18.	20th Century Wars	Eric Warde	224
19.	Memories of the 20th Century	Local Residents	261

The Principal Authors

David Bick A retired Chartered Engineer who designed hydraulic equipment for aircraft and industry. He has written many books on aspects of local history including the Hereford and Gloucester Canal and the Metal Mines of Mid-Wales. He founded Newent Local History Society and is a vintage car enthusiast.

Len Millar A former handicraft teacher at Newent School and Chairman of the Civic Society. Sadly Len died during the production of the book and his contribution to the Education chapter is gratefully acknowledged.

Derek Pearce A retired Chartered Engineer from the water industry and author of books on water supply and motorsport history. He has helped transcribe the Parish Registers and record the Churchyard inscriptions and is presently the Treasurer of Newent Local History Society. He is a classic car enthusiast.

Frances Penney worked at the top secret Bletchley Park code-breaking centre during World War II. She has written many historical articles for local publications, and helped transcribe the Parish Registers and record the Churchyard inscriptions. She served on the Gloucestershire Local History Committee for many years and is presently the Chairman of Newent Local History Society.

Kathleen Setters is a humanist and an optimist. She came to Newent in 1998 and very much appreciates the friendliness and unpretentiousness of Newent people. Having brought up four children she has since been trying to improve her education in other ways. She is a former Secretary of Newent Local History Society.

Don Sherratt A farmer from Taynton, who was educated at Newent Grammar School. He is a keen amateur historian with a hands-on approach, specializing in metal detection and field walking. He is the author of a number of articles on recent Saxon, Roman, and Neolithic discoveries.

Dr Kenneth Tomlinson A doctor in Newent for many years before his retirement. He is the author of a number of articles on local history including the famous "Edmonds Case". A former guide to Gloucester Cathedral and a Past President of Newent Local History Society.

Eric Warde A retired Chartered Chemical Engineer and author of the Pool Hill history "They Didn't Walk Far". Since retirement he has worked with schools to encourage pupils to enter the chemical engineering profession. Other interests include Jazz.

Illustrations

1. Flint cores from Boulsdon
2. Flint arrow points and blades from Boulsdon
3. Neolithic tools from the Newent area
4. Bronze age Palstave Axe and late iron age brooch from Nelfield Farm
5. Bloomery slag from Roman iron smelting
6. Roman coins and brooch from Newent Business Park
7. Roman coins and pottery from Newent Business Park
8. Roman pottery from Newent Business park
9. Anglo Saxon gold thrysma from Boulsdon
10. Plan of Newent, c1900 showing important buildings
11. Map of Newent, c1720
12. Field map of south west Newent, c1770
13. The old Rectory
14. The Tanhouse
15. Newent Court Lodge House
16. 30-32 Church Street
17. 62-70 Culver Street
18. Former Picklenash School, Ross Road.
19. Thatched Cottage, Bradfords Lane
20. Newent High Street in the 1930s
21. Newent Cattle Market, c1910
22. Stardens, c1950
23. Moat Farm, c1910
24. The Old Court, c1910
25. Newent Union Workhouse, c1910
26. George Freeman's Hosiery Shop in Lewall Street, c1930
27. Part of the 1624 Survey of the Manor of Newent
28. James Henry Frowde, circus clown
29. James Henry Frowde, Mason
30. Family tree of William Fitz Osbern
31. Family tree of the Foley and Onslow families
32. Family tree of the Bisco family
33. Family tree of the Rogers, Beale, Bearcroft and De Visme families
34. Family tree of the Bower family
35. Newent Waterworks steam engine, built in 1897
36. Felling the Waterworks chimney, 1956
37. Gas street lamp in Culver Street, 1909

38. Laying water mains in Church Street, 1909
39. Accounts of the Newent Gas Light and Coke Co Ltd, 1852
40. Private Boys School, Newent, c1920
41. Mrs J Perillo (née Orme) and her school class, c1928
42. Picklenash School, Group V, 1926
43. Picklenash School, Standard 3, 1929
44. A fireback cast at Newent 1655
45. A fireback 1671
46. Coalpits, and water supplies for Newent Ironworks
47. Artists impression of Newent Colliery 1879
48. Lancaster Sawmills, Newent c1960
49. The face of a Newent clock 1820
50. A page from the Newent Ironworks accounts, 1749
51. Transcription of the Newent Ironworks accounts, 1749
52. Sign of the Glassshouse Inn
53. Site of one of the Glass Kilns
54. Glass fragments from Moses Meadow
55. Crucible fragments from Moses meadow
56. 17th century silver bodkin from Moses Meadow
57. Silver coins from Moses meadow
58. Pottery shards from HillyField
59. Newent Glasshouse pottery
60. A Newent Glasshouse Pot
61. A Newent Glasshouse dish
62. Part of the Latin Cartulary of Newent Priory, 1242
63. Newent Bishops Transcripts, 1599
64. St Mary's Parish Church dating from the 13th century
65. United Reformed Church, 1846
66. 14th century tomb in St Mary's Church
67. Catholic Church, Ross Road, built in 1959
68. Wesleyan Chapel, Culver Street, 1855
69. Tannery building used by the Plymouth Brethren, built in 1695
70. The will of Thomas Avenant, Vicar of Newent, 1726
71. Part of the Probate Inventory of Symon Parsons of Hayes, 1709
72. Part of the Probate Inventory of Edward Tayler, 1702
73. An old milestone between Newent and Ross
74. Bob Beachus in his 1910 Belsize Taxi, c1920
75. Partly restored canal near Oxenhall tunnel
76. Lock Cottage, Oxenhall

77. Letter notifying Corp Phillpots death, 1918
78. Andy Russo in his Italian Army uniform
79. Joe Perillo in his Italian Army uniform
80. Letter from Newent Parish Council about F/Lt Eric Jones DFC
81. F/Lt Eric Jones with his crew in front of his WW II Lancaster
82. Royston Cadle, 1945
83. The Hooke family tree
84. The Cadle Family tree
85. Newent Court before the fire of 1942
86. Newent Court Quoits Team, c1900
87. Pupils of Ribston Hall School at Newent Court, 1950
88. Decorated float at the Holts garden party, c1924
89. Francis Chamberlain and his dog c1900
90. The Carnival Queen and attendants 1953
91. The Coronation Carnival beer tent 1953
92. Conservative Fete fancy dress competition 1953
93. Mr Hobart at work at the LSA, c1955
94. Queen Mary visiting the LSA 1944
95. Richard Phillips with his BEM 1969
96. Laying the foundation stone of the Church Vestry, 1912
97. Annie James
98. The James family tree
99. Newent Mens hockey team 1927/8
100. Black Dog darts team c1950
101. F W Dickinson, headmaster of Newent Grammar School
102. Frank Jenkins blacksmith's shop, Wharf Pitch, c1920
103. John Jones and son Eric in front of his shoe shop in the 1920s
104. W Wildsmith & Son Ltd., works outing 1953

1. Newent's Early History
Don Sherratt

The Stone Age, 10,000 BC to 2,000 BC

At the end of the last Ice Age ten to twelve thousand years ago, the Newent area would have been covered with forest and vegetation. Britain's land mass was still joined to Europe and men and animals began to re-occupy the land moving over vast areas in the hunt for food. Many flint tools have been found in and around Newent confirming that for thousands of years humans wandered and sometimes settled in this area. They camped here, produced and fashioned their flint tools and weapons, hunted and may even have started to clear some of the forest.

Flint is not a naturally occurring material in this part of Britain therefore we know that it has been brought in from a considerable distance by prehistoric man. The nearest sources are Wiltshire and Wales but the better quality flint comes from the eastern part of Britain, Grimes Graves in Norfolk being a source of the best quality. It is possible that the very earliest form of trading was with flint being gift exchanged or bartered for other goods such as animal skins. Flint would have been a very highly valued commodity as it was the hardest material available at that time, metals had still not been discovered. It was used for such tasks as killing and butchering animals, cutting bone, scraping and cutting skins to make articles and clothing. Many of the flint tools found have edges so sharp that after thousands of years in the ground they will still cut like a knife, some have sharp points for boring holes while others have been found with circular grooves possibly for shaping arrows.

Flint is formed in limestone rocks that were laid down countless millions of years ago. Liquids containing silica from decaying sea creatures seeped into holes in the chalk deposits of the sea bed and solidified into irregular rounded shapes known as "nodules". When dug from the ground these lumps of flint are surrounded with a coating known as the cortex. On some flints found in the Newent area the cortex can be seen which suggests they were brought in as nodules and fashioned into tools on site as required, although it is possible that some may have been traded as ready made tools. Flint is extremely hard and has the unusual characteristic that when struck sharply pieces flake off that have razor sharp edges. Flint tools were made by striking nodules in a precise way using bone or a large pebble. The flint flakes produced were then fashioned into knives, scrapers, awls, arrowheads etc. Worked flint is often characterized by having one or more of its edges finely chipped to make a serrated edge. The whole flint knapping process needed a good deal of skill to get the maximum number of useful tools from each nodule. Eventually some lumps of flint would be discarded from which no more tools could be produced, these are known as flint cores. Amongst the many flint artefacts found in and around Newent numerous cores have been found.

Fig.1 Two flint cores from which no more useful tools could be obtained. From Boulsdon, 2002

Broken nodule of flint showing cortex. From Boulsdon 2002

In 1990 an early Mesolithic (Middle Stone Age) camp site believed to date between 8000 BC and 6000 BC was found by the side of the stream that divides Newent and Taynton parishes. It was discovered by Norman Webley and is considered to be one of the most important prehistoric camp sites found in recent years and the only site in west Gloucestershire that was exclusively Mesolithic. Around five hundred flints were found there at that time and a further one hundred and fifty flints have been recovered since then. They include arrow heads, scrapers, piercing and cutting tools and a very rare Creswellian-type arrow point. Several different qualities of worked flint were amongst them showing that they had come from a number of different sources including some good quality imported flint (1).

Nearer to Newent town on Common Fields and on fields to the west well over five hundred Mesolithic flints have been found and four camp sites identified. The main concentrations of flints were on the higher ground where no doubt family groups gathered for safety, but close enough to an abundance of springs and streams. The area would have been ideal hunting ground for wild boar, deer, elk, bear and many other wild animals that inhabited Britain during that period. At the most southerly tip of Newent parish in the vicinity of The Glasshouse a Mesolithic camp site was discovered in 1996. Over 100 flints were found there close to a stream and at the junction of possible ancient trackways.

Flint tools and debris have been found on about ninety per cent of the farm land so far investigated around Newent. This includes land at Malswick, Cugley, Anthony's Cross, Boulsdon, Oxenhall, Conigree, Kilcot, Cleeve Mill, The Scarr, Brand Green, Culver Street, Huntley Lane and Southend Lane.

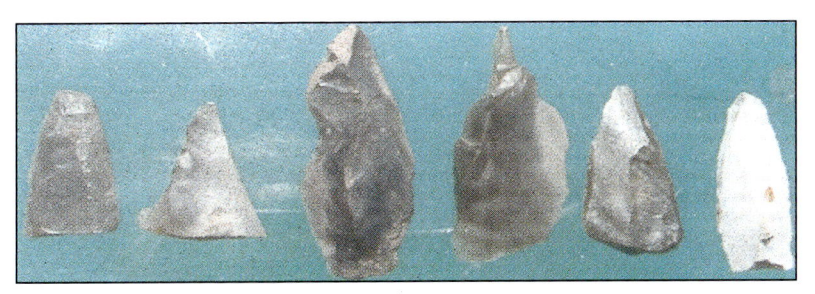

Fig.2 Flint arrow points, notched blade and awl from a Mesolithic camp site at Boulsdon

Neolithic flint arrow head found at Fordhouse Lane

Flint spear head showing how it may be used

During the Neolithic (New Stone Age) period 4000 BC to 2000 BC man started to become more skilled and civilized; the nomadic ways of the past began to give way to a more settled existence and so primitive farming had begun. He started to clear areas of forest for growing crops and grazing animals and his flint tools began to become more finely crafted and specialized. A large number of Neolithic flints have been found over the past few years close to the Newent border on Irelands Hill, Taynton. An interesting find was a barbed and tanged flint spear head crafted so that on entering the animal it could not easily be retracted. Two smaller barbed and tanged arrow heads have also been found; one in a garden at Ross Road, Newent and another on the outskirts of the town at Fordhouse Lane (2).

In 2001 a large flint blade was found by the author at Conigree Court Farm, Newent. It showed marks that indicated that it may have been used as a sickle for cutting crops. In 1998 just over the Newent border at Taynton Court Farm David Hutton found a Neolithic polished flint axe lying in a plough furrow. It had a chipped cutting edge and showed it must have been used for chopping.

Fig. 3 Neolithic polished stone axe found at Oxenhall by David Bick in 1980
Actual length 13.5 cm.

Neolithic flint reaping/cutting tool found at Conigree, Newent by D Sherratt, 1998

Neolithic barbed and tanged flint spear head from Taynton. Found by D. Sherratt, 1980

A similar axe head was found in 1951 at Conigree Rocks, Newent. This one also had a chipped cutting edge and is now in Gloucester City Museum (3). During building work on the Foley Road estate several flint tools were discovered and in 1993 during work on the Newent Business Park David Hutton discovered a number of flint tools including a large knife and part of a Neolithic polished stone axe. The axe, thought to date between 3000 BC and 2000 BC was made from Pembrokeshire volcanic rock but the cutting edge showed no signs of use. It is thought that it may have been kept as a status symbol or to have been used as a ceremonial or votive offering.

In 1980 a complete Neolithic polished stone axe was found by David Bick whilst walking in a field below Oxenhall Church. This axe was identified as being made from igneous rocks known as augyte granophyre, from the "Neolithic axe factory" at Penmaenmawr in Caernarvonshire. These finds indicate that long distance trading must have been taking place (4).

The Bronze Age, Iron Age and Celtic period 2000 BC to 43 AD

During the Late Neolithic/Early Bronze Age period (c2000 BC) man learnt to smelt copper and tin and by adding about 10% tin to the copper he discovered bronze. Proof of man's existence in the Newent area in the Bronze Age first came to light in 1854 with the discovery of a Bronze Age spear head with two basal loops together with a flat axehead with chevron decoration. They were found in Kilcot Woods but unfortunately their present whereabouts are unknown. In 1961 a Middle Bronze Age palstave axe was found by the Crown House Cottages in Newent and another was found at Kilcot also in the 1960's (4). The only Bronze Age copper object ever found in the whole of the Forest of Dean area was a knife found at Taynton in the 1980's (5).

In 1999 an unusual late Iron Age brooch was found at Nelfields Farm, Newent. It was very similar to the so called "Birdlip Brooch" that was discovered in an Iron Age grave at Birdlip in 1879 and believed to date c40 AD. During 2001 a complete iron age glass bead was found at Rudford and part of one was found on the Taynton/Newent border at Ploddy House Farm.

It is believed that prior to the Roman invasion of Britain in 43 AD the country was divided up between at least twenty Celtic tribes. This part of Britain came under the jurisdiction of the Dobunni with a major settlement at Bagendon near Cirencester. Their territory stretched over Gloucestershire, Hereford and Worcester and into parts of Somerset, Wiltshire and Gwent. Evidence of their presence in the Newent area came in 1906 when a gold Dobunnic coin known as a Stater was found near the south end of Culver Street.

It was inscribed EISV and believed to be of the tribal leader EISVRIG, 15 BC to 30 AD. It is now in the British Museum (6).

In 1998 David Hutton found a gold Dobunnic Stater thought to be of the leader Corio, 30 BC to 50 AD, at Tibberton. Surprisingly, at the time of writing a mysterious coin that may be a Celtic Potin of about 100 BC has been found in a field off Culver Street. This coin-like object is made of lead alloy but despite expert examination it has so far not been positively identified.

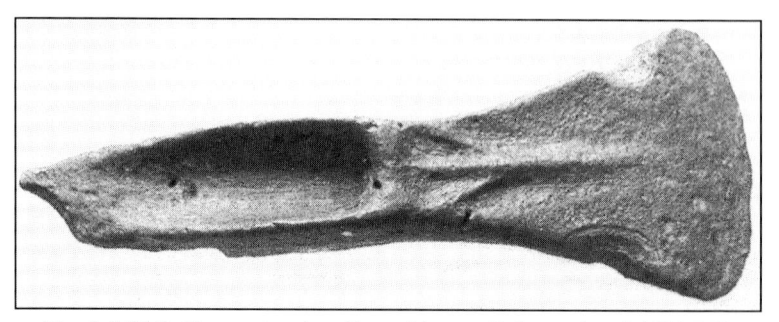

Fig. 4 Middle Bronze Age low flanged bronze Palstave Axe (c1000 BC) Found at Crown House Cottages, Newent in 1961.
Courtesy of Susan Byrne, Gloucester City Museum

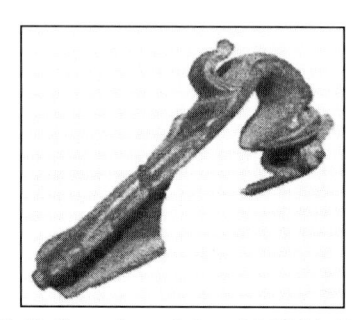

"Birdlip" type brooch from Nelfields Farm
Identified as late Iron Age by Gloucester City Museum

What has so far been unearthed must be but a small fraction of what must still lie buried below the plough depth, under woodland and in areas unfit for cultivation such as steep hill land and marsh. This region of the country would have been very attractive to our early ancestors; no doubt they would have found lush vegetation and an abundance of wildlife, and the dry sandy soil would have enabled them to hunt here all the year round. From what has already been discovered it is certain that this area witnessed the emergence of human-kind from primitive beings to civilized man. It is highly probable that some of our present roads and lanes follow the hunting and trading routes formed thousands of years ago and so in some small way they helped shape the Newent landscape that we know today.

The Romans 43 AD to 410 AD

The use of iron in Britain is believed to have started between 700 BC and 500 BC and as it became more plentiful the use of copper and bronze for making tools and weapons began to decline. A very extensive iron making industry began to develop in the area due to the large deposits of iron ore that could be found locally and in the Forest of Dean, and also due to an abundance of timber for making charcoal with which to fire the furnaces. In 1990 evidence of a major Roman iron working and pottery making site was discovered just south of Newent, east of Moat farm, the whole site extending to well over 100 acres. Iron slag was found scattered over a wide area, pottery shards, lead and bronze artefacts and Roman coins were also discovered. In two locations there were quantities of roof tile fragments believed to have come from a Roman building. The dating of the artefacts suggests that this site was in occupation during the first and second centuries AD (7).

According to archaeologists the iron was made in a simple furnace known as a shaft furnace. A cylinder of clay was built about a metre high with an arch at the bottom to allow slag to run off. Charcoal and iron ore were put into the furnace in layers. Some form of bellows would have been needed to raise a temperature of 1,300°C. in order to form a bloom (a mixture of molten iron and waste materials). This crude iron mixture would then be taken out of the furnace, and heated and hammered until all the rubbish had been driven off, producing wrought iron. This was then used for making tools and weapons and the waste left behind is what we now call bloomery slag or cinders. It was estimated by archaeologists that about 175,000 tons of iron ore would have been smelted at the Newent site.

There would have been many of these small furnaces and kilns operating at the same time filling the area with dense smoke and through this it is believed that the name for Newent in Roman times may have been Dolocindo. Soon after 700 AD an anonymous Ravenna cleric listed 300 geographical locations with Dolocindo named as being not far from Glevum Colonia (Gloucester). It is believed by Bryan Walters that the name may have originated from Dolo (stream-side meadow) and Cindo (smoke) making "smoky meadow". There could have been no more apt description of the extensive Newent industrial settlement than "smoky meadow". The acres of concentrated iron smelting and kiln sites together with the pottery kiln sites would have produced smoke visible for many miles around (8).

Due to the inefficient extraction methods used by the Romans, bloomery slag still contained a high percentage of iron and thousands of tons were left piled up at the smelting sites. In the 17th and 18th centuries it was collected and re-smelted at the new and more efficient furnaces that came into being. Most of the local slag would have gone to Elmbridge Furnace in Furnace Lane, Newent owned by the Foley family. Their old accounts record the quantities and costs of hauling cinders (slag) from Newent and Tibberton (9). Mention is made that Roman coins of Nerva, Vespasian and Constantine and fine pieces of pottery were found among the cinders at that time (10).

Fig. 5 Bloomery Slag from Roman iron smelting operations at Newent

In 1992 a rectangular parcel of land consisting of 3.5 hectares known as Square Field was designated for industrial development. In early 1993 topsoil was bulldozed to the perimeter to form a protective barrier in order to deter travellers and itinerants from occupying the site. David Hutton visited the site and discovered a considerable quantity of artefacts in this mound of soil and the surrounding area. Amongst the objects found were Neolithic implements, Roman coins, brooches and pottery. It soon became obvious that this had been an important Roman settlement. When contractors moved on to the site and began removing the remaining topsoil, Mr Hutton kept a close watch and on one occasion noticed a "circular hearth" with its base made from rammed iron-smelting slag, thought to be the floor of an iron smelting furnace, but by the next day it had been obliterated by a bulldozer.

Large quantities of broken pottery were found scattered around the site. In one particular area there was a large concentration of shards, possibly an ancient rubbish tip. The bottom halves of two urns were found, the tops having been sliced off by the earth moving machinery; one contained a near mint condition coin of Carausius, 287-293 AD. Among other coins found were a silver Denarius of Maximinus I 235-238 AD, a Sestertius of Faustina Junior 145-175 AD and a Denarius of Trajan 98-117 AD. In total about thirty Roman coins were found. The date range indicated that the site must have seen Roman occupation during the 1st to 3rd centuries. Among other finds was a panther brooch with one glass eye still in place, the foot from a statuette and two nearly complete fibula brooches.

The pottery was identified by experts at Gloucester City Museum and also by the Dean Archaeology Group. It included Severn Valley Ware, Bead-Rimmed Pottery, Black Burnished and Samian Ware. It was possible to reconstruct a two handled drinking cup or tankard, the only complete Roman vessel known to exist from Newent. One piece of Samian Ware pottery showed the name SABINUM, which may be the name of a potter who is known to have been working c50-70 AD. Mr Alf Webb Director of Archaeology of the Dean Archaeological Group believed it to be the Roman name for the River Severn (Sabrina) and that the pottery was being made locally.

On further investigation, the existence of a large building became evident. Two archaeologist members of the Dean Archaeological Group, Brian and Mark Walters, surveyed the site. They identified and recorded the postholes of a timber building that would have been at least 16 metres long and 6 metres wide. Large quantities of iron slag were found by the postholes and scattered throughout the site, showing evidence that there had been a substantial Roman iron smelting industry there. In addition to the Roman finds, the Neolithic stone axe, referred to earlier, and several other flint tools were also found there. This suggests that the site may have been occupied long before the Romans arrived, the Romans may well have taken over an already established iron smelting industry.

In September 1994 the Gloucester Archaeological Service carried out an excavation at the site. Hundreds of Roman pottery shards were found and identified as Grey Severn Valley Ware, Black Burnished Ware, Samian Ware and White Mortarium. The shards were recorded as being the remains of Roman bowls, storage jars, tankards, platters and amphora. Several of the pots were recorded as "having recently been crushed by the wheels of heavy earth moving machinery". Large quantities of iron slag were also unearthed. The concentration in one area was check weighed and amounted to as much as 56 kg per sq. m. Several postholes were found, one of them being of a particularly large diameter, thus giving further support to the earlier findings by Hutton and Walters of a large building having been there at one time (11).

Fig. 6 Marcus Ulpius Trajanus 98-117 AD
From Newent Business Park 1992

Julius Verus Maximinus I
235-238 AD. From Newent
Business Park 1992

2nd century Panther Brooch found at
Newent Business Park by D Hutton in 1992

During 2000/01 a further small salvage excavation was carried out by D. Hutton and D. Sherratt on an area of land on the Business Park still awaiting development but from which much of the topsoil had been removed. The area excavated measured approximately fifteen square metres and produced several hundred Roman pottery shards. It was possible to partly reconstruct a pot, a dish and a bowl. Amongst the pottery were some fragments of 1st/2nd century Samian Ware believed to have been imported from Central Gaul. One piece shows the head of a wild boar possibly from a hunting scene while another piece showed what appeared to be dancing girls. In addition to the pottery two copper bracelets, a child's ring, numerous iron nails, horse teeth and three coins were found. One of the coins was of the emperor Maximianus 286-305 AD and was found underneath what may have been a cremation urn. Another, a silver Denarius was of the emperor Severus Alexander 227 AD and the third was unidentifiable, but of a large flat type that predates 250 AD (12).

Fig.7 Rare bronze Antoninianus of Maximianus, minted between 287-293AD
On the reverse:- PAX-standing holding olive branch and sceptre - the symbols of peace.

Silver Denarius of Severus Alexander 227 AD.
On the reverse:- Aequitas (Equity), standing holding the scales of justice and a Cornucopia (horn of plenty) - symbols of fairness, justice and prosperity.
Both found at Newent Business Park in February 2000

Roman coins and pottery have been found at several other locations in and around Newent. A Denarius of the emperor Septimus Severus 210 AD was found at Scarr Road in 1968. Gloucester Museum have a record of a coin of the emperor Nero 54-68 AD being found at Gorsley in 1982 and a coin of Constantine 307-337 AD was discovered in a garden at Bury Bar, Newent, in the 1990's (12). Interestingly, the names Bury or Berry are known to have strong Roman connotations. There are fields near Newent named Berry Field, Greasy Romans, Stony Romans (near Kilcot), Cinders Meadow and Cinder Field (Malswick). These names may well indicate Roman activity and if explored could one day shed more light on Newent's Roman past.

A few years ago a number of Roman coins were unearthed at Lyne House Farm, Newent, when a posthole was being dug. There is evidence of an ancient settlement nearby that is worthy of investigation and one day may prove to be of Roman origin. Two interesting named fields opposite called Town Field and Cinder Pits may well have turned up some important historical information, but unfortunately they are now built over by a garden centre, it is recorded that a Roman coin was found there some years ago. It is generally known that Dymock was a Roman settlement and many coins, artefacts and some Roman skeletons have been found there. Rudford, Tibberton and Taynton are local villages where Roman finds have also been uncovered in recent years.

Fig.8 Roman Severn Valley Ware two handled tankard from Newent Business Park. The only complete Roman vessel from Newent.
Found by D. Hutton 1994

Much of the Roman pottery found at the Business Park and elsewhere may well have been made locally. In 1996 an intensive pottery-making site was discovered by Robert Phelps at Nelfields Farm, Newent. Large quantities of Roman pottery including Severn Ware, Grey Ware and Oxford Mortarium shards were found scattered over the fields. A large pit on the site is thought to have been the source of the clay (13).

Due to the discoveries at Moat farm and particularly at the Business Park, Newent is now recognized on the Roman map of Britain as a Roman settlement. The big question is where did the population live. Is there a settlement area yet to be discovered or has it all been swept away over time? During the development of the Cleeve Mill Business Park in the late 1980's some bloomery slag and pottery was uncovered. In 2002 a square metre exploration hole was dug in a field close to Newent Business Park, in it were several fragments of Roman pottery and over 23 kg of iron smelting waste. From the foregoing it seems highly probable that there are more discoveries yet to be made.

The Dark Ages to the Saxons. 410 AD to 1000 AD

Despite the prosperity and culture that the Romans brought to Britain, by the late fourth and early fifth centuries the country began to suffer great unrest. Britain was under almost constant attack by the Picts and the Scots, and from Europe came the Angles and the Saxons. By 410 AD most of the Roman regular soldiers had left Britain and the country was left to fend for itself. For nearly two centuries Britain went through a time of turmoil and anarchy often referred to as the Dark Ages. Despite this, Newent settlement survived and continued to expand under the new rulers. It is recorded that the Saxons took Gloucester in 577 AD and eventually they must have pushed west into the Vale of the Severn and into the Forest of Dean. Evidence that they penetrated into the Newent area came to light in 1998 when a very rare Anglo-Saxon gold coin known as a "Wuneeton Type" Thrysma was found at Boulsdon (Fig.9). It is the first coin of its type ever found in this part of Britain and provides an important link in our history as Roman influence is apparent in its design. The cross on the reverse may be one of the first indications of the arrival of Christianity into Anglo-Saxon England. This unique find is among the very first English coins minted and is believed to date between 630 AD and 650 AD, it is now in Gloucester City Museum.

At the same find spot a small section of a trefoil brooch was also found indicating that both objects may have come from a yet undiscovered Saxon grave. Newent church is believed to be of Saxon origin and the details of this can be found under the history of the church, chapter 15.

Fig.9 Anglo-Saxon gold Thrysma 630-650 AD from Boulsdon, Newent. Found by D.Hutton in 1998. Courtesy of Susan Byrne Glos City Museum

References

1. Walters. B. 1992 Ancient Dean and Wye Valley, p12
2. Glos City Museum Ref: A3102. (CM 37 Ail)
3. Glos City Museum Ref: A2993. (CM 37 Ah2)
4. Hart. C 1967 Archaeology in Dean pp 11,12 Glos City Museum (A5124). Glos: SMR Area 5187 MBA Spearhead
5. Walters. B 1992 Ancient Dean and Wye Valley, p36
6. Glos. SMR Area 5380. Dobunnic stater, inscribed EISV found c1961 Newent. Now in British Museum. Evans Type XVIII
7. Walters. B 1992 Ancient Dean and Wye Valley, p83
8. Dean Archaeology 1991 No.4, p29
9. Bick. D 1987 The Mines of Newent and Ross, chpt. 2
10. Rudder. S 1779 A New History of Gloucestershire, p562
11. Erskine. J 1994 Gloucestershire County Council, an Archaeological Excavation
12. Sherratt. D 1998 Newent's Roman Past and The History of The Newent Glasshouse
13. Dean Archaeology 1996 No.9, p18

I wish to acknowledge the following for their assistance:-
Tim Grubb, SMR Gloucestershire County Council Archaeology Service
Susan Byrne, Archaeology Officer (Collections) Gloucester City Museum
Derek Pearce, Newent Local History Society
David Hutton, my metal detecting colleague
The many farmers who have allowed us access to their land

2. Buildings
Derek Pearce

Newent is an ancient town, which is mentioned in the Domesday Book. As a working market town the buildings have been continually adapted and changed over the centuries. Many of the timber framed buildings have been encased, or fronted, in brick as this became fashionable, giving the town a later appearance.

Behind the facade many buildings are older than they look, and some have medieval features hidden from view such as roof timbers and cellar vaulting. It is not possible to mention every construction but the following will give the reader an insight into the Town's antiquity.

The Market House, a scheduled ancient monument, is the most striking building for the casual visitor. It was built in 1668 (1) as a butter market and has undergone a number of restorations over the years; in the late 17th century or early 18th century, in 1864, 1937, 1975, and 1991. The "signature" of the Dutch builder, a ball and flute carving, can be seen on the underbeams. The 1864 restoration was carried out by the Lord of the Manor, Richard Foley Onslow, who also added the southern extension. His and his wife's family coats of arms are in the internal stained glass window. There was a second staircase to the ante-room but this has now been removed.

At the beginning of the 20th century the ground level of the building was used to house the town fire pump. The building and the adjacent cattle market were sold by the Onslow family in 1913. The Market House was bought by Henry Bruton, who then presented it to the town. The town council still hold meetings here. Until the 20th century the stocks and a whipping post were situated near by.

The Market House has also been the focus of attention on important occasions. For example the proclamation of King George IV on 9th February 1820. (19) The principal inhabitants of the town assembled in the church vestry and went in procession down the aisle, through the great door and along Church Street to a platform that had been previously erected in front of the Market House. In the procession were the two Beadles (with black staves), a band of music playing "God Save the King", the Constables, the Parish Clerk, the Surveyor of the Highways, the Guardian of the Poor, the Organist, the Churchwardens (with white staves), the Sheriff, two Magistrates and the Clerk, the Clergymen in their gowns, and the Gentlemen and principal inhabitants of the Town. On arrival at the Market House, the Constables went to the front of the platform while the rest of the procession went on it. The Sheriff read the Proclamation and immediately on the conclusion of it the air was rent with

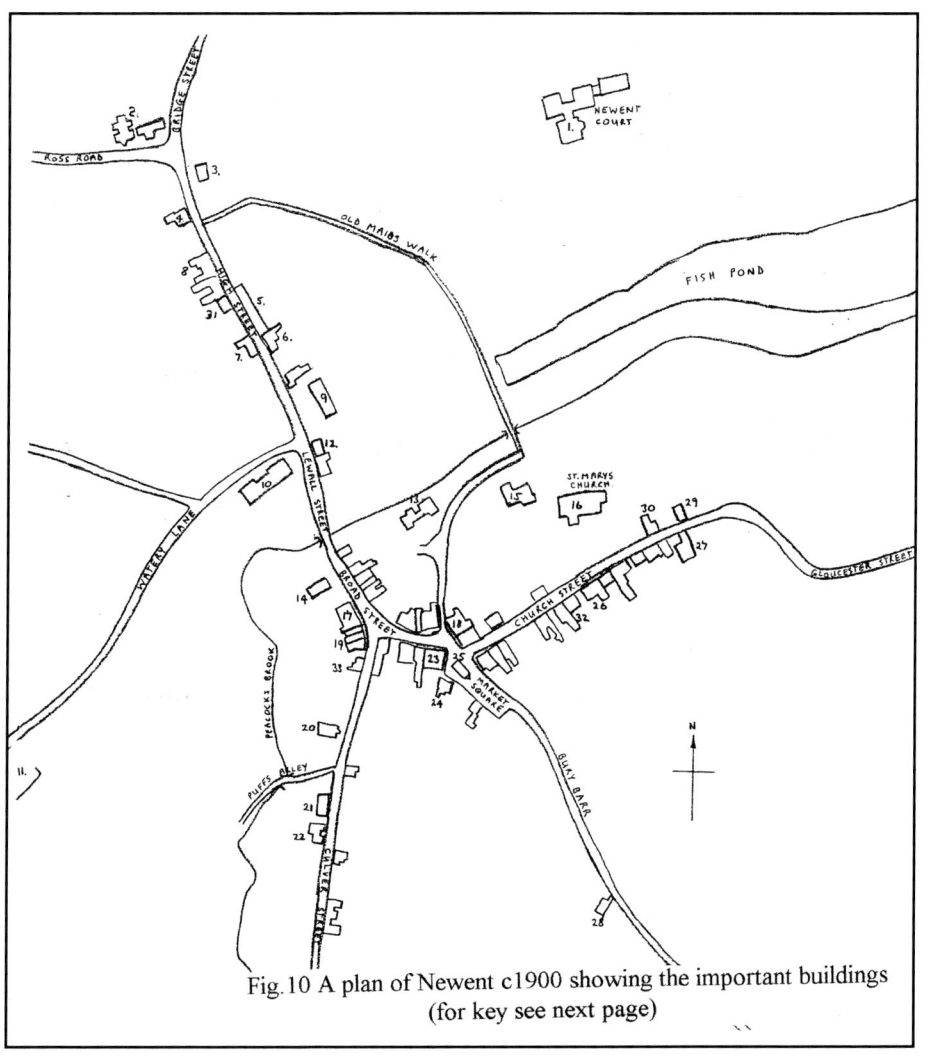

Fig.10 A plan of Newent c1900 showing the important buildings
(for key see next page)

Key to the plan of Newent as it was about 1900

1. Newent Court — built c1810, demolished 1960s
2. Union Workhouse — built prior to 1768, enlarged c1868
3. Lodge House to Newent Court — demolished 1960s
4. Crown House
5. Nanfan & Dobyn Almshouses — Originally built 1639, demolished 1970s
6. Devonia — early 18th century, grade II listed
7. Noent House — 17th century, grade II listed
8. Shirley House — early 18th century, grade II listed
9. Rectory — Early 18th century
10. The Holts — Demolished
11. Gas Works — built 1850, now a private house
12. Parish Rooms — 16th century, grade II listed
13. Police Station — 19th century, on site of tithe barn
14. United Reformed Church — built 1846, grade II listed
15. The Old Court — on the site of the Priory
16. St Mary's Church — dating from 13th century, grade I listed
17. Bennions garage — mid 18th century
18. Costcutter Stores (part) — 15th century, grade II* listed
19. Shop — dated 1465, grade II listed
20. Wesleyan Chapel — dated 1855
21. Barn — dated 1695, grade II listed
22. Tan House — late 17th century, grade II listed
23. Red Lion — 17th or 18th century, grade II listed
24. Harwood House — early 17th century, grade II listed
25. Market House — built 1668, grade II listed
26. Post Office — early 18th century, grade II listed
27. The Black Dog — early 17th century, grade II listed
28. Bury Bar House — mid 19th century
29. 32, Church Street — 15th century, grade II listed
30. 28, Church Street, Church House — Partly 17th century, grade II listed
31. Malt House — early 18th century, grade II listed
32. George Hotel — dated c1649, grade II listed
33. 1, Culver Street — 17th century, grade II listed

shouts of "Long live King George the Fourth". His Majesty's health was drunk by the Gentlemen in bumpers of wine (given in abundance by Archdeacon Onslow and Dr Richardson) and by the populace in old cider from a hogshead bought by the Vestry for £4-4s-0d.

There are a number of public houses in the town, some of which were coaching Inns. The George Hotel is dated c1649, and had the distinction of receiving the first load of coal from the Newent Colliery (2). Being the main coaching inn in the Town it was often used for public events. In 1823 when John Ellis was the landlord it was the scene of the auction to operate the five toll-gates around Newent. The previous year the profit from this operation was £270 (3). There were three toll houses; at the Travellers Rest on the Gloucester Road, at the bottom of Culver Street, and at Elmbridge on the Dymock Road. In addition there were two gates on the Ross Road beyond Mantley House, and Horsefair Lane (21). The Black Dog was Home Farm until 1831 and one of the adjacent buildings was used by Colonel Mynne as his headquarters for a time during the Civil War, but it is uncertain which one (4). Colonel Mynne was killed in a battle at Redmarley.

The Red Lion appears to date from the first half of the 19th century but is much older. Crown House at the north end of the High Street was also a Public House, called The Crown, and was owned by the Bower family in the 18th Century (5). It was listed as a Temperance Hotel in 1927 (6) and is now a private house. The other public house in the town, The Kings Arms, on the Ross Road is later (7). To the east of the town, on the Gloucester Road, is the Traveller's Rest.

In 1844 the public houses and their licencees were listed as :- The Bull (Edward Colley), The Crown (John Jennings), The George (John Ellis), The Kings Arms (Alfred Haskins), The Red Lion (Joseph Lewis), and The Royal Oak (William Powell).

In the 1851 Census the following public houses are listed together with their landlords:- The Mitre in Upper Church Street (Thomas Bundy), The Red Lion (Frederick Bisco), The Royal Oak, now called Toad Hall, in the Market Square (George Smith), The George Hotel (Edward Pocock), The Bull Inn (William Walduck), and the Crown (John Hogan). Also listed is Sarah Bailey, a beerhouse keeper, in Broad Street.

Barclays Bank on the corner of Culver Street and Broad Street was also a former pub, the Nag's Head, which dates from 1723, but was taken over by the Women's Institute in the 1930s (14). Church House on the east side of the churchyard was a public house called the New Inn, and later the King's Head. No.1 Church Street, on the corner of Market Square and Church Street, was the

Bull Inn at the beginning of the 20th century. There were also The Yew Tree Inn and the Anchor opposite each other on the Dymock road. The Yew Tree was thatched.

In the 20th century there was a Plough Inn on the north side of the Cinema in Culver Street, but this closed after World War II (15), and Noent House in the High Street was the New Inn but this also closed between the World Wars. The Chain public house existed at the bottom of Culver Street and got its name from the chain across the road for collecting tolls. The Bell was in Church Street, and one of the buildings opposite the present library, in what was then Lewall Street, was a public house called the Hat, before 1819. Once owned by Edward Baron, the Hat became a dye house or colouring house and was two cottages joined together.

The George Hotel was owned by the Lodge family for over 100 years until the death of Percy Lodge in 1963. His grandparents Mr and Mrs West had originally bought it in 1852 and it was sold for £11,500 on December 5th 1963. Prior to the sale Walter Forty had been the handyman there for over 60 years.

According to J Douglas in his Historical Notes of Newent (1912) there was an Inn called the King's Head which stood across the entrance drive to the Old Court and joined up to the churchyard wall and the great gates of the churchyard. These may have been the old priory gates onto Court Lane which were still there at the beginning of the 19th century.

There are four churches currently in use in Newent although several other buildings have been used for religious purposes. (see chapter 15). The main church, St Mary's, is built on the site of a pre-conquest building. This is evident from the 9th century cross shaft discovered in 1907, on display in the church entrance (8) and also an 11th century pillow stone, found in 1912 when the new vestry was being built. This is on show inside the church together with replicas of other early carved stones found in the church wall when a window was being modified. Two 7th century gravestones also stand in the church entrance

The present church dates from the 13th century with many later alterations, the major one being after the roof of the nave collapsed in 1674 (see chapter 15). The monumental inscriptions have been recorded from both the churchyard (9) and within the church which is useful for those wishing to know what is beneath the carpet (10).

A fine alabaster tomb of a knight and his lady has been dated between 1370-1385 and may be of the Grandison family. The 14th century spire is 153 ft high.

The United Reformed Church in Broad Street, a grade II listed building, was built in 1864 as the Newent Congregational Church (11). The Sunday

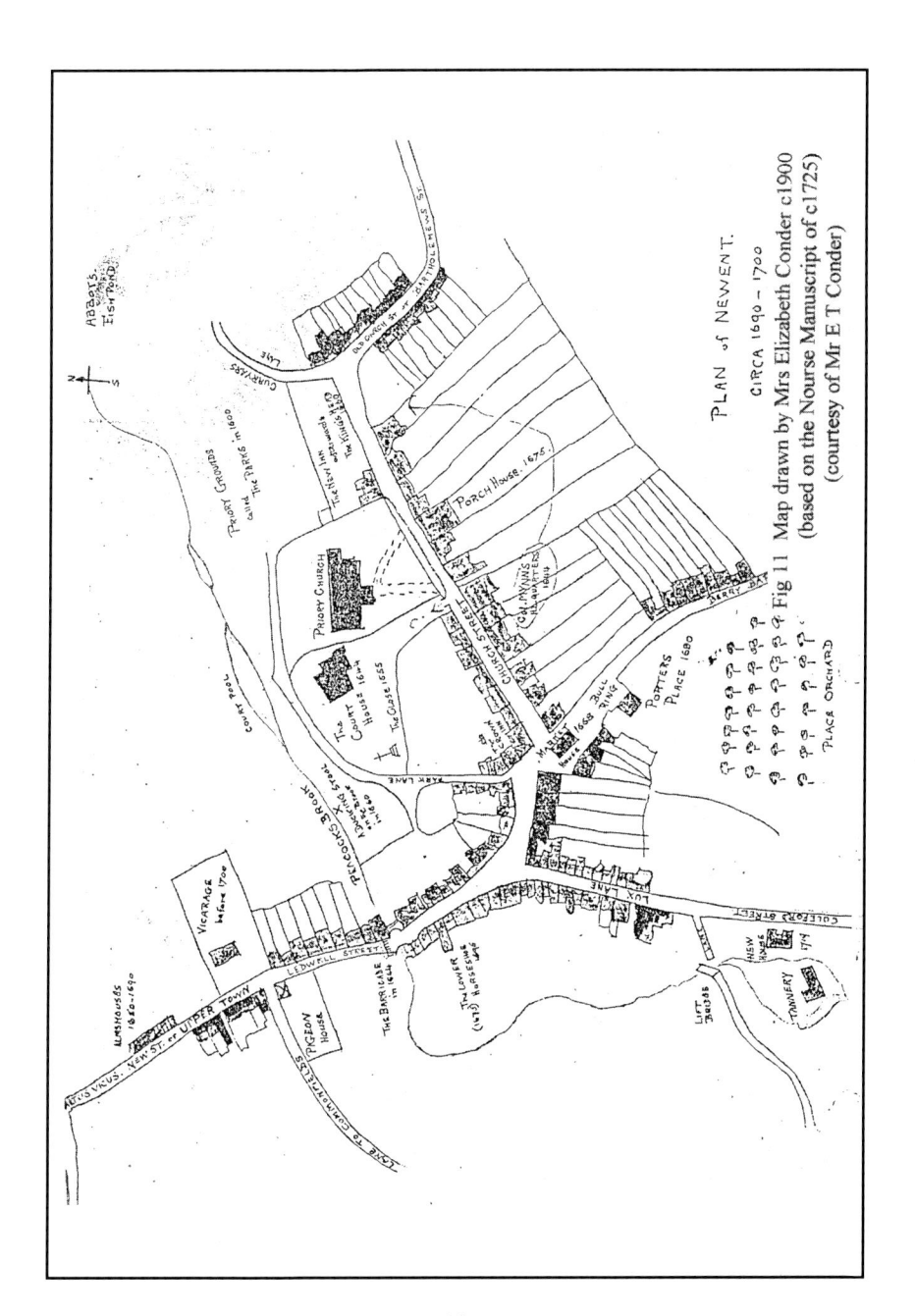

Fig 11 Map drawn by Mrs Elizabeth Conder c1900 (based on the Nourse Manuscript of c1725) (courtesy of Mr E T Conder)

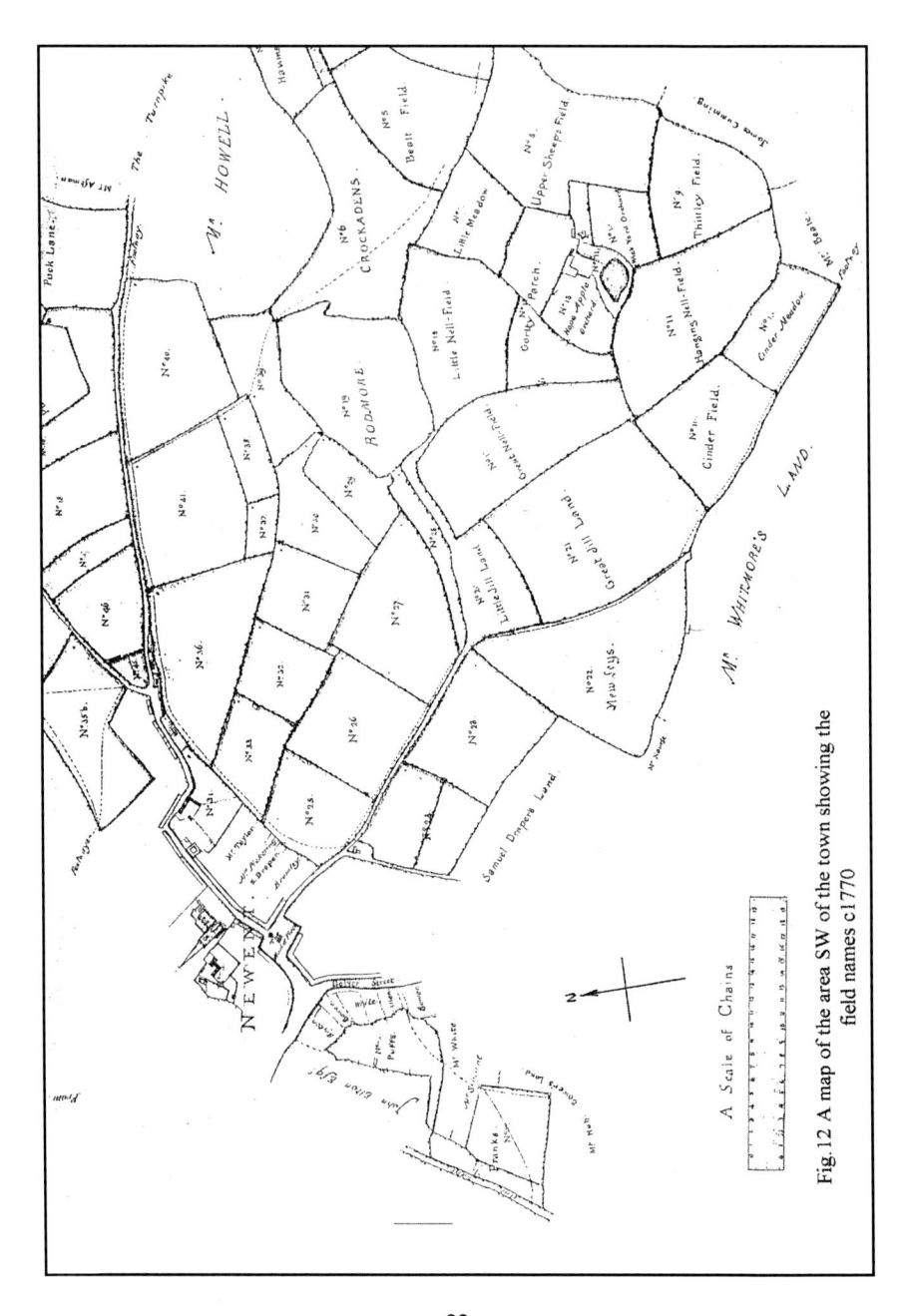

Fig.12 A map of the area SW of the town showing the field names c1770

School extension at the rear of the building was added later (See chapter 15). It was formerly the site of a Public House called The Lower Horseshoe, which dated from 1675, then the New Horseshoe in 1718 and later The Swan.

The Wesleyan Methodist Church in Culver Street was built in 1855 but is now used as an auction room. The Mortuary Chapel in Watery Lane was built in 1863 by Jacques and Son to serve the needs of the new graveyard when burials ceased at St Mary's Church. The two acres of ground and the Lodge House cost £1300 (14).

The Catholic Church in Ross Road and the Gospel Chapel in Glebe Road are late 20th century buildings.

There are a number of 15th and 16th century buildings in the Town. The oldest are 30 & 32 Church Street (fig.16), and the Fish and Chip Shop at the junction of Culver Street and Broad Street dated 1465. No.32 Church Street gained a degree of fame in 1999 when it was put up for sale. Part of the building had a spider's web spun across the ceiling measuring 16ft by 14ft and was claimed to be the largest spider's web ever recorded. It even warranted a mention on the television news. Part of No.1 Broad Street, which is now a supermarket on the ground floor, is of medieval construction originally dating from the 15th century. It has a particularly fine roof structure which is unfortunately not normally open to public viewing. It was originally thatched and in the late Middle Ages was the town's boothhall and court house.

31 & 33 Broad Street and 2 & 4 Church Street are all 16th century timber framed buildings(a) and Nos 5 and 7 Culver Street have massive cruck beams hidden behind a more modern looking exterior.

There are a large number of 17th century buildings in the town (1). Most are timber framed with later brick frontages. They include the following:-

Broad Street	-	Nos. 7, 9-17,
Church Street	-	Nos. 1,3,6,8,25,27,37,39,41,45,47
Culver Street	-	Nos. 1,32,50,52,62-70
High Street	-	Linwood House, Noent House (formerly the New Inn)
Market Square	-	No. 4 (Harwood House), Pound House

18th Century buildings include the following (1):-

Broad Street	-	Nos. 4,6,8,12,16,27,29,39
Church Street	-	Nos.7,17,19,20,29,31(Post Office), 35 (Porch House)
High Street	-	The Poplars, Devonia, Good News & house adjoining, Shirley House

The Good News Centre was formerly the parish room (14). The rectory opposite Watery Lane, was built in the early 18th century and between 1762 and 1865 was occupied by incumbents of the Foley and Onslow families. In the 20th century it became council offices and has now been converted back into housing accommodation (fig.13).

Other buildings have an industrial background (see chapter 13). The Tan House in Culver Street is late 17th century and was owned by the Bower family (fig.14). A deed of 1652 refers to a *"newly erected Tanhouse"* purchased by Thomas Fletcher. He sold it to Edward Bower in 1671. The barn on the north side, now offices for the glassworks, is dated 1695 with the initials HB (Hubert Bower) inscribed (see chapter 5) and was used as a meeting place for the Plymouth Brethren for a number of years. In the early 19th century the tannery was run by Mr Herbert but when he died his wife put the property up for sale in 1834, with the stipulation that she would be allowed to carry on living there. She was 82 at the time and did not want the upheaval of moving house (c). It went through several ownerships including Mr Hatton, two brothers called Lee, and then Arthur Clark. It was listed as disused in 1923. In the middle of the 20th century it was used as a doctors surgery. Until the 1980s the tannery buildings at the rear were still distinguishable, but have since been converted into living accommodation.

No. 125 Watery Lane is now a private house and hides the fact that it was the office of the town gas works built in 1850.

The Malt House, High Street, dates from the early 18th century and at the rear are more or less complete c1800 maltings with perforated tile floor and fireplaces for heating the barley. They had fallen into disuse by 1900.

At the end of Furnace Lane on the north side of the town is the site of the Newent or Elmbridge ironworks (see chapter 13). The furnace building itself was originally a corn mill (1624) but became a blast furnace by 1639(b). It was turned back into a corn mill in the early 20th century and is now a farm building. Behind it is a substantial sandstone barn-like building with massive buttresses, which was used as a charcoal store for the ironworks between 1639-1751. It seems an elaborate construction just for a charcoal store and may have had some earlier monastic purpose.

The Community Centre in Ross Road was originally the Workhouse which was established c1768 by taking over an existing house (on the right of Fig. 25). It was enlarged in 1868 by demolishing two cottages and the left hand part built at a cost of £1,488. It was mostly rebuilt and became Newent Grammar School in 1925. The second storey was added in 1957/8 It ceased as a school when the new Comprehensive School was built in Watery Lane (see chapter 11). At the back of the building is a capped dry stone lined well.

A number of other notable buildings have been demolished and redeveloped in the 20th century. The Nanfan and Dobyn almshouses on the east side of the High Street were built in 1639 but were demolished in the 1970s. (fig 20). Porters Place, a 16th century house owned by the Porter family, once stood near the Market Square. Later it was owned and rebuilt by John Nourse Morse who died in 1830, aged 90. When this house was demolished the cast iron windows were used above the new brick frontage of 6 and 8 Church Street. One of the glass panes has the inscription "Mary Matthews 1836" scratched in it. She is believed to be the grand-daughter of John Nourse Morse.

Newent Court, not to be confused with The Old Court, stood where the Lakeside housing development now stands. Its construction began about 1810 with landscaped gardens formed around the lake, which was made out of the silted up monastic fish ponds. It was built by a Scotsman James de Visme J.P., and the bricks were made from clay dug on the site. In 1833 it was put up for sale by George Reed together with 70 acres of grounds, but remained empty for some years before Mr Burland bought it. From the late 1870s The Court was owned by Andrew Knowles, a coal owner from Lancashire, and in 1906 it was again put up for sale. It is said that the building was haunted by Mr Knowles daughter. She had wished to marry a man "from downstairs" and to prevent this she was locked in the room to the left of the front door. The night before the wedding she escaped and ran away with her lover.

Andrew Knowles J.P.,D.L died on 25th November 1909 and his wife Catherine decided to sell all of the Newent estate. It was put up for auction at the Bell Hotel, Gloucester on 17th September 1910 in 43 separate lots.

The estate consisted of several farms in the Newent, Taynton and Linton area, as well as numerous properties in the town. It included the Court, as well as the Old Court. The total estate came to approximately 2,000 acres with a value of nearly £50,000, a considerable sum in those days. Seven lots were withdrawn, not having reached their reserve, and two lots received no bids. The following is a list of some of the lots in Newent Parish, the price paid and the buyer, together with the tenant and the annual rent:-

Lot No	Title	Price	Purchaser	Tenant	Rental
5	Newent Court, 54 acres	£4,800	withdrawn	-	-
6	Poykes Farm, 67 acres	£2,900	Robert Vines	Charles Nash	£140-10s
11	Old Court, 2 acres	£1,000	Miss Hutchinson	Miss Hutchinson	£60
22	Churchyard Cottage	£60	John Davis	Ellen England	£5-4s
24	Moat Farm, 341 acres	£7850	withdrawn	Ernest Bellamy	£520
25	Caerwents Farm, 176 acres	£3,150	Fred Cowles	Fred Cowles	£140
26	Nelfields Farm, 176 acres	£2,900	T S Brewer	J G Spry	£173
28	Malswick Farm, 84 acres	£2,000	W Cummins	W Cummins	£113
31	Rymes Place, 130 acres	£2,750	John Smith	A King	£130
34	Kents Green Farm & House, 55 acres	£2,700	Walley	C Walker/F Smith	£115

Fig.13 The Old Rectory, early 18th century

Fig .14 The Tanhouse, Culver St., late 17th century

Fig.15 Lodge House to Newent Court (demolished 1966)

Fig.16 30-32 Church Street, 15th century

Eventually Newent Court and grounds were sold to Edward Charles de Peyer, a wealthy Swiss, in 1911 for £3,500. This was less than the figure it was withdrawn at during the auction. The house had 21 bedrooms, a billiard room and 3 tennis courts. It became unoccupied again in 1926.

Colonel Parkinson owned it before World War II but it suffered from a serious fire on February 26th 1942 and the main part of the house was abandoned. The surviving buildings were used by Ribston Hall School (15) for a time but were finally demolished in the 1960s. Part of the walled garden boundary is all that remains of this imposing building. In recent years the lake has been dredged and the surrounding area landscaped to form an excellent amenity for the town. A fountain was installed in 2002 to commemorate the Golden Jubilee of Queen Elizabeth II.

The Old Court, next to St Mary's Church, is built on the site of an 11th century priory and dates from the Georgian period. It was bought by William Rogers, c1650, and occupied by the Beale family in the 18th century.(see family tree fig.30) At the beginning of the 19th century *"An ancient gateway and some smaller fragments of the Monastic buildings yet remain"* (16). These have also now disappeared. In the 18th and early 19th centuries it was owned by the Foleys.

Pigeon House, later called the Holts, stood on the site of the present Health Centre and was the scene of the tragic death of Anna Edmonds in 1867. Her husband was later tried for her murder but acquitted (12). Edmonds was a prominent solicitor in the town and part owner of the gas works, as well as being the largest consumer of gas in 1851. The clock on the south wall of the Health Centre was designed by a pupil at Newent School, Carol Roberts, for the 1977 Queen's Silver Jubilee and was unveiled by the Chairman of the Parish Council Mrs Cynthia Offord. It was made by Smiths of Derby at a cost of £800.

To the west of the town is Conigree Court, built on the site of a Roman settlement, which was the scene of a skirmish during the civil war in 1645, when the owner Elizabeth Horton was killed (6). Several cannon balls have been dug up in the vicinity after it came under fire in 1642. It is said that a secret passage led from Conigree Court to Crockett's Hole, where the martyr Edward Horne hid in the 16th century, but no trace was found when Byard and Piper excavated it in c1888. The distance makes this story seem unlikely. A more likely explanation is that the tunnel led out near to the Ross Road, a much shorter distance, and forms part of the cellars. Edward Conder owned Conigree in the early 1900s and the house was considerably improved in 1897. It remained in the Conder family well into the 20th century before becoming the home of Major Dobbins, and later Lady Chick.

Bury Bar House (not the present building of that name) was owned by Mr Morse who let it to Joshua Fry, an uncle of the Bristol chocolate maker. Later Mr Morse's daughter, Mrs Beale, lived there.

Other interesting buildings of considerable antiquity are The Moat, a moated farmhouse close to the Huntley road, and Poydresses, another farm a little further south which was the home of an old Newent family of the same name for several centuries. The Moat Farm was purchased by the Woodward family, c1600, from Sir Arthur Porter Lord of Boulsdon manor. It was acquired through marriage by Mr Chinn in 1732 and in turn sold to Mr Fowke in 1802 (fig.23). James Richardson was the owner towards the end of the Victorian age, and in 1912 Charles Priday was living there. It is now the residence of the Keen family. At the end of Southend Lane is another old farmhouse called Southerns owned by the Nourse family and occupied by Cornelius Draper in 1757. John Nourse Morse bought it in 1789. In 1926 it was used as a guest house called "Brittains Guest House" run by Samuel George Brittain.

On the north side of the parish stands Walden Court, a 16th century timber-framed building. In 1619 it was the property of the Pooles of Pauntley Court and was leased to Lawrence Pauncefoote. By the second half of the 19th century a James Henry Frowde a retired Major of the Gloucestershire Yeomanry had acquired it (17). The outside was covered in plaster but in 1939 this was removed to expose the timbers. One of the Newent turnpike gates was bought by Major Frowde and erected at the main entrance drive. The building was renovated in the 1980s.

Also just to the north of the Town is Stardens, a name found in the 1327 Subsidy Roll. In 1826 it was owned by John Hill and passed through several owners/occupiers including Sir John Wintour (Lord of Newent manor 1619-1659), Rev Richard Francis Onslow and his son Richard Foley Onslow. It was considerably extended in Neo-Gothic style in 1865. Mr F A Wilson was living there in 1897, but it was sold with the remainder of the Onslow estate in 1910. The sale particulars show the estate to have been a little over 2410 acres with an estimated rental value of £1929 per annum. Col. William Noel was the owner in 1923 and the sale particulars of the following year stated that it was lit by electricity. This must have been by generator as electricity did not come to Newent until some years later. Alfred Daniels, the Sheriff of Gloucester, was the next owner and he sold it for £8,000 after World War II to a rogue named Frank James White, alias Eustace Hamilton Ian Stewart-Hargreaves (see chapter 5). Later in the 20th century Stardens became a hotel and night club, but suffered a serious fire in 1980. It is now divided into flats. (fig.22).

There was an old grange at the Scarr, encircled by a moat, but it was

Fig.17   62-70 Culver Street, 17th century

Fig.18   The former Picklenash School, Ross Road

Fig.19 Thatched cottage in Bradfords Lane

Fig.20 Newent High Street in the 1930s

demolished in late Victorian times. It was also called Waters End or Atherlords Place and belonged to Samuel Dobyns. According to Walter Nourse a barn there was burnt down in 1717 and later rebuilt in brick. It passed through several owners including Mr Sargeant (1779), Jeremiah and Ann Herbert (c1800), and Mr Hankins (1807). Jeremiah and Ann Herbert (nee Stockley) had nine children who were educated at Mr Beale's school in Newent. According to their granddaughter, Martha Roberts, in her Victorian diary, *" The Scarr was a great rambling old house with what my aunts used to call galleries; passages I think they must have been. Whether it had ever withstood a siege, I cannot say, but they used to speak of cannon-balls that lay about in the disused rooms and how, as children, they used to bowl them from end to end of one of those long galleries disturbing nobody because no one was near enough to hear."*

Until the late 19th century a moated farmhouse, formerly the home of the Rogers family, existed at Okle Clifford, a mile east of the town. It is listed on the 1840 Tithe map with 310 acres of land. It was demolished in the 1880s and the present red brick farmhouse built to one side. The moated area was turned into a garden. The cast iron fireback from the original building, dated 1710, is in the Gloucester Folk Museum (18).

In the South part of the parish, near the Glasshouse, is Clifford Manor which boasted a nudist colony in the 1950s. It was built of stone from Clifford's Mesne in 1882 by Col. Philip Reginald Cocks, who became Baron Somers in 1883. When he died in 1899 it was bought by T D Grimke-Drayton, the High Sheriff of Gloucestershire. Two of his sons died tragically and he lost a lot of money in the failure of the Stepney Wheel Company. The house was auctioned in 1912. It is now divided into several dwellings.

Mantley House just off the Ross Road was owned by Lord and Lady Raikes, a descendant of Robert Raikes the founder of the first Sunday School, in Gloucester. It was built prior to the first World War and initially occupied by Mrs Conder in 1912.

In the 1980s Newent Local History Society made a survey of many of the old barns in the parish as part of a national survey for the Society for the Protection of Ancient Buildings (13).

The building opposite the old Wesleyan Chapel in Culver Street, which is now "Perpetua Press", was previously a cinema. It was called "The Plaza" and was in use in 1922, over 8 years before electricity was laid on. Originally it began life as a Wesleyan Chapel and Cornelius Thurston extended it to form a Temperance Hall. Travelling artists used to perform there before the first World War, and in the 1920s Miss Hartland played the piano during silent films. The stage curtain had a fine painting of Symonds Yat. Newent Amateur Dramatic

Society used it for one week a year for their annual production, the last time in 1938. The hall was updated in 1937 when Benjamin Longfield leased it. A new stage was installed, together with a sloping floor and electrically operated curtains. The balcony was enlarged so that the total capacity was increased to 272. Heating was by gas heated oil filled radiators. It was open as a cinema for six days a week and in 1951 the seats were priced at 2/4d, 1/10d and 10d. The last film to be shown before it closed down was "Soldier Blue" . The present occupier "Perpetua Press" started in 1976.

The red sandstone in Bury Bar is very close to the surface and some of the houses have their cellars carved out of the bedrock. The Memorial Hall on the south side of the Market Square was built in the early 1950s by W. Wildsmith & Son Ltd, building contractors, using materials from disused wartime buildings. The roof covering was damaged in a storm in 2002 and had to be replaced.

The Crime Museum building, adjacent to the main car park, was built in 1878 as a Police Station and Court Room. It was constructed on the site of the old Tithe Barn, and later became the national headquarters of the 18 Plus Club.

St Bartholomews "grouped" accommodation in Gloucester Street was built in 1967 and Ross Willis Court, containing flats built by the Royal British Legion, was opened by Princess Anne in 1979.

In former times a lot of houses in the town had thatched roofs. Most of these have been replaced with slate or tiles which require less maintenance. A small number however do survive; the best known is at the southern end of Bradfords Lane (fig.19). Another is at the southern end of Culver Street, with a well in the front garden, and a third in Cleeve Lane which was severely damaged by fire in January 2003. There are over 20 other thatched houses in adjacent parishes west of the River Severn. Cleeve Mill was originally thatched. There are letters in the Foley Estate papers regarding a complaint from Isaac Moore, the new tenant, in November 1666 that the house belonging to the mill and the outhouses want thatching. There has been a mill on this site since at least 1291 and Mr Lawrence, the miller in the 20th century, claimed that the foundations dated from before the Norman Conquest. Mrs Maud Florence Jones was the owner in 1927 and it remained in operation until the 1950s.

Another mill, "The Tuckmill", recorded from 1482, existed at the eastern end of the present lake, where the bypass now runs, but this had been demolished and is not shown on the canal plan of 1791. The Tuckmill Pool is listed in the 1840 Tithe Assessment as being over 2 acres in area, but was probably filled in when the railway was built in the 19th century.

Fig.21 Newent Cattle Market c1910. Now the Memorial Hall car park
(photo R J Bisco)

Fig.22   Stardens c1950

Fig.23 The Moat Farm c1910

Fig.24 The Old Court c1910

Among the less interesting structures that have existed in the town were some cast iron toilets in the Market Square at the beginning of the 20th century, in the same place that the Bull Ring existed some time before.

The derivation and history of some of the place names in Newent are as follows:-

Picklenash means "Goblin in the Ash tree"

The area north of the Market House was known as "Golden Square"

"Graces Pitch" is said to be where the famous cricketer W G Grace once played. The corner of Church St and Broad St. was known as Clark's Corner after Arthur Clark's printing shop which once occupied the site.

"Old Maid's Walk" was so called because the old and infirm from the Workhouse would use it as a short cut to the Church on a Sunday.

The northern end of Culver Street was originally called Lux Lane and is recorded from 1333, but the name is no longer used. Culver Street was originally called Colford Lane in the 16th century, then it changed to Culvert Street, and was later shortened to its present format.

Lewall Street dates from before the civil war in the 17th century. Curriers Lane dating from 1683 (meaning leather dresser) was at the eastern end of Church Street. It was called Curryard Lane in 1624 but no longer exists.

Stardens is a name mentioned in the 1327 Subsidy Roll, and Ford House is mentioned as early as 1515. Brass Mill was converted from a corn mill in 1646. Anthony's Cross is said to take its name from a man who hanged himself from an oak tree which grew on Free Bromage Oak Green near by, known as Brummagen Green (21) in 1912, but now just called The Green.

Until the 20th century all house building was privately financed, but as councils became wealthier they addressed the need for low cost housing. Before World War II the council built a hostel for homeless families in Bradfords Lane. During the war the huts were used as a prisoner of war camp and were not finally demolished until the end of the 20th century. The first council houses in Newent were built in 1932, when they constructed 12 semi-detached dwellings at Lancaster Terrace, at the end of Cleeve Mill Lane. In 1937 they built a further 16 in Watery Lane and commenced an estate of 50 houses at the Tythings in 1939, before the war intervened. After the war 42 houses were built in Vauxhall and Bradfords Close and another 42 in Glebe Road. Private enterprise contributed a further 100 houses making over 250 new homes in the town in just 30 years.

In the second half of the 20th Century many more houses have been built at Lakeside and Foley Road, considerably expanding the population.

An interesting sketch map exists in the Gloucester Record Office

(Fig.11). It is thought to have been drawn by Mrs Elizabeth Conder in 1898 and based on information from William Baron, the parish clerk, and the original Nourse manuscript. It has some interesting features. It shows the position of a ducking stool on Peacock Brook and a "lift bridge" over the same brook in what is now Puffs Alley. It also shows a cross in the grounds of Old Court. Perhaps this was the original site of the Saxon cross shaft now in the church porch. The Bull Ring is shown in the Market Square.

The original Nourse manuscript was in the possession of Mrs Elizabeth Parlour of Cliffords Mesne at the beginning of the 20th century, but is now lost. Mrs Parlour was a direct descendant of Mr Nourse.

The centre of Newent is now a Conservation area and at the end of the 20th century considerable discussion took place on the merits of building a new Co-op supermarket off Market Square. In the end after many protests the new store was constructed, but the scheme did not receive universal approval, mainly due to the heavy increase in traffic through the town.

Fig.25 Newent Union Workhouse c1910

Fig.26 George Freemans hosiery shop in Lewall Street c1930
The assistant standing on the right is Miss Forty

References

1. Gloucestershire Sites and Monuments Record
2. D Bick 1987 The Mines of Newent and Ross
3. Gloucester Citizen advertisements 1823/34
4. Wyedean Tourist Board Civil War information sheet No 23
5. Parish Register 1672-1766
6. Kelly's Directory 1927
7. Ordnance Survey map 1880
8. R M Bradfield 1999 The Newent Carved Stones Unravell'd
9. F Penney 1987 St Mary's Churchyard
10. F Penney 1988 Memorial inscriptions of Newent Church
11. Newent United Reformed Church Souvenir Booklet
12. K M Tomlinson 1995 Transactions of Bristol and Glos. Arch. Soc.
13. Newent Local History Society Barn Survey 1985
14. T Ward 1994 Around Newent
15. M Thurston 2001 A Brush with the past
16. Britton, Brayley, & Brewer 1816 Beauties of England and Wales
17. Eric Warde 2000 They didn't Walk Far
18. R E Bailey 2002 The History of the Bailey family
19. F Penney 1965 Parish magazine article
20. Bruton Knowles 1910 Newent Court Estate sale particulars
21. Plan of Newent area toll roads GRO D2210/15
22. J Douglas 1912 Historical Notes on Newent
    Maurice Carter Other information on planning matters

3. Newent in the 18th and 19th centuries
Frances Penney

In the 18th century and into the 19th century the main unit of local government was the parish, of which the governing body was the Vestry, comprising all the rate payers of the parish. The Vestry's duties were many: the repair and maintenance of the church, excluding the chancel which was the Vicar's responsibility; the relief of the poor; the maintenance of law and order; the upkeep of highways and bridges; the destruction of vermin; and the control of parochial charities. The officers who carried out the decisions of the vestry were the Churchwardens, the Overseers of the Poor, the Town Constable, and the Surveyor of the Highways.

Newent Vestry meetings were held at frequent but irregular intervals and the minutes of the meetings were recorded by the parish clerk whose salary was £15 a year. These minutes (5) are available from 1768 onwards, the earlier documents having unfortunately disappeared.

Meetings were not always calm. In 1773 a note, at the end of a meeting at which various orders were passed, tells us that those present *" all agree and are for the above orders but none will sign the book (on account of some little dispute that arose) except J.N.Morse and Sam Wood"*. In the same year it was recorded that great inconvenience was caused by non-attendance at meetings and twenty-two members agreed to attend regularly *"under the penalty of half-a-crown unless we can assign proper reasons to be allowed by the Gentlemen present and we do empower the Overseer for the time being to call upon us for the said money"*. In 1790 this fine for non-attendance was raised to one guinea.

In 1793 the Rev William Beale refused to sign the order authorizing the payment of *"one penny for each full grown rat, three pence a dozen for young ones and two pence a dozen for sparrows, and all small birds, crows, rooks etc"*. The Churchwardens' accounts are not available for this particular year but later accounts show that they paid one shilling to *"Warren for a fox"* in 1795 and to T.Sysom in 1806.

In 1790 there is a note that *"several dogs have lately run mad"*, so a proclamation was to be cried for three successive days *"to desire every person that keeps a dog to chain them up"*. Beside this order is written *"Done"*. Things ordered were not always done. John Nurthen, who was Beadle in 1772, was to be informed in October that *"except he clears the Town of Vagabonds and executes his office in a better manner he will be discharged"*. He was also instructed to survey the streets and *"correct the boys that are found flinging* stones or doing any other mischief in the Church Yard or in the Streets, particularly on a Sunday". Evidently he paid little attention to the warning for he was dismissed at Christmas 1773. Perhaps it was his son, John Nurthen Junior, who was established as a Beadle in February 1788, with a new hat and coat and the wages of *"one shilling a week so long as he execute the said office in all its branches"*.

Breaches of the peace were sometimes referred to the higher authority of the Justice of the Peace, as in 1788 when, on April 2nd, it was noted that the Vestry had applied for a *"warrant against John Skinner for abusing Richard Waite"*. And on April 16th it was recorded that *"Mr Chinn used Richard Waite cruel by whipping him with stinging nettles and twigs"*. The same John Skinner had helped him, so a warrant was sought from a J.P. to *"deal with Mr Chinn and John Skinner as the law directs"*.

The Vestry had the power to levy rates; in 1770 there was a sixpenny rate for the repair of the Almshouses and in 1781 another to raise money to clothe the poor. But these were special ones; the poor rate was levied regularly and was often a source of annoyance. The most notable dispute arose in 1816 when John Nourse Morse, of Southerns, gave the Vestry notice that he was going to appeal against his assessment at the Quarter Sessions. He maintained that others were assessed *"not properly in proportion to me"* for he was rated higher than the yearly rents of his estates and others were not rated to their yearly rents. A committee was immediately appointed to look into the matter but not, however, to help Mr Morse. Their instructions were *"not to lower any charge..... but to raise those that appeared to be under rated"*. He can hardly have been popular with his fellow landowners! Three very poorly attended meetings were held, at which additions were made to the rateable values, but these were later said to be *"at random and in error"* because the committee did not know the quantity of acres of the premises that were altered. On 27th August, when the new rate book had been produced, John Hale and Mr Morse were leaving the committee room when Mr James Cummins came in and said that if the charge on his estate of *"Casswalls"* were not put back from £6-10s-0d to the original amount of £5-10s-0d he would pay no poor rate at all. The other two noted in the minute book *"We find ourselves somewhat indignant by being deserted by our officers and propose that the rate above mentioned shall be produced at a public meeting...... allowing appeals to those who think themselves aggrieved"*. Unfortunately there is no record of this public meeting so we do not know how the story ended.

Problems continued. In 1817 parish bills were not paid until the end of the year because there was not enough money. The Vestry resolved that half the poor rate then being levied should be used to pay off old bills *"until all are discharged"*, leaving half for current expenses. In the future the bills were to be audited and settled once a month.

As was to be expected, additional rates had to be levied in 1817 and 1818 to balance the accounts. In 1819 the minutes show that *"Nine rates at 6d in the pound"* raised a total of £1,587-3s-0d. Of this £1,436-12s-2d was spent on the maintenance of the poor, £52-2s-3d went to *"Paupers employed on the Highways"* and £10-1s-0d to a *"woman who taught children to head pins"*.

There had been complaints about rates before. In April 1784, at a very full meeting of the parishioners, a committee of ten persons had been appointed to *"examine the accounts and form a plan for reducing the expenses of the Parish which have of late years been increasing at so rapid a rate as to threaten the most alarming and serious consequences to the payers"*. The committee suggested that relief granted to the poor should be more strictly controlled and that the poor should lose their relief entirely unless they wore the Parish badge "P" (for pauper) on their shoulders; that the expenses allowed the Parish Officers should be reduced; that *"all strollers and vagabonds should be discountenanced"* (the Town Constable was to drive them out); that goods for the Workhouse should be bought from ratepayers of the parish *"in preference to all others supposing they will serve the house upon equal term"*; and that a committee should be appointed to manage the affairs of the Parish for the coming year, reporting every three months. In 1793 another committee was appointed to make a new poor rate on the grounds that the present one was *"partial and unequal"*. The Committee adjourned to the Bull *"to make the Church Rate and the Poor Rate in a just and equitable and convenient manner"*. This manner of levying rates has still to be found!

The Local Government Act of 1894 allowed the formation of an elected Parish Council which then took over from the Vestry. The Rural District Council, successor of the Newent Union, eventually set up offices after World War II in the Old Rectory opposite the end of Watery Lane until 1974 when a further reorganization saw them swallowed up by the larger Forest of Dean District Council. Magistrates courts were held in Newent until 1976.

Surveyor of the Highways

Maintenance of the highways was yet another duty laid on the Parish, by the Highway Act of 1555, and each year the Vestry elected one of its members to be the Surveyor of the Highways. Newent Vestry elected a Surveyor for the Town Liberty and one for each of the five Tithings. The Surveyor had to inspect the roads three times a year, appoint four days a year between Easter and Midsummer for road mending and supervise the work carried out, without payment, by the parishioners. By statute landowners had to provide a cart, a team and two men, while cottagers worked themselves on the four days. The Surveyor's other duties were reporting defaulters to the Justices, collecting dues and keeping accounts to be presented to the Justices at the end of his year of office; if he refused this thankless task he was fined five pounds.

But statute labour did not necessarily provide good roads and when Rudder came to Newent, about 1770, he found the *"roads so intolerable it was necessary to desert his horse and to travel with a guide on foot"*.(1)

By the beginning of the 19th century roads throughout the country were in such a bad condition that it was decided that repairing them could provide work for the paupers; the account kept by the Surveyor for Newent Town and Kilcot for the period 1805-1825 show that the men were paid a shilling a day. The stone for the road, quarried in the district, some at Gorsley, cost about nine pence a ton, but the cost of hauling it varied from 1s-6d to 2s-9d a ton. It then had to be broken before being carried in baskets or wheelbarrows and laid on the dirt roads. The accounts also show payments for extra work such as *"getting bricks out of a gutter at Caises, 3s-6d. Planting quick on the Kilcot road, 9s, work in Wyats Road, £1"*. Larger jobs included *"lowering the side of the road between the Turnpike and Kilcot, £10. Stoning 260 yards of road at Kilcot Hill at 1s-3d per yard, £15-3s-4d; making a drain across the said road, 10s-6d and pitching 126 yards of gritting at 4d, £2-2s-0d"*

The money used for the upkeep of the roads was raised by a Highway Rate, levied on the yearly rent of the property. In November 1791 it was recorded *"Book of sixpence in the pound granted and a loud* [allowed] *to be expended on the road leading from Newent to Ross and being within the Liberty of Cugley and Killcoats"*; and in July 1812 the Surveyors reported that a sixpenny rate was not enough to keep the highway in a proper state of repair, so an extra threepenny rate was allowed.

From 1812 to 1815 there were several complaints about the state of the roads. The cost of repairs, which had averaged £230 a year for the town and Kilcot for the years 1806 to 1812, rose steeply during the next three years, reaching £840-4s-9.¾d in 1815. At a meeting of the Vestry on 22nd November 1812 John Ford reported that the road from Elmbridge to Fordhouse was not wide enough, being too narrow to admit two carriages abreast, and was *"out of repair"*. He hoped he would not have to resort to *"an indictment as the only means of obtaining a safe road to his house"*. The Surveyor of the Highway for the Tything of Compton was ordered to make a contract to have the road widened and repaired and to levy an extra threepenny rate annually until the expenses were paid. The accounts show payments, totalling £120-15s-0d made in April and May 1814 to *"Mr Hartle for widening the road in the Compton Tything"*.

The state of the highways in Malswick and Cugley was considered at a meeting on 22nd August 1813, when it was noted that the Vestry was *"threatened with immediate indictment by the Collector of Excise unless the road from Newent to Taynton be put into proper state of repair"*.

This was not the only trouble; Mr Bisco had said that *"unless the road leading to his farm at Kent's Green is repaired he shall be under the necessity of indicting the Parish of Newent"*. The Vestry agreed to repair immediately *"the worst and most founderous parts of the road leading from Anthony's Cross to Kent's Green"* and to have the main work done the following summer. The meeting was then adjourned until after Morning Service the next Sunday when estimates for the Newent to Taynton road would be considered and a report made by the Surveyor. But the estimates presented on 29th August were not comparable, having been obtained *"at different times and under different constructions"*, and Messrs. Dale and Hartle were asked to *"measure, mark and describe the different parts of the said road which are to be repaired and widened"*. The new estimates would be received the following Thursday *"in a sealed cover"*.

The meeting held on Friday 3rd September 1813 at the George Inn at 10 O'clock in the morning was attended by Jonathan Wintle, surveyor of Taynton as well as the Newent Vestry. He came to report that Taynton would allow £10 towards the *"expenses of building a bridge over the brook at the bottom of Abon's Hill if a meer* [boundary] *stone were put at the boundary of the Parish of Newent"*. The following estimates were then considered:-

Thomas Hartle	£340-7s-7.3/4d
Thomas Dale	£277-3s-10d
William Thornbury	£266-3s-6d
John Probyn	£267-12s-0d
Robert Apperley	£467-9s-6d
Benjamin James	£217-1s-6d

The majority decided *"to give a preference to William Thornbury's estimate"* and ordered the Surveyor to enter into a contract with him and said a Highway rate of sixpence would be made immediately.

By January 1815 the Highways were in such a bad state that a meeting was called to consider *"the best means of extricating the Parish out of the existing difficulties respecting their maintenance and repair"*. On 13th January Thomas Dale, Mercer, was appointed General Surveyor for the whole parish at an annual salary of £40. There was difficulty too over financing the work; the latest assessment had not produced enough money and it was suggested that parishioners should advance sums of £5, these advances to bear interest and part to be paid off annually by lot as the *"funds of the highways will permit"*. When it became obvious that the Surveyor could not find enough subscribers the plan had to be dropped and the Vestry applied to some of the Gloucester Banks to advance the *"sum of £300 on the security of ten of the Principal Parishioners in the Parish of Newent"*.

With the creation of Turnpike Trusts, the main roads between towns gradually became the responsibility of Trustees, who raised money for the construction of new roads and the improvement of existing ones by tolls levied on those who used the roads. An Act of 1726 set up the Gloucester to Hereford Turnpike Trust to *"widen and improve"* the roads between these two towns, including the road that ran through Newent. One of the Trustees was Miles Beale of Newent and in 1728, when the General Surveyor resigned, he became the Surveyor for the road from the bottom of Rodway Hill to Newent. There were regulations concerning the traffic to use the roads; wide wheels were preferred on carts as they did less damage to the road surface than narrow ones, and there was a limit to the number of horses allowed to pull a cart. In April 1740 the Trustees ordered that the Surveyor and Keeper of the Turnpike *"do seize all and every horse or horses above the number of six that they shall find drawing in any waggon or carriage for hire"*.

Tolls were let by public auction to the highest bidder who had to pay a quarter's rent in advance and give security for the payment of the remainder; those in Newent District were let in July 1786 for a yearly rent of £93.

Meetings of the Trustees were held in various districts in rotation, those in Newent being held in the Horseshoe, the Bell or the George. At first meetings were well attended but there was one period. from 3rd August 1731 to 22nd May 1733, when twelve consecutive meetings were attended by insufficient numbers and no business could be transacted.

Since the roads were so bad and, in 1792, it was noted that there was no coach or regular carrier to the town, it must have been with some excitement that the people of Newent heard that an Act of Parliament had been passed in 1791 to allow the construction of a canal from Hereford to Gloucester with a cut to Newent. But this was never a real success (see chapter 14).

Churchwardens.

The duties of the Churchwardens were numerous. They had the responsibility for the maintenance of the fabric of the Church. In January 1806, Thomas Stone received 3s-4d for *"one day repairing Vestry"* and 2s-9d for the lime and tile he had supplied for the job. They supervised such details as provision of *"green bays for the Vestry table"* at a cost of 5s-6d, of a lock for the

Church chest which contained all the Parish documents, and of a *"cobweb brush and carriage"* which cost 3s-8d. The clearing of snow cost one shilling in February 1795 and three shillings in 1819, whilst in May 1814 two men were paid six shillings for *"mowing the Churchyard and raking it"*. The fence was replenished with *"half a hundred of quick"* at a cost of sixpence in November 1805 and in March 1819 sixteen shillings was paid for gravel for the walks.

The Churchwardens bought prayer books, one for the Minister in 1819 cost £2-12-6d and one for the Clerk £2-8s-0d, and in 1795 they bought an *"Almanac for Church"*, and a new map for 1s-2d. They also provided the sacramental bread and wine as these entries in the minutes show; *"£3-1s-6d to Mr Cook for two dozen of wine"* in October 1794 and two shillings for *"sacramental bread for two years"* in April 1809.

In 1812 the Vestry ordered that the children were to be instructed in Psalmody, the instructor's salary of £10-10s-0d a year to be paid from the Church rate. When the organ needed repair, in November of the same year, it was decided that it formed part of the fabric of the Church, consequently the cost of repair fell on the Parish and the money was to be found by subscription, helped by the Church rate. The organ was then described as a *"solemn instrument properly adapted to assist the congregation in the ancient practice of psalmody"*. An account of £62-11s-2.5d was paid in December 1813 to *"James for timber work at organ, etc"* and in May 1814 a *"new swell in organ and other repairs"* cost £26-5s-0d.

There is no record of the number of bellringers at this time but they were paid 15 shillings every year on May 29th and five shillings on June 4th, when they rang a peal to celebrate the King's birthday. They also received special payments of one pound on October 25th 1809, this being the Jubilee day and five shillings in June 1815 after the Battle of Waterloo. There is only one entry in the Vestry minutes concerning the repair of the bells, two shillings was paid to Hirem Jenkins in January 1795, though the work done is not specified.

Farming.

Farming was the occupation of the greater part of the population in the 18th century. Sir Robert Atkyns (7), in his book published in 1712, described the land as *"good pasture and arable"*, and Rudder (1), in 1779, said it was mainly *"pasturage and orcharding"*.

The open field system was not practised here; the land was already enclosed and divided into separate farms as advertisements in the Gloucester Journal show. In August 1730 The Mote, at Malswick, was to let at £30 a year, *"it being about 82 acres of good tillable and pasture-ground, and well planted"*.

In February 1733 there were two farms to let at *"the yearly value of £140 or thereabouts"*; these were *"The Moate and Poydras's Farm, adjoining each other, consisting of arable, meadow and pasture grounds, well planted and in good husbandry and the houses and outhouses in good repair"*. The name Poydresses comes from one Christopher Poydres, a butcher, to whom a cottage and three acres of land in Cugley were let in 1716.

Waterdines, *"consisting of about 70 acres of arable, meadow and pasture land, well fruited, with a good house, barns, stables, and all other conveniences"* was to be let from Candlemas 1735 at £30 a year. The farmstead has long since disappeared completely. The Fordhouse, with 220 acres of arable, meadow and pasture land, was advertised in February 1788 as a *"freehold estate, with a new built brick house"* to be sold by private treaty (3).

Newent Vestry owned land, known as *"Poor's Land"*, which was let, usually by auction, the rent being used for the relief of the poor. At an auction in October 1772 Christopher Roberts became tenant of land *"near Cliffords Meen for a term of twenty one years at two pounds fifteen shillings yearly......and a couple of fat pullets every year if demanded"*. He had to *"hall five waggon loads of lime and ten waggon load of muck in the last three years, also to hall no hay nor grass off"*.

There was a second area of Poor's Land in the Common field, a third in Boulsdon and a fourth *"near the squirrel"*. The tenants of each were subject to the same conditions as those imposed on Christopher Roberts and all tenants had *"to give a bond of performance of the covenants"*.

Crop yields per acre were low by present standards, the land being over-cropped and underfed. Fields were manured by allowing cattle and sheep to feed on the stubble after harvest and left to lie fallow after every two crops. The main crops grown were wheat, oats, barley, rye, peas, and beans. In 1709 prices for crops, ready to thrash, were 8/- a bushel for wheat, barley 4/6 and rye 5/6. There is no record of potatoes which did not become popular as a farm crop until the latter half of the 18th century.

Farmers possessed ploughs, carts, waggons or wains, dungcarts, harrows, rollers, corncarts and drays; their lighter implements were picks, bills, rakes, and wheel-barrows.

Horses were the most commonly owned, and most important animals at this time; they were needed for ploughing and harvesting, for taking produce to market and for travelling from place to place. They varied in price from £3 to £4 generally, although Cornelius Draper owned, in 1757, a *"Hackney mare"* valued at £10. Pigs were kept, even in households that had no other animals at all, to provide meat to be eaten fresh in summer and preserved in salt for winter use.

A few farmers kept pigs for breeding, but mainly they were listed as *"store piggs"* valued at approximately 10/- each. Sheep were well worth keeping; they manured the land, provided wool and meat, and milk to make into cheese, and cost 5/- each. Farmers kept many more sheep than cattle. Winter feed being a problem, particularly at the beginning of the century before the introduction of root crops, the beasts were raised mainly for beef and there was very little dairy farming. Cows were valued at approximately £3, heifers at £2 and bulls at £5. In considering all the prices we should remember that a farm labourer's average wage at this time was only six to seven shillings a week.

Probate Inventories, lists of a man's total possessions at the time of his death, have been a valuable source of information about crops, growing and stored, livestock owned, and implements used in Newent during the early part of the 18th century. Unfortunately they do not often give the name of the farm, *"Jasper James of Newent"* being sufficient in those days to identify a man. Only in four cases can the farm be identified and described; these are Hayes, Athelord Place (or the Scarr), Carswells and Southerns.

Simon Parsons, who farmed at Hayes, met with a violent death, recorded in the entry in the Parish Register for 11th February 1709. He was shot by John Hill (see chapter.5). The inventory compiled on 25th February shows that he grew wheat, barley, rye, oats and peas; he had *"44 acres of wheat and rye on the ground at £1-5s an acre but 16 acres is sorry"*. His livestock included *"old sorry mares and geldings, 4 small oxen, 2 small cows, 8 store piggs and 83 sheep"*. There was a *"dayery house"* containing milk skeels (wooden buckets), six milk pans and churns, a milk strainer and a set of *"butter scales and waits"*, together valued at 18/-. In his cheese chamber, where the hardened cheese was stored separately from the new, moist cheese, he had *"six and twenty small cheeses"*. In one of the rooms in the farmhouse he had a store of *"one and twenty stone and nine pounds of wool"* valued at £14-14s-0d.

Athelord Place must have been a large farm where, in September 1709, Samuel Dobyns had *"corne of all sorts, growing and housed"*, valued at £228, together with a store of hay and clover. He owned *"four bullocks, four yearlings and four calves; eight cows, five heifers and one bull; thirteen horses, mares and colts of all sorts; thirty pigs and stores and nine suckers"*.

In March 1711 William Jones had, at Carswells, *"corne of all sorts now growing"* valued at £42 and corn *"in the houses"* worth £51. His inventory listed *"5 horse, 2 colts, saddles and geares; 13 cowes, 8 calves and 6 heifers; 6 oxen and 12 two year old beasts; 9 yearlings and 8 store pigs; 2 sows and 17 piggs; sheep and lambs"*. Cornelius Draper grew *"wheat, barley, beans and pease, and clover seed"* at Southerns in 1757 and also had a store of hay. He owned *"6 horses, 3 mares and colts and a Hackney mare; 24 piggs; 28 cattle of all kinds; 155 sheep"*. He had *"a corn screen and three scives"* used during threshing, and *"a half bushel"* to measure the grain. In the dairy were a cheese press, a cheese cowl (or cooler), 7 cheese *"vates"* and a butter board as well as churns, milk pails and scales.

One record of a luxury crop has been found in a private garden. An advertisement in the Gloucester Journal for 31st July 1733 says *"whereas the garden of Hubert Bower at Newent was robbed of some early peaches on Saturday 21 instant, this is to give notice that whoever will discover the person or persons concerned in the said fact so as they may be brought to justice shall receive a guinea reward"*.

Leisure and Entertainment.

It is difficult to name the books that Newent people read in their leisure time, most of them could not read at all. Of all the local inventories only five mentioned books and only one gave the titles in detail. These books were the property of Rev. Thomas Vaughan who died in 1726; he had a collection of religious works, volumes of Ovid, Virgil, Juvenal and Horace, a Greek Testament and Lexicon, Blackwell's Introduction to the Classics, the Clergyman's Companion and a copy of Addison's Poems. All the books were valued, from a "Historical Dixonary" at fourpence to a large Bible at ten shillings.

From April 1722 the Gloucester Journal was available. Published weekly, on Monday, it consisted of four pages, cost twopence and gave national and international news as well as local advertisements. These were of houses, farms, and Inns to be let or sold, of cock fights and horse races. Horse racing was held in a meadow near the river in Gloucester in September 1734, to be followed by an assembly with dancing in the evening. Travelling stage companies advertised, like Mr Murrell's Company of Comedians who appeared at the Boothall in 1734. There were sometimes small illustrations; one showed a stage coach pulled by six horses above an advertisement for a journey from Cirencester to London in one day.

Husbands advertised for wives who had "eloped" from home; Richard Sysum, Innholder of Newent, announced in 1732 that he would not pay any debts contracted by his runaway wife, Anne. Masters advertised for missing apprentices; Thomas Newton offered a reward of ten shillings in 1735 for information about his apprentice Thomas Davis, and said the boy would be kindly received on his return if he behaved himself well.

There were numerous notices about missing animals, stolen or strayed, but the Rev. Edward Draper of Newent minced no words in the advertisement he inserted in February 1724 about his greyhound dog *"stolen on Friday at midnight being the 20th December last"*. The dog was yellow and white with a *"white garland round his neck......and a handsome tail always curled at the end"*. In March with the dog still missing, he said he had *"good grounds to suspect that the dog was stolen and privately conveyed away by Jonathan Dalimore and Jonathan Hitchens, or by one Filladans and Danford, or by some or by all of them, who are all inhabitants of Dursley Town.....some of which at least are thought to be poachers and unlawful destroyers of Qualified Gentlemen's game"*. He promised at least half a guinea reward to anyone who could bring proof of the guilt of the *"aforesaid persons"*.

The Gloucester Journal also gave accounts of the Gloucester Assizes and the Quarter Sessions, at which those convicted of crimes were sentenced to death, transportation (see chapter 9), burning in the hand or whipping. A number of Newent Residents were mentioned.

Exceptional weather was recorded and in November 1770 the floods around Gloucester, caused by violent rains, were the worst for over a century. The man with the letters for Ledbury was drowned. These floods were also mentioned in a letter by Sybil Beale of the Court House, who wrote that Newent was cut off from Gloucester. (4) On 22nd December 1788 it was reported that *"In this climate no winter has been remembered to set in with the severity of the present season. The Severn is one continued sheet of ice, from Shropshire to a place some miles below this city* [Gloucester] *, and affords fine skating"*.

The chief places for entertainment for the poor were the ale-houses. These were regarded as a nuisance by the Vestry who, in 1784, sent a petition to the magistrates that no licence should be granted *"for establishment of an alehouse at Eaton's Hill or any other place in the Parish"* and it appears, from the comments on the poor in 1788, that poverty was no bar to drunkenness.

At some of the Inns there were other attractions; shuffle-board (a form of shove-ha'penny) was played at the Horseshoe, and the Crown had *"a very good cock-pit"*. Here, in 1743, a Cock-Match was *"to be fought between the Gentlemen of Gloucestershire and Herefordshire. To show thirty-one Cocks in the Main for four guineas a battle, and forty guineas the odd battle; also ten By-battles, for two guineas a battle. To weigh on Monday 18th day of April next, and fight the three following days"*.

Behind the Market House was a Bull-ring, in which bull-baiting provided a spectacle for all the townspeople. The churchyard, too, became a playground for there was a fives-court against the east wall of the chancel.

A popular activity of the wealthy during the 18th century was visiting spas to take the waters. There was a spa in Newent about half a mile east-north-east of the church.(see chapter 10)

Fairs, feasts and general rejoicings were always appreciated, bringing as they did a break in routine and a little gaiety into the hard lives of the working people. Four fairs a year were held in Newent; on the Wednesday before Easter, the Wednesday before Whitsuntide, August 12th and the Friday after 9th September (2). In recent years the last one has been revived as the Onion Fair. William Baron, born in 1821, who was once the Parish Clerk, remembered in 1900 that on August 12th in his boyhood *"the whole street was full of sheep and horses right up to the workhouse"* (6) But livestock was not the only thing on sale at the fair; there would be fripperies and luxuries not normally obtainable in the Town, sideshows, dancing and plenty to drink. Newent Feast Day was the Sunday after August 12th. The feast was held in the Churchyard, gingerbread and cakes being laid out on the flat tombstones and, again, there was plenty to drink for, to quote Baron, *"men were drunk in the afternoon"*. Extra constables were always hired on feast day and paid half a crown each.

Great national events were always commemorated locally. When King George III died at the end of January 1820 the Vestry decided on certain ceremonies to *"show every proper mark of affection and respect to the memory of the late venerable Sovereign and to proclaim his present Majesty George the Fourth"*. The bells were to toll from 8 to 9 p.m. each day until the day of the funeral and on that day (February 16th) there was a special service at 3-00 p.m. with a funeral sermon. The pulpit, reading desk and organ loft were hung with black cloth and the sconces and pillars near the door with black crape. The material for this cost £14-5s-0d. The bells rang a muffled peal, the ringers receiving £2-17s-6d for all their extra work during this time.

References
1. S Rudder   1779   New History of Gloucesteshire, p561
2. Universal British Directory   1792 GRO
3. Gloucester Journal   County Collection, Gloucester library
4. Beale correspondence   Nat. Register of Archives
5. Newent Vestry Minutes   GRO
6. Conder MS   c1900   GRO D.412/Z3
7. Sir Robert Atkyns   1712   The Ancient and Present State of Gloucestershire

4. Population and Occupations
Frances Penney

There are no reliable records of population until the first census in 1801, at which time there were 2351 people living in Newent. Calculations based on the number of baptisms show around 1300 in the 17th century, and in the 18th century historians record 1100 in 1712 (1) and 1560 in 1779 (2).

By 1851 there was a population of 3,306, after which time the numbers fell to 3,168 in 1871, 2,605 in 1891 and 2,485 in 1901. With the building of new estates in the second half of the 20th century the population rose steadily to reach 4,669 in 1981.

For occupations in the 17th and 18th centuries the Parish Register is a valuable source of information, the father's occupation being frequently given in baptismal records. Occupations are sometimes shown on tombstones, and they are also given in the lists of youths apprenticed by the Walter Nourse and Timothy Nourse charities, and in leases granted by the Foley Estate (3).

The Register of Apprentices of the City of Gloucester, 1595-1700, (4) show that some of these came from Newent. They were trained in apprenticeships of 7 or 8 years to become tanners, curriers, cordwainers, mercers, vintners, silk weavers, broadweavers, pin makers, and chandlers. These records also show the occupations of their fathers, mainly the same as those of the apprentices, but two more unusual ones were those of matmaker (1661) and coalman (1676).

Until the end of the 18th century Newent was a self-supporting town providing all its daily needs with weekly markets and four annual fairs. As Newent was mainly agricultural there were all the trades connected with it. The corn had to be ground into flour. In 1615 the Foley papers describe Cleeve Mill as "ancient" and in 1666 Isaac Moore, the new tenant, complained that the house and outhouse needed thatching. In 1685 John Poyke, the miller, rented Cleeve Mill for 21 years at £33 a year. By 1725 the mill was known as Poyke's Mill and was advertised in the Gloucester Journal as *"a grist mill with three pair of stones"*.

There were blacksmiths - John Godsall took a charity apprentice in 1727 - a plough carpenter in 1739 and a wheelwright in 1785.

Barley was turned into malt by a maltster; Thomas Clarke was one in 1664, and in 1709 Simon Parsons had sent *"12 bushells of barley mow to be made into malt by Mr Skinner"* as recorded in his probate inventory.

Beef cattle were raised by graziers, of whom there were 15 listed in a directory of 1792, who also acted as butchers. In the early 18th century they were claiming *"they kill twice as many beasts weekly in season as they do in the City of Gloucester"* (5). If this claim is true it is not surprising that a leather industry should have developed. The Bower family (Edward and Hubert in the 17th century) had their tannery in Culver Street. It was in use until 1911.

Ancillary trades were those of fellmongers, who dealt in the skins; curriers who softened and coloured the rough tanned leather; cordwainers who worked in fine leather; shoemakers and glovers. Anthony Edmunds was a glover and his inventory, taken after his death in 1722 lists:- *"twelve stone of wool, skins, cat and dog skins, six pair of men's britches, four pair of boys breeches, twenty pair of gloves, one horse hide, and a colts skin"*.

In 1712 there were 270 houses in the town and 459 in 1801.

Carpenters were the earliest craftsmen recorded in the Parish Register (6) with William Wheeler and John Bower in 1632. The best known carpenter was Edward Taylor who was responsible for the *"contriving and building"* of the roof of the church in 1675-9. The inventory of his son Edward who died in 1702 lists all a carpenter's tools - planes, augers, saws, axes, adzes, chisels, one gimblet and bits, hammers, compasses and one "hold fast", presumably a vice.

There were masons listed in 1672 and 1668 and later bricklayers, plumbers, and glaziers. John Green who died in 1780 and his son, also John, worked at this trade until 1826. John's widow, Elizabeth, is recorded as taking an apprentice in 1832. Possibly she ran the firm and one of her staff taught the apprentice (7).

There were always Innkeepers in Newent who brewed their own beer and the utensils for brewing are listed in several inventories. There were bakers, Samuel Pace had this occupation recorded on his tombstone in 1697 (8). An advertisement in the Gloucester Journal in 1725 showed *"a very good oven for a baker"*.

Material for clothing was produced in the town. There was plenty of wool, prepared for spinning by a woolcomber, and probably spun by the women, woven by the weavers (Joseph Pitt was one in 1670) and made into clothes by the tailors, such as Richard Elton and John Wadlie in 1667.

Flax was grown in the town as early as the 17th century because Peter Hopkins was listed as a flaxdresser in 1694 when he took Joseph Billy as an apprentice. By 1707 Joseph Billy was able to take Samuell Suffell as his apprentice.

John Bradford and William Jones advertised flax seed for sale in 1725 in the Gloucester Journal.

Other trades were those of dyers - Samuel Osborne in 1663 and Anthony Meek in 1701(8), and hosiers - Richard Draper in 1607(3). By 1792 according to the Universal British Directory the gentlemen of Newent could call upon the services of a breeches maker, a hatter, five shoemakers and a perruke-maker. Wigs were worn during most of the 18th century and in 1733 Joseph Owner, a barber, had in his shop *"one wig trough and one powder box"* for the treatment of wigs.

Shops were probably the front rooms of houses with conversions to large window frontages in the 19th century when shops selling clothes were listed. Benjamin Green was a draper in 1842 and C Cadle a mercer in 1842. The stock of Joseph Loggins, draper, was advertised for sale by auction in 1796 and included: woollen cloths, chinz and cotton gown pieces, calicos and muslins. He also stocked handkerchiefs, gloves, buttons, and ready made clothes.

In the 19th century there is more evidence of professional occupations such as solicitors, doctors, surgeons and veterinary surgeons. The 1851 census lists all of these, together with an Inland Revenue Officer, auctioneers, fire and office agents and a postmaster aged 89. There was a Registrar of births and deaths, the Treasurer and the Surveyor of the turnpike road from Newent to Aston Ingham. With the opening of the canal there was work for the clerk to the canal company, two boat owners, a wharfinger, a dealer in marine stores, and four watermen, two of these were in each of two barges at the wharf on census day.

The census also shows that Newent had a Police Sergeant and two officers based in a police house (or Station) in the Market Square. That Saturday night four young agricultural labourers were housed there as prisoners. Had they been taken in drunk? It is probable because there were eleven inns in the centre of town.

References
1.	Sir Robert Atkyns	1712	The Ancient and Present State of Gloucestershire
2.	S Rudder	1779	History of Gloucestershire
3.	Foley Estate papers		Hereford Record Office
4.	Register of Apprentices of City of Gloucester	1597-1700	Bristol & Glos Arch Soc, Vol 14
5.	William Green Manuscript		GRO
6.	Parish register	1672-1766	GRO P225
7.	List of Apprentices		GRO P225 CH3/2
8.	Frances Penney	1988	Newent Churchyard Survey

5. People
Derek Pearce

In earlier times the majority of people for whom a record survives were the wealthy. The Lords of the Manor were the major landowners and they give us some of the earliest names. In 1779 Rudder (1) lists them as follows:-

Lords of the Manor of Newent (the list is not complete)

King Edward the Confessor	until 1066
Roger FitzOsbern	
Abbey of Cormeilles (Normandy)	Prior to 1086
King Edward III	
Sir John Devereux	From 1382
College of Fotheringhay, Northamptonshire	From 1415
Sir Richard Lee	From 1548
Sir Nicholas Arnold	
Sir William Wintour	From 1567
Sir Edward Wintour	From 1589
Sir John Wintour	From 1619
Thomas Foley	From 1659
Paul Foley	c1670
Thomas Foley	From 1699
Thomas Lord Foley	In possession 1779

Also listed are the owners of five Tithings/hamlets

1. Compton also called Compton House or Walden Court
   Owned by Reginald Bray and sold to Edward Rogers before 1779

   Carswell mentioned in the Domesday Book

Owned by Ulfel	Up to 1066
Roger de Laci	In possession in 1086
Pauncefoot family	
Mr Bromley and Mr Smith	In possession in 1779

   The Scarr also called Atherlord's Place or Waters End

Mr Dobyns	Prior to 1779
Mr Sergeant	In possession in 1779

   The Hays

Walter de Laci "as a portion with his niece"	In 1086
Wall family	Prior to 1779
Mr Pritchard	In possession in 1779

2. Malswick
Philippa, widow of Henry Masham	Okeley Until 1407
Elizabeth widow of Robert Lovell	Okely-Grandison Until 1438
Sir James Ormond and his wife Amice	Okely-Grandison Until 1457
James Earl of Wiltshire	Until 1461
Thomas Duke of Norfolk	Okely-Grandison Until 1545
Thomas Brook	Okely-Grandison Until 1547
Joan Arrowsmith, sister of Thomas Brook	Okely-Grandison Until 1548
Mr Rogers	Okely c1700
Mr Bearcroft	
Mr Jones	
George Smith	Okely Pritchard in possession 1779

3. Cugley
William Gerand of Matisden, & Catherine his wife	In possession 1315
Woodward family	
Mr Chin of The Moat	In possession 1779

4. Boulsdon
John Atwood	Until 1301
Thomas Boulsdon	Until 1475
Thomas Porter	Until 1558
The Nourse family	1630- until mid 1700s
Lord Foley	In possession 1779

5. Kilcot
Ansfrid de Cormeliis "holds one hide"	In 1086
Robert de Musgrose	Until 1254
Bogo de Knovil	Until 1339
Thomas Moine	Until 1364
Beatrix Burly, wife of Richard	Until 1393
Walter Nourse	1686
Mr Lewis	In possession 1779

Ansfrid of Cormeilles married the niece of Walter de Lacey.

Earl Roger, who was the Lord of the Manor after Edward the Confessor, was the son of William Fitz Osbern. William founded the Benedictine Abbey of Cormeilles in Normandy in about 1060, where he was Lord, and fought at the battle of Hastings in 1066 (2). Six hides of land in Newent that had never been taxed, being a portion of the Royal Demesne as mentioned under "Terra Regis" (in the Domesday Book) were given to the monks of Cormeilles by Earl Roger for the good of his father's soul, with the consent of King William. This donation occurred between 1072 and 1074, and as a result the monks established a priory in Newent.

William Fitz Osbern, who was Earl of Hereford, was buried in the Abbey of Cormeilles. His son Roger was imprisoned for treason in 1074 and forfeited his lands. He died in prison after 1087 (3). The early family tree (Fig.30) shows the relationship between William Fitz Osbern and William the Conqueror

The Domesday Book of 1086 is the earliest reference to Newent, on page 166a:-

St Mary's Church of Cormeilles holds Noent [Newent] *King Edward held it 6 hides did not pay tax   Earl Roger gave it to his church for his father's soul, with King William's assent   In Lordship 3 ploughs; 9 villagers and 9 smallholders with 12 ploughs; A Reeve who has 1.5 villagers and 5 smallholders; between them they have 5 ploughs and a mill at 20d*
2 slaves; 2 mills at 6s 8d; from the woodland 30d
Durand holds 1 hide of this land from the Abbot, he has 1 plough and 5 smallholders and 2 slaves with 2 ploughs
2 hedged enclosures of which the King has taken possession
Value of the whole Manor before 1066 £4; now 100s; of Durand's hide 12s
William son of Baderon holds 1 virgate of this manor's land by force.

Although there were variations one hide is estimated to be about 120 acres, and a virgate about 30 acres. The value of the land means the rental value payable to the Lord

Durand was the Sheriff of Gloucester in 1086. In the reign of Henry III there was a bailiff in Newent. A deed for half a yard-land called Totteland, was granted by Nicholas son of John de Camma, to the Abbey of Cormeilles, and to the bailiff. It was witnessed by Reginald de Acle then Sheriff of Gloucester. The last Bailiff was William White towards the end of the 17th century.

The next source of early names is the list of Ministers of the church who are (4):-

1301	Hugh de la Grave	1663	Thomas Jackman
1311	Hugh de Marcelye	1684	Thomas Avenant (see note)
1344	William de Sterdone	1728	John Craister
1363	Robert de Ratford	1737	James Griffith
1363	John Lilic	1762	Robert Foley
1370	Reginald Mile, or Milo	1783	John Foley
1390	Reginald Clifton	1803	Richard Francis Onslow
1393	Robert Hoke	1850	Arthur Andrew Onslow
1434	John Hoke	1865	Frederick Wood
1484	John Taylour	1870	Benjamin Ruck Keene
1524	William Porter	1878	Peter Almeric Leheupwood
1524	Thomas Byrde	1897	Samuel Bentley
1537	John Warde	1906	William Higgin Connor
1550	John Cutler	1925	Cyril Joseph Kildare Burnell
1564	Henry Donne	1949	William Charles Hodgins
1605	Nathaniel Dodd	1961	Herbert Lewis Owen Davies
1617	William Diston	1969	Charles Walter Earle
1627	Francis Singleton	1976	Iain Marchant
1642	John Wilse	1993	Robert Simpson
1663	Henry Kirkham		

Note:- The list in the Church says Thomas Avenant became vicar in 1691. Thomas Jackman died in 1690 but Thomas Avenant has signed as vicar from 1684 for reasons which are unclear.

The Gloucestershire Subsidy Roll dated 1327 (5) contains the following names of Newent residents and the tax they paid :- (the names have been modernized where possible)

John Payne	19d	Adam Barefoot	5/-
Roger Mammeline	6.25d	John Parley	6.5d
Roger Chesare	6.5d	Henry Bythway	6.5d
Edward Mercer	6d	Gilbert Caple	19d
Roger Webb	16d	John Caple	18.5d
John Hobyes	12d	William Broom	6d
Walter Dyer	6d	John Brown	6d
William Wint	13d	John Home	18d
John Hull	6d	Richard Cross	20d

Peter Hugh	13d	William Fekard	6d
David Pistor	6d	Reginald Coppe	12.5d
Richard Flawe	6d	William Emelot	18d
Walter Maynard	2/1.5d	Henry Emelot	7d
Walter Compton	12d	John Ploddy	18.5d
Thomas Coppe	12.5d	Richard Ploddy	12d
John Hartland	10d	Walter Farley	2/2.25d
Stephen Birch	6d	Robert Farley	10d
Allen Bythway	18.5d	Robert Birch	7d
Robert Hugh	7d	Hugh Swan	18.25d
Dyonis Pirie	6d	Nicholas Dodde	6d
Thomas Hall	18d	Henry Tyler	12d
John Ardarne	2/-	Adam Ely	13d
Henry Bradenore	18d	Thomas Hull	18.5d
John Staurton	3/0.25d	Richard Oldbrook	20d
Geoffrey Wint	2/-	Richard Hartsley	18.5d
Lucia Sotherby	2/2d	Sybil Day	6.5d
John Jones	18.5d		

The list shows 53 names and should be multiplied by about 4.5 to give an approximate population, say 240 people. A further list of the surrounding area gives another 46 names :-

John Shaw	9.5d	Alice Chappell	18.5d
Walter Starden	9.25d	Audlee Ocle	2/1d
William Bolesdon	5/0.5d	Richard Craswell	6/-
John Ross	6.25d	John Slouz	18.5d
John Hall	6d	Nicholas Cowmeadow	12.5d
Thomas Kilcot	9d	John Bytheway	3/-
Richard Holdare	7d	Thomas Liewe	6/-
Walter Hull	7.5d	Robert Ely	16d
Richard Budel	6d	William Rene	2/-
John Dylewy	7d	Nicholas Hoke	15d
Roger Wallis	11d	Nicholas Starden	2/0.25d
John Coke	7.5d	Walter Hoke	6d
Walter Putte	9d	Richard Mile	6.25d
Henry Fab	13d	Randolph Pole	6.5d
Peter Coke	2/8d	John son of Peter Ocle	2/0.5d
Thomas Ethelard	14.5d	Isabel Garden	6d
William Coppe	7d	Matilda Ocle	12d

Geoffrey Crompe	7d	Margaret Mere	7d
John Hyne	7.25d	John Green	11d
Edith Bond	7d	John Wallis	9d
Henry Bishop	6d	Agnes Anketel	6.25d
Reginald Cornis	9d	Richard Hartland	4/0.5d
Edith Bolloke	7d	William More	7.5d

This appears to show a population of around 450 people in Newent Parish in 1327. A number of the names have survived to the present day and some are from local place names. The money collected was one of the highest in Gloucestershire, which gives some indication of the town's prosperity at the time.

The Gloucestershire Inquisition Post Mortem documents include a number of references to Newent and people who owned land in the area.(15). In the reign of Henry III (1216-1272) it states :- *The abbot* [of Cormel] *holds 3 carucates of land in the Manor of Newent demesne, whereof each is worth by the year 20s when stocked. Also in rents of assize 11 marks, 7s 10.5d. Also 2 mills, 3 marks. Also in villeinage 5 virgates of land, whereof each is worth half a mark and a quarter, 10d.*

Sum of the Manor of Newent, £14 - 9s - 6.5d and there can be no stock there because there is neither pasture nor land lying idle (wavetum).

Also the same Abbot holds the church of Newent and Dymoc with the chapel of Panteleg to his own use. Of the land of Normans and Aliens they know nothing"

The document is signed by 12 people :- Robert Dobyn, Henry Haket, Robert de Leden, William de Boifeld, Nicholas de Strongeford, Henry de Acle, Henry Calni, Robert de Strunling, Robert de Dyke, Robert Anunden, John de Bosco, Osbert de Boclinton.

In 1283 King Edward I granted that Bogo de Knouvile might cut down large oaks in all his wood of Kyllicote (Kilcot). The King would be damaged by 10s per year. William de Astonene (Rector of Aston) would be damaged by 5s per year, and Thomas de Bolesdon by 5s per year. Bogo de Knouvile died in 1307 when his son and heir, also Bogo, was 24 years old.

In 1297 Robert de Stallinge held the following tenements of the Prior of Newent "*in chief by the service of riding in the service of the said Prior wheresoever he wished in England at the cost of the Prior*" :- 1 messuage with a garden and curtilage, and they are worth per annum 12d. He also had there 40 acres of arable land, and each acre is worth per year 2d. Sum 6s 8d. Also 2 acres of meadow, and they are worth by the year 2s. And 1 acre of pasture and it is worth by the year 4d. Also of the rent of assize by the year 16s-7.5d. And 0.5 acre of wood, and it is worth by the year 3d. The pleas and perquisites of the Court are worth per annum 12d.

The alabaster tomb of a Knight and his Lady in the church are said to be members of the Grandison family, possibly Thomas de Grandison who died in 1375 and his wife Margaret. He was a relative of Peter de Grandison who died on 10th August 1358, (aged 53) holding the manors of Dymock and Oxenhall. Peter left the majority of his estate to his elder brother Sir John de Grandison, Bishop of Exeter, but he left the Manor of Oxenhall to Thomas. When Sir John died in 1369 he made his nephew Thomas his heir. Peter and Thomas were the children of William de Grandison who died in 1335 (15).

The Hooke family have been residents in the Newent area for several hundred years. Their wealth came from a gift of King Henry V for saving his life before the battle of Agincourt (see chapter 6). The family home is Crookes Farm, formerly in Pauntley Parish but now in Oxenhall. His son, also Thomas, married Margaret the daughter of Sir Guy Whittington in 1435, a close relative of the more famous Dick Whittington, Mayor of London (17). Margaret brought with her a dowry of 100 marks, a considerable sum in those days.

A later member of the family, another Thomas Hooke, died on 7th March 1628 leaving a widow Isabella and a son Edward. His estate in the Newent area is listed as :- Crookes (now in Oxenhall) and 60 acres

80 acres of land, meadow pasture , wood and underwood called Callow Hills
40 acres of land and pasture called Cleeveleyes and Lyllies in Compton
28 acres of land, meadow and pasture called Mauntleyes
1 acre of land in the common field called Bowlsden field
1 several field called Picklenash field, containing 17 acres of land and pasture
2 acres of land called Slades alias Lyllies.

As well as the list of lands a number of people farming it are also mentioned :- John Wintour, Richard Estcourt, Walter Nourse, Henry Atkinson, and John Keyse.

During the civil war some of Cromwell's troops were billeted at Crookes Farm, and some culverin balls have been found in the nearby fields. At the coronation of Charles I Edward Hooke was fined £17-10s for refusing a knighthood (33).

Many of the place names in the Newent area have their origins in antiquity. The 1624 survey of the Manor of Newent runs into over 50 pages (34) and lists all the fields and buildings rented out by the Lord of the Manor. Each field has a name and many of the place names can be identified today, as the following list shows :-

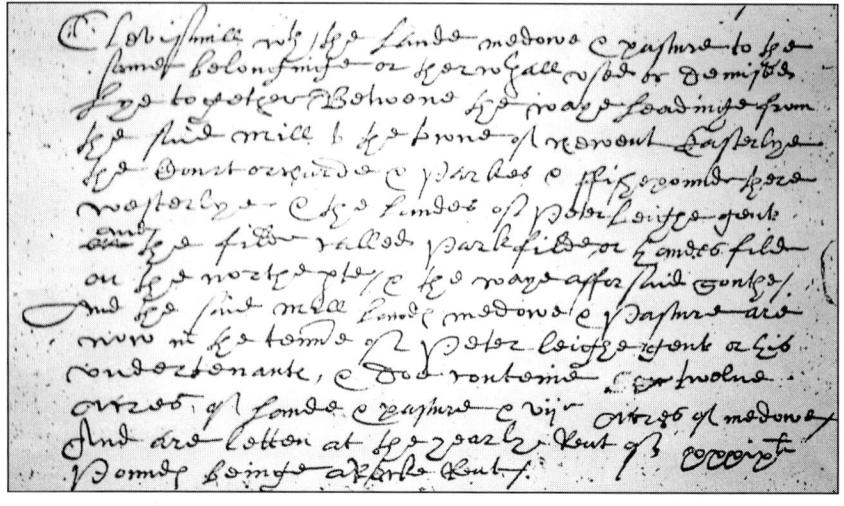

Fig.27 Part of the first page of the 1624 Survey of the Manor of Newent

Transcribed it reads :-

       "Clevsmill wth the lande medowe & pasture to the
       same belonginge or therwithall used or demised
       lye together betwene the waye leading from
       the said mill & the towne of Newent easterlye
       the Court orc yarde & Parkes & fishepound there
       westerlye & the landes of Peter Leighe gent
       and the filde called Park Filde or Handes fild
       on the northe pte / & the waye afforsaid southe /
       and the said mill lande medowe & pasture are
       now in the tende of Peter Leighe gent or his
       undertenant & doe contenue sextwene
       acres of lande & pasture & VII acres of medowe
       and are letten at the yearly rent of XXXIX
       pounds being a rack rent /

Anthoneys Cross	Court House (Old Court)	Nelfield
Boothall (now a supermarket)	Cugley	New Street
Brand Green	Ford House	Peacocks Brook
Carswells	Glasshouse	Picklenash
Cleeve Mill	Kents Green	Ploddy House
Colford Street (Culver St.)	Kilcot	Puffs
Compton Green	Malswick	Yartleton Wood

It is perhaps a misguided impression that Lords of the Manor were hard and oppressive on their tenants, the 1624 survey shows a dozen properties being occupied rent free e.g. *"Widow Baylis holdeth a cottage and garden enclosed out of Yartleton Waste, a quarter of an acre rent free, an almswoman"*. It also shows that some people encroached upon the land in the hope they would not be noticed e.g. *"Charles Quarrell encrotched and built a cottage in the waste in Malswick near Deadmans Cross"*. In 1624 Yartleton Wood on the side of May Hill was estimated to be 700 acres.

It was not uncommon for some rents to include payments in kind e.g. *"William Willys in the right of Elizabeth, aged 62, his wife for her life only, holdeth by copy of Court Rolls bearing date the 8th day of August in the 23rd year of our late sovereign Lady Queen Elizabeth* [1581] *one messuage & diverse lands, tenement, meadow, & pasture with their appurtenance by rent 12 shillings & 2 capons"*

According to the survey the Manor totalled over 2,250 acres and was worth per year just over £570. The exact figures are difficult to determine because small parts of the document are unclear or incomplete. If the wood and common land are ignored the remaining productive land was worth on average approximately 3 shillings and 8 pence per acre.

Over 170 people are recorded in the survey. The ages of some of the tenants are mentioned; this helps to pinpoint their year of birth, something which is difficult for genealogists in the time before the existing Parish records. It also records the relationships of some family members. Those listed with their ages are as follows:-

Jo Adys, 30	Thoms Cox, 30	Johane Reading, 60
Tho Adys, 34	Willm Cuffe, 42	Elizabeth Renton, 67
Anne Astman, 65	Alys Giles, 46	Richard Tyler, 46
Ruthe Astman, 22	Thomas Giles, 52	Thomas Underwood, 62
Thomas Astman, 54	Guy Hall, 26	Ann Wall, 42
Alys Baker, 50	Maulde Hill, 60	John Wall, 40
Anne Baker, 46	Richard Hill, 26	Jo Williams, 32
John Bullocke, 36	Tho Hill, 60	John Williams, 62

John Bullocke, 69	Tho Hill, 71	William Williams, 30
John Bullock, 70	Willm Hill, 36	Elizabeth Willys, 62
Julian Bullocke, 54	Henry Hopkins, 42	Christopher
Johane Clerck, 64	Willm Kirrye, 16	Woodwarde, 17
Tho Clerck, 40	Willm Lane, 46	Johane Woodwarde,
Tho Cox, 62	Jeffrey Palmer, 26	widow, 56
		John Woodwarde, 23

Thomas Dobbins, gent, died on 1st January 1634. He owned a house called Hull Hey at Compton together with 20 acres of land, 2 acres of meadow, and 10 acres of pasture. It was left to his son Thomas who was *"aged 17 or more"*.

The Manor of Newent was acquired by Thomas Foley of Witley in 1659 from Sir John Wyntor and his son William for the sum of £8,640. During the second half of the 17th century numerous properties in Oxenhall, Pauntley and Longhope were added to the estate. This was done primarily to give control of the iron ore, wood and water necessary for the family ironworks at Elmbridge (called Elsbridge in some early documents).

Many of the deeds and documents relating to the Foley Estate are held at Herefordshire Record Office, but special permission is required to examine them. They mention many of the Newent residents and the lands and property associated with them.

One of the earliest, dated 1399, lists Richard Coldewell and his wife Lucy, the daughter of the late William Geffrey of Kempley. In the same year a John Marcle and his wife Katerina of Oxenhall, and Peter Heynns are also mentioned. In a 1464 document the following Newent people are mentioned :-

John Ballarde and his wife Margery
Thomas Porter
John Wyllys
Margaret Chefan
Lady Cecilia Whityngton and her son Richard
Thomas Hoke
Thomas Hathewy
William Philyppe
Henry Hobys
Thomas Puddyng

The Court Leet, or Manorial Court imposed justice in earlier times. In the 1396 Court Roll (31) there is a record of fines being imposed. John Caerwents was summoned for making the road near his property dangerous, and

Matilda Oxenhall was fined for disturbing the peace. John Davey's offence was pulling manure in Bury Bar Street.

Local bye-laws were made by the Leet, for example in 1777 it was ordered that *"all persons within this Borough to throw up the dirt that shall be opposite their doors, carry away the same every fortnight on pain of ten shillings. That no person shall singe any pigs or make any fire under the Market House. That all persons shall yoke and ring their pigs before they turn or suffer them to go out."* They also ordered *"that no butchers within this Manor shall burn any bull flesh without burning a candle in his shop or standing, during the sale thereof for better distinguishing the meat and preventing imposition on persons intending to buy beef on pain of 13/4 for each bull and each person offending".* At the same time they appointed Samuel Wood to be Taster of ale, fish, flesh and fowl. He was also appointed Hayward of the Manor.

In 1824 William Cummins, Thomas Hayes, Joseph Clark and Revd. Wm Beale were all summoned before the Court for enclosing land, and were ordered to *"throw up"* the land by January 1st on penalty of one shilling *"if he make default"*

Thomas Porter may have been an ancestor of Arthur Porter who is mentioned in a document dated 1526, together with his wife Alice, the daughter of John Arnold of Highnam. The Porter Family were prominent members of Newent society for many years. They originally came from Tickenham in Somerset in the late 15th century. Roger Porter lived at Porters Place on the south side of the Market Square (now demolished). He was a Justice of the Peace and died on 15th April 1523. His brass in-laid gravestone has been relocated and now stands against the wall of the Lady Chapel (21). He was married twice, firstly to Margaret Arthur and then to Johanne (22). He was also cited in the Hereford Consistory Court for adultery (23).

Roger's brother William, was vicar of Newent until his death in 1524. The wills of both Roger and William are held by the Public Record Office at Kew. In Roger's will he states:- *"To be buryed in our Lady Chapel afore the image of our Lady at the alters end. For my tythes forgotten I will that two oxen be eaten amongst my neighbours at my burying with bread and ale according. Wife allowed to keep all she brought at our marriage e.g. plate, bedding, napery, girdles, beads. To my brother William my pot of silver with knap of golden on the cover enamelled. Gowns various."*

Their uncle, John Hayward, was the Prior of Llanthony in Gloucester. Probably because of this, Arthur Porter, Roger's son by his first wife, came into possession of several manors and lands previously held by Llanthony Priory. At the dissolution of the monasteries by Henry VIII he became Lord of the Manors of Alvington and Quedgley and owned lands in St Briavels, Hempsted and Boulsdon as well as a fishery in the Severn (1). In 1538 he bought Llanthony Priory and associated property for £723-16s-8d (28). Sir Arthur Porter died at Llanthony in 1630 leaving his only daughter, Elizabeth Scudamore, his heir.

In 1624 there is a Court Roll entitled *"True returne of the names of the inhabitans within the town and burrow of Nwewnte"* which contains 180 names, all men. This indicates that the population of Newent at this time was about 800.

As well as the people of Newent the papers also mention some of the street names existing in 1540 :- Church Street, Lewall Street, Lux Lane, Culfarde Land, and Cleve Mill Lane, the last one helping to prove the antiquity of Cleeve Mill (20).

The Bower family were prominent members of the Newent community from Elizabethan times. A John Bower and his wife Ann (née Nanfan) have an elaborate tomb in Gloucester Cathedral depicting themselves and their 16 children. John was an apothecary and in 1572 was elected surgeon to St Bartholomews Hospital in Gloucester. He bought some land in Newent in 1593 and the conveyance in Gloucestershire Record Office states:- *"between John Bower apothecary of Gloucester, and Thomas Good of Clyffords Inn, London, conveyance of land in Old Church St, Newent, between the lands of Jacob Collwall on the east and Arthur Dunne on the west, and extending to Burris Field on the north, formerly held by Philip Bower, Consideration £8"*

A John Bower is recorded as occupying the Porch House in 1582 although it is not certain if this is the same person. Unfortunately the English Civil War during the middle of 17th century caused a lot of information to be lost and it is unclear if the later Bower families are descended from the above, although it seems likely.

The Newent family had members who owned the Tanhouse in Culver Street. The adjoining building bears the initials "HB" (Hubert Bower) and the date 1695. Later members of the family became Warden of the Tanners Company, Sheriff of Gloucester (1729), Mayor of Gloucester (1833) as well as Newent butchers, cordwainers, Innholders (The Crown, High St), surgeons, and churchwardens (1669).

One later member of the family, Hubert Bower (born 1835) wrote a book in 1873 entitled "History of the Town and Parish of Newent in the County of Gloucestershire" but it appears never to have been published. He wrote another in 1876 on "The Bower Family of Gloucestershire" but unfortunately the only known copy which was held by the British Library in London has been "mislaid" all except the last page.

There was a degree of inter-marriage within the family and a number of Bowers are buried in the Church (graves 46,84,97) and in the Churchyard (graves G42, G51 & G52). The family tree is shown in Fig.34.

Despite the lack of medical knowledge in earlier times some residents of the town lived a long time. The Parish register of 1602 (now lost) recorded the death of Ann Wilson, aged 115 (25). An exceptional achievement even today.

According to J Douglas (36) in August 1720 a Newent bricklayer's wife gave birth to quadruplets, all boys, however the event is not recorded in the parish register. Maybe they all died before being christened. When Jane Abbot (née Mayo) died in 1705 she was so fat that it took 12 men to carry the coffin to the church, and it was necessary to break down the wall of her house to bring her out.

The census counts began in 1801 but it was not until 1841 that the actual names of the people were recorded. However in Newent the names of male residents aged between 12 and 60 were recorded for the collection of a 1d tithe. These records mostly still exist between 1802 and 1827 (30). In the year 1809 they show the following numbers in each tything :- Compton 56, Cugley 46, Malswick 50, and Newent Town 185. Although the figures varied each year by multiplying by 4.5 we can obtain an approximate population for the Parish at this time of 1,517.

The 1831/2 Gloucestershire Electoral Roll lists 128 people from Newent. The qualification for being able to vote was being the owner, tenant, or leaseholder of land, and although some of those listed were absentees, most would have been Newent residents.

The Newent Tithe Assessments of 1840 list all the landholders in the parish (29). The total area of the Parish was 7,803 acres of which 965 acres was woodland. The following is a list of owners of more than 30 acres with an approximate acreage of the land each one held :-

Isabella Beale	182	Joseph Hooper	59
John Cox Bower	142	Ellen Hull/Jane Perry	104
William Cadle	39	John Morse	191
James Clarke	59	Thomas Morse	174
Thomas Beale Cooper	206	Henry Thompson	82
John Cadle	117	John Matthews	51
William Dyke	130	James Matthews	51
Edmund Nelson Dean	101	Mary Matthews	62
Elizabeth Foley	1,507	Roston Sarah Ann Nash	63
Paul Hawkins Fisher	309	Rev R F Onslow	41
Elizabeth Green	37	William Priday	278

William Green	32	Richard Osman	182
Thomas Grosvenor	53	Mary Elizabeth Rees	98
John Hill	134	James De Visme	464
James Humpidge	36	John White	201
Thomas Hankins	451	John Wood	250
Benjamin Hook	172	Thomas Woodyate	127
Thomas Hartland	141	Rabshekah Wicks	35
William Hartland	130	Edward Gibbon Wakefield	220
John Hartland	67	Trustees of John Markey	63
Thomas Haynes	33	Frederick Stokes	125

This indicates that just 42 people owned 89.6% of the Parish.

John Morse was living at Southends Farm in 1830 and was the only son of John Nourse Morse, who died in 1830. John Morse, senr., was Lord of the Manors of Great Boulsdon and Kilcot and in his will he refers specifically to the crab apple and pear stocks growing in his nurseries (35). He issued tokens to his workmen, in lieu of wages, advertising his trade. On the one side is a tree laden with fruit with the motto *"Industry leads to Honour"*. On the other side is a strange spiral inscription :- *"Several thousand young healthy and fine crab apple & pear stocks raised from the kernel to be sold by J Morse Newent Gloucestershire 1796"*. The estate produced 100-150 hogsheads of cider and perry each year. (1 hogshead = 52.5 gallons).

The Morse family were associated with Newent for over 250 years, and several members became clergy. Abraham Morse (1651-1726) the son of a Newent property owner, another Abraham, was Rector of Huntley. His son Jackman Morse (1690-1765) and his son John Morse (1738-1797) both succeeded to the position. Jackman Morse took his rather unusual christian name after Thomas Jackman, vicar of Newent, a witness to his grandfather's will. Edward Morse (1688-1759) another son of Abraham, junr., became a mercer and tallow chandler in Newent and married a Newent woman, Jane Stone, in 1736. Their son John Nourse Morse lived to the age of 90.

Eleanor Martha Morse (1808-1854), granddaughter of John Nourse Morse, married Thomas Hankins, owner of Walden Court and the Scarr, and her brother John became vicar of Oxenhall, although he later emigrated to Australia.

Some of the bequests in the will of Abraham Morse, junr., dated 1724 are interesting. Amongst other things he left his son Abraham The Boothall in Lewall Street, Newent. He left each of his six children a mourning ring, and his son Jackman *"the six silver spoons, which were his late deceased mother's"*. He left his daughter Deborah Fowle *"the silver watch, which was her late deceased mother's"*. It would be nice to think that later members of the family still own these cherished heirlooms. Their mother was Deborah (née Knowles).

The wealth of the family declined dramatically in the Victorian era as land values fell and by the 1881 census there was no one with the Morse or Hankins family name living in Newent (38).

Tragedies

A number of Newent people have met an untimely death. Some have been murdered and others have died in accidents, whilst others suffered execution.

On November 15th 1558, in the reign of Queen Mary, Edward Horne was burnt at the stake for his religious convictions in the grounds of Old Court. The indictment read *"for reading the bible and for refusing to attend mass"*. In an attempt to escape from this persecution he hid for a time in a mysterious underground chamber near Cugley with another man named Crockett. The chamber then became known as Crockett's Hole. He was given away when a party was held to celebrate the baptism of his child. His wife saved some meat from the meal to feed her husband and this was noticed by the midwife. A search was made and he was found *"concealed under a vessel with the head out"*. He was led to his execution singing the 146th psalm.

Shortly afterwards when Queen Elizabeth I came to the throne the women of Newent, who were incensed by the execution, tied the priest, who was the chief accuser, backwards on his horse and drove him out of town. Some years later, in about 1665, a disbanded soldier from London called Fairfax *"assisted by Lilly the astrologer"* opened up Crockett's Hole in the hope of discovering riches. This drew a large crowd, some of whom had been drinking. A number went into the hole *"and told incredible things concerning it"*. The whole episode came to an unfortunate conclusion when a drunken man named Witcombe went in and died. A long tunnel which led from the chamber was explored by Stephen Ballard the canal engineer, in 1834 (6). It was again excavated in about 1888 by T Byard of Newent and Mr Piper of Ledbury but without any remarkable revelations. It has now collapsed and is just a depression in the ground (grid reference 719232).

The gallows was sited in "Pinchin Field" at Squirrel Corner on the Ross Road. It is said that one of the gibbet beams was used in the construction of Squirrel cottage.

In 1645 Elizabeth Horton, the widow of Thomas Horton Esq. of Conigree Court was killed by Parliamentary troops whilst attempting to retrieve some of her possessions from her occupied home. It seems she had refused to give any financial support for the war effort (8).

In 1728 Thomas Nash was executed *"for breaking open a house in the Parish of Newent and stealing £6 and upwards in money"* (14). In 1770 Timothy Phillips was sentenced to death for stealing two sheep belonging to Thomas Brassington, but he was later reprieved.

On July 13th 1699 (21) John Bower, a wealthy businessman and the owner of the Tanhouse, was returning late at night from Huntley on his horse. As he approached the southern end of Culver Street, near the entrance drive to the Moat House, he wandered off the road in the dark and was thrown off and killed (8). He is buried in the Church.

The early Bishop's Transcripts and the Parish Register list a number of unfortunate departures, some of which are not fully explained.

An interesting entry appears for January 28th 1600 relating to the death of Henry Held the illegitimate son of Joane Held. *"And for that it was doubted that this child came to his death by som mischaunce, the body was viewed and serched by Thomas Hill then constable Roger Comyn clerck and certen women present at the death of the said childe"* This is a fairly lengthy report on an unexplained death when compared with that of James Harman later the same year who is simply reported *"slayne"*.

On June 4th 1664 Ursula Arters was buried *"beinge killed with a gune"* (9) and on the 3rd August 1670 Phillip Matlie was buried *"being killed by a blow with a cuggell"*. On 11th February 1710 Simon Parsons was buried *"churchwarden, shot with a slugg of three quarters ounze weight from a pistol, by one John Hill (Mason) on Friday 10th February, about 12 at noon, was buried 11th February, the inquest being upon February 20th after"* (10). He was shot in the back yard of the Bell Inn in Church Street.

Although not a resident of Newent the death of John Hale in 1692 was rather unusual. The burial entry appears in the Hartpury Parish register :-

"John the son of William Hale senr of the Grove, yeoman, by Sara his wife, lately deceased. Killed by Newent's third bell as he and others were ringing. He was buried here September 11" His gravestone in Hartpury churchyard records that he was the village blacksmith aged 24yrs 4 months and that the accident happened on September 9th.

A number of people accidentally drowned at various places in the parish. On 26th June 1688 John Burnell, a yeoman, was buried *"being drowned"* (9) and on Whit Sunday 1704 John the son of Elizabeth Suffell was drowned while learning to swim in Southend's pool (8). Francis Thomas was also *"drowned in a pool at Gorsley"* in March 1708 (10), and Charles Smith was *"drowned in the Tuckmill Pool"* in May 1739 (10). The Tuckmill Pool was at the eastern end of the present Newent Lake, where the bypass now runs.

Some people died in falls such as John Bayley who was working on the construction of Mr Beale's house, the Old Court, when he was killed after falling off a ladder in December 1717.

In 1720 John Hill, the son of another John Hill, a tailor, was killed after he fell down the cellar steps of the Crown Inn (now Crown House), which was run at the time by his cousin James Hill. He was a Prestbyterian and often spoke out against King Charles I, and had been drinking heavily. It was thought by some to be divine justice.

Several murders have taken place in Newent although the culprit has not always been caught. The parish register says that John Phillips *"was murdered on October 10th"* 1747 and in November 1712 a strange entry says John George *"an apprentice at Edward Long a farmer slaine by me"*. It is uncertain who "me" was and almost reads like a confession.

In about 1830 when the road between Cleeve Mill and Hill Top was widened a skeleton was found. It was said by Mrs Conder to be the miller who went missing in 1780 *"whom Dee killed"*(11).

Some people chose to end their lives by their own hand. In about 1820 a woman named White poisoned herself and was buried at Anthony's Cross (11) but the local residents feared she might come back and haunt the spot so they exhumed her body at night and re-buried it in the churchyard. Her father also committed suicide. He was imprisoned in Gloucester Gaol awaiting trial for the murder of a Newent woman named Barnes, in the yard opposite the vicarage. His wife visited him in prison and is said to have given the poison which he used before the trial came to court.

On 24th February 1867 Anna Edmonds died at Pigeon House (the site of the present health centre in Watery Lane). Five years later her body was exhumed for a re-examination as rumours had circulated around the Town that her husband, Edmund, had murdered her. He was arrested and tried, but acquitted, despite the inquest jury returning a verdict of manslaughter (12).

Even in the 20th century there were a number of tragic accidents. Bill Barker was killed in the machinery at Lancaster's saw mills (now Ladder and Fencing Newent Ltd in Horsefair Lane) (13).

One Newent tragedy happened on the day of a Royal visit to the City of Gloucester. A young 21 year old woman, Ethel May Ford, and her sister Mabel were waiting in the rain in Eastgate Street, Gloucester on 23rd June 1909 to see King Edward VII. Miss Ford had moved from Newent to Victoria Street, Gloucester to become a dressmaker. They were standing with two friends sheltering under umbrellas outside the Co-operative Building. It appears that the flag on top of the building had become heavy with rainwater and wrapped itself around the decorative masonry. This was a piece of Painswick stone carved into a globe and mounted on four balls. The 11 lb globe became dislodged and crashed down on Miss Ford's umbrella striking her a fatal blow. She died instantly and was pronounced dead at the scene by Dr J.A.Bell. Whilst not admitting liability the Co-operative Society offered to pay the funeral expenses. The family were Wesleyans and the funeral ceremony was held at Ryecroft Weslyan Chapel followed by burial in Newent, where Miss Ford had been born and where her widowed mother was still living (27). Her mother, Elizabeth, was later buried in the same grave in 1949, although there is no headstone.

On 12th February 1922, 17 year old Geoffrey Awford was drowned in Newent lake after falling through the ice whilst skating. Many of the school children, who were also there, tied their scarves together to make a rescue rope, but to no avail. He had been assistant projectionist at the cinema in Culver Street.

In 1933 Sidney Huggins, an employee of the Co-op, was killed in a motorcycle accident on the road to Chepstow, and in December 1934 George Freeman, senior, died after being struck by a car in Gloucester Road, near the junction with Foley Road. He was unloading a cattle lorry in heavy rain which was said to have reduced visibility. He was the owner of a hosiery shop in Lewall Street. In the late 1960s Jack Price, a Newent RDC rent collector, was killed in a road accident whilst riding his bicycle at the north end of High Street.

These are just some of the tragedies that have occurred in Newent over the years which have helped the residents to realize just how fragile life actually is.

Charities. A number of local people have given money for the benefit of the church or the poor of the Parish. The earliest was a grant of 12 pence by Adam Humphrey of Dymock in the 13th century for the lighting of the church (16).

The Parochial charities came from various people. Ten almshouses in the High Street (shown on the left of fig.20) were given by John Nanfan (1635), Randolph Dobyns (1639) and William Rogers. They were demolished in the 1970s.

Apprenticeship charities were provided for in the wills of Walter Nourse (1652), William Rogers (1690), and Timothy Nourse (1699).

Eleanor Green left 10 shillings to be paid to the incumbent to preach a sermon annually on 29th January, the anniversary of when the Church roof fell down in 1674.

In 1836 John Harvey Olney Esq, left £200, the dividends from which were to be distributed in coal and blankets at Christmas.

Over a dozen small charities for the benefit of the poor, totalling £57 per annum were amalgamated in 1972 and are now administered by the Trustees as the Newent United Charity. Some of the benefactors are recorded on panels in the church entrance.

In 1954 John Henry Court of Salisbury, Southern Rhodesia, left £10,000 to the church. He had been in the choir in his youth.

Newent has two people who became well known in the field of music. Probably the most famous was "Joe" (Robert George) Meek the composer of the 1962 hit tune "Telstar". He was born in a house in Market Square and worked with many famous musical personalities. Sadly in 1967 he murdered his landlady with a shotgun and then committed suicide. He is buried in Newent cemetery. Since his death over 20 extended play collections of his work have been released (18).

The second well known musician and composer was Rutland Boughton (1878-1960) who wrote the opera "The Immortal Hour". He lived the last 30 years of his life at Kilcot (19).

In the literary field a number of Newent residents have published books in the 20th century but in the days when this was less common Timothy Nourse published "Compania Faelix" a discourse of the benefits and improvements of husbandry, in 1700. He was the uncle of Walter Nourse who wrote the historic notes on Newent. Although not a Newent resident, Paul Hawkins Fisher, the writer of "Notes and Recollections of Stroud" had Newent connections. He is listed on the Newent Electoral Roll of 1831/2 and his mother, Margaret (née White), was the daughter of Joshua White a Newent tanner. The White family were tanners for over 100 years.

The Rev. John Lightfoot, a celebrated botanist and author of "Flora Scotia" was born at Nelfields in 1735.

In the field of dishonesty Newent is not alone in having numerous residents who have fallen foul of the law. One of the most notable in the 20th century was Frank James White. He was brought up in London during the first World War and between the wars he started a number of business ventures which were more than a little dubious. He served three terms of imprisonment starting in 1933 (5 years), 1939 (12 months), and 1943 (3 years).

After his first prison sentence he married and changed his name to Eustace Hamilton Ian Stewart-Hargreaves. In 1945 he was released, and with only £100 to his name he set up the Cotswold Cider Company, a mail order company delivering barrels of cider all over Britain. Initially the company prospered and he bought Stardens (fig.22) on the north side of Newent, in 1946, for £8,000.

Unfortunately, despite his apparent good intentions, the business failed and the police arrived once again, in January 1952. He was granted bail by the

Newent magistrate, but before the case could come to court, he left the country on a forged passport in the name of his gardener, Wilfrid Wadley. He was arrested by the French police in Paris, but later found his way to Tangier. After various adventures he was captured and taken to Gibraltar prison before being returned to Gloucester for trial in March 1953. He was sentenced to 8 years imprisonment and died just before the end of his sentence. Whilst in Tangier he wrote an account of his life entitled "The Hargreaves' Story" but the book was withdrawn from sale on a legal technicality and only a few copies went into circulation (32). An even scarcer book is his "Man on the Run" published by Allan Wingate Ltd in 1957.

The Hengler Dynasty of the 19th century became a power to be recognized in the circus world. The arrival of Michael Hengler, a Lieutenant in the Hanovarian Artillery from Kronberg, in the late 18th century enabled the foundations of the dynasty to be created. He was both an equestrian and a firework artiste. His marriage to Sarah just after his arrival in London was the starting point of the Hengler Circus that evolved and developed under family guidance and ownership throughout the following century. This was the golden age for the Hengler family, but by 1901 the touring circus was all but extinct.

Michael's grandson, Frederick Charles, owned Hengler's "Colossal Moving Hippodrome" that played at Gloucester in August 1851 and Cheltenham in December 1855. The Hengler tented circus also played in many Gloucestershire towns during the intervening years, such as Bristol, Dursley, Minchinhampton and Tetbury. One of the key members of the "Ring" team was James Henry Frowde, a buffoon who was firmly established as "Frowde the Proud", a clown, contortionist and bottle equilibrist (fig.28). His maternal uncle, Frederick Charles, had taken James Henry under his wing some years before after the demise of his sister, James Henry's late mother, in 1838.

James Frowde, a descendant of an old Devonian family, married Michael Hengler's grand-daughter Georgina Margaretta in 1830 at Lambeth. Georgina had played in the family circus as a tight-rope walker. Regrettably Georgina died giving birth to her fifth child in 1837. Consequently James Henry Frowde, the eldest child, joined his uncle's circus in Stamford in 1847 and started to work his way up the ladder to fame. Some ten years later he married Elizabeth, the daughter of the Rev. Christopher Hayden, but sadly she too died in childbirth the following year.

James Henry continued to tour with his uncle's circus and continued to receive rave reviews of his acts. In 1859 he set up his own circus "Frowde's Cirque Modele", but it only ran for three months before he handed control of the show over to an uncle, John Henderson, who played as "Henderson's Grand

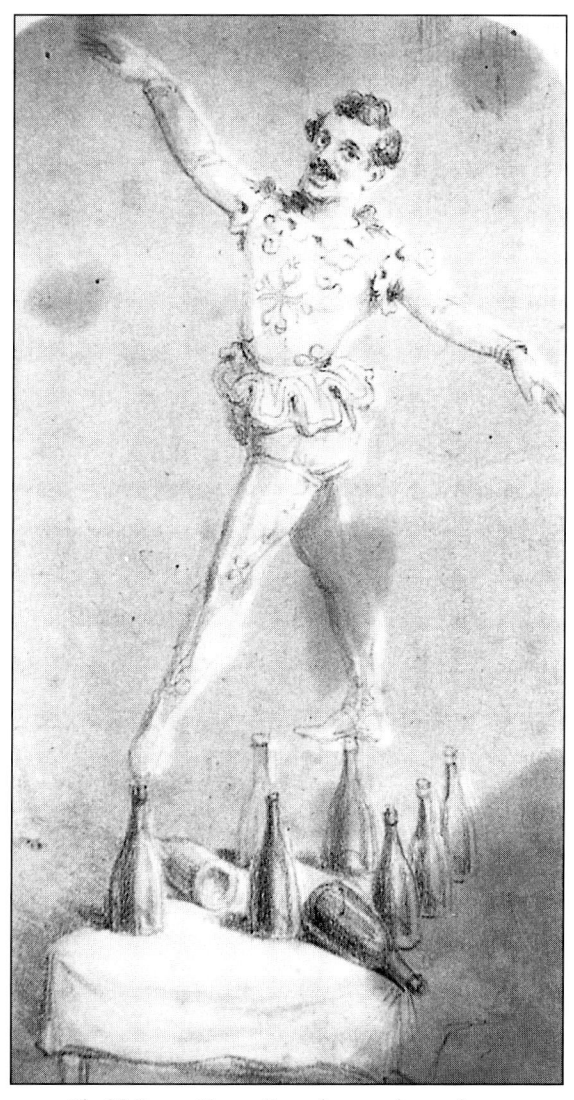

Fig.28 James Henry Frowde as a circus clown
(Photo David Stabb)

Fig.29 James Henry Frowde, Mason and founder of the Zetland Lodge.
(Photo R F Cryer, Gloucester)

Cirque Variety". Early in 1860 James Henry returned to Hengler's Circus but changed his allegiance later that year to "William Cooke's Equestrian Establishment". He finally left circus life when he married the daughter of the Rev William Harrison, Susan Mary, in 1861.

He then embarked on a new career, that of Country Gentleman, Farmer, Preacher, Mason, Philanthropist and general "do-gooder" as a result of his new mother-in-law purchasing Hayes Farm, Newent, in March 1863. Susan Mary inherited Hayes on the death of her mother in 1863.

James Henry became a Mason (fig.29). In May 1864, together with Henry Symonds, a 39 year old Newent farmer, Richard Oliver Cromwell, a Newent chemist (a direct descendant of the former Lord Protector) and F Bisco, Landlord of the King's Arms they set up the Zetland Lodge based on the King's Arms. The Landlord was responsible for the exclusion of intruders, and together with his wife for the provision of a meal for the membership. The Lodge later moved to Gloucester and is still operating today (39).

The Frowde family also owned Walden Court, Aylesmore and a parcel of land at Malswick, which, together with Hayes, were sold to John Leather Stelfox in 1902 for £9,000.

There were several Hengler circuses trading under the brand name "Hengler's" run by various members of the family at different times, and in the late Victorian times they frequently wintered their circus in the Newent area, at Little Cugley, and Ploddy House. Several members of the family came to live in the area (40).

The motor vehicle is a relatively modern invention in historical terms but it is interesting to know the types of car or motor-cycle that were in Newent at the beginning of the automobile age, and who owned them. Some of the records still survive (41).

In 1905 Mr T Grimke-Drayton of Clifford Manor had a green 3 seater 6.5 h.p. Humberette (Registration No AD 544). It seems he liked Humbers as in 1906 he bought a 16/20 h.p. green Landaulet (registration No AD 726) and then the following year acquired a 15 h.p. tourer.

In 1906 Edith de Vere Beechley, of The Holts, had a 20 h.p. red Humber Tourer (registration No AD 690).

Mrs Vine-Bradford, of Taynton, had a grey 12/16 h.p. Peugeot tourer in 1907 and Mr A Longden, of The Gables, rode a 2.25 h.p. F N motor-cycle (registration No AD 644) in 1911. The Post Master was someone who definitely needed transport and in 1912 Mr R H Bisco was riding a 5 h.p. AJS motor-cycle (registration No AD 492).

In 1912 Mr A McKilbin, of Kents Green House, had a 5/6 h.p. Clyno motor-cycle and side-car (registration No AD 875). The first motor car in Aston Ingham was a 4 litre, 4 cylinder Mercedes Benz owned by Walter Walters who later ran his own taxi business. During World War I Walter became a driver in the Royal Army Service Corps and later a Chauffeur for the Thomson family at Aston Ingham Court (26).

No doubt all of these vehicles would have been seen in and around Newent before the first World War.

In the late 1920s C & F Thurstons used a Willys Overland Whippet motor van for deliveries (24). This American vehicle was built by Crossley of Manchester under licence.

A number of people have started businesses in Newent that have helped to provide employment and build the reputation of the town. One company with Newent associations is G R Lane Health Products Ltd, of Gloucester. The company was founded by Mr Gilbert Lane and his wife Grace. Mr Lane was a teacher at Newent Grammar School in the 1930s, and his particular area of interest was the relationship between health and diet. He started a small business from home and wrote a series of booklets, "Common Sense Eating" for a variety of conditions. The most popular was "Common Sense Eating for Rheumatism". In 1938 Mr lane was offered a Head Teacher's post, but he decided to turn it down and concentrate on the growing herbal treatment business. Shortly afterwards the firm relocated to Gloucester and after several moves is now located in Sisson Road. They employ over 100 staff and one of their best known products is the decongestant "Olbas Oil" (37).

In early Victorian times William Hartland was a grocer in the town and also acted as a Bankers Agent until the work got too much for him. About this time the Gloucestershire Banking Company opened in Newent and on 16th March 1866 they bought the premises now occupied by Lloyds Bank, from Joseph Burgham. The building had previously been a boys school in the 1820s run by the Revd William Beale. A Mr Nash came to Newent in 1862/3 and became the first manager of the bank, being affectionately known as "Banker Nash". He was a keen farmer and farmed land at Conigree Court and later at Poykes Farm. Mr Nash would ride into Newent on his horse which he kept in a stable at the back of the bank. Because there was no access to the rear of the bank he would take his horse up the entrance steps and through the building. "Banker Nash" died in 1917 at Bury Bar House.

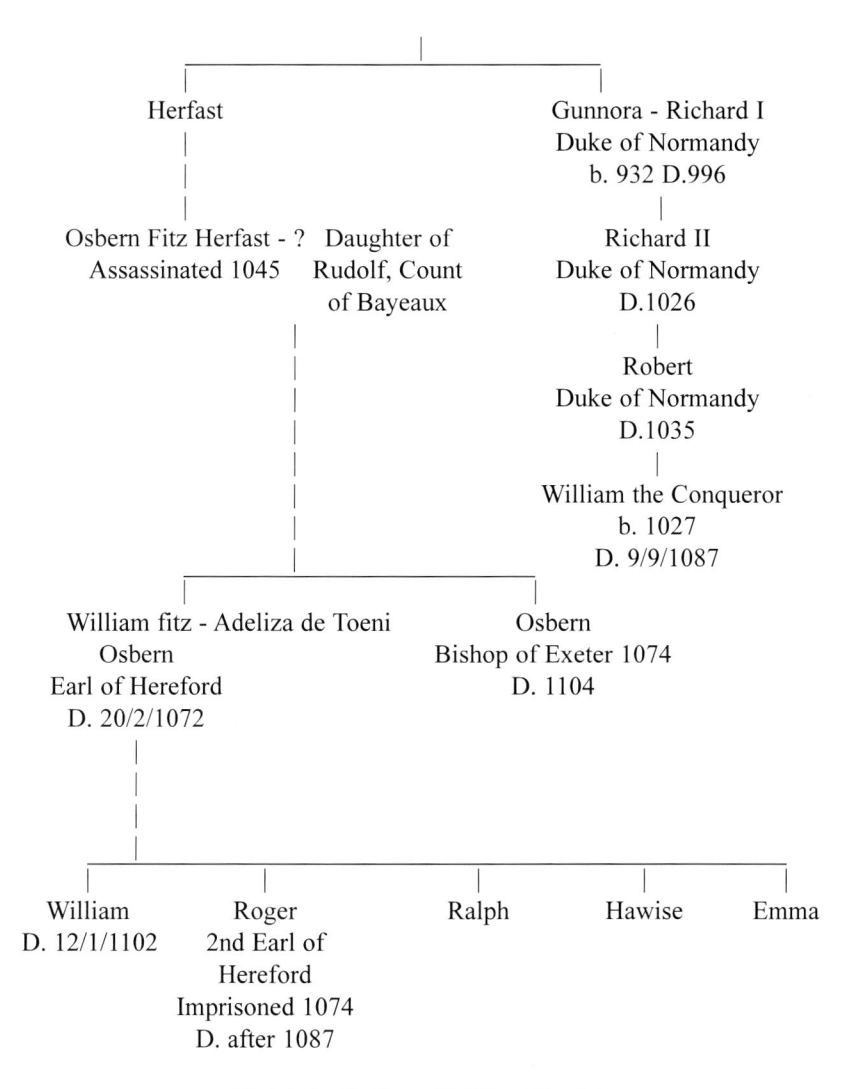

```
                          |
        _____
        |                                  |
     Herfast                         Gunnora - Richard I
        |                                Duke of Normandy
        |                                  b. 932 D.996
        |                                      |
  Osbern Fitz Herfast - ? Daughter of       Richard II
   Assassinated 1045     Rudolf, Count    Duke of Normandy
                         of Bayeaux            D.1026
                              |                  |
                              |               Robert
                              |           Duke of Normandy
                              |                D.1035
                              |                  |
                              |          William the Conqueror
                              |                b. 1027
                              |              D. 9/9/1087
                    _____|_____
                    |                   |
   William fitz - Adeliza de Toeni   Osbern
      Osbern                    Bishop of Exeter 1074
   Earl of Hereford                  D. 1104
   D. 20/2/1072
        |
        |
   _____|_____
   |          |            |         |          |
William      Roger        Ralph    Hawise      Emma
D. 12/1/1102 2nd Earl of
             Hereford
             Imprisoned 1074
             D. after 1087
```

Fig.30 Family Tree of William Fitz Osbern

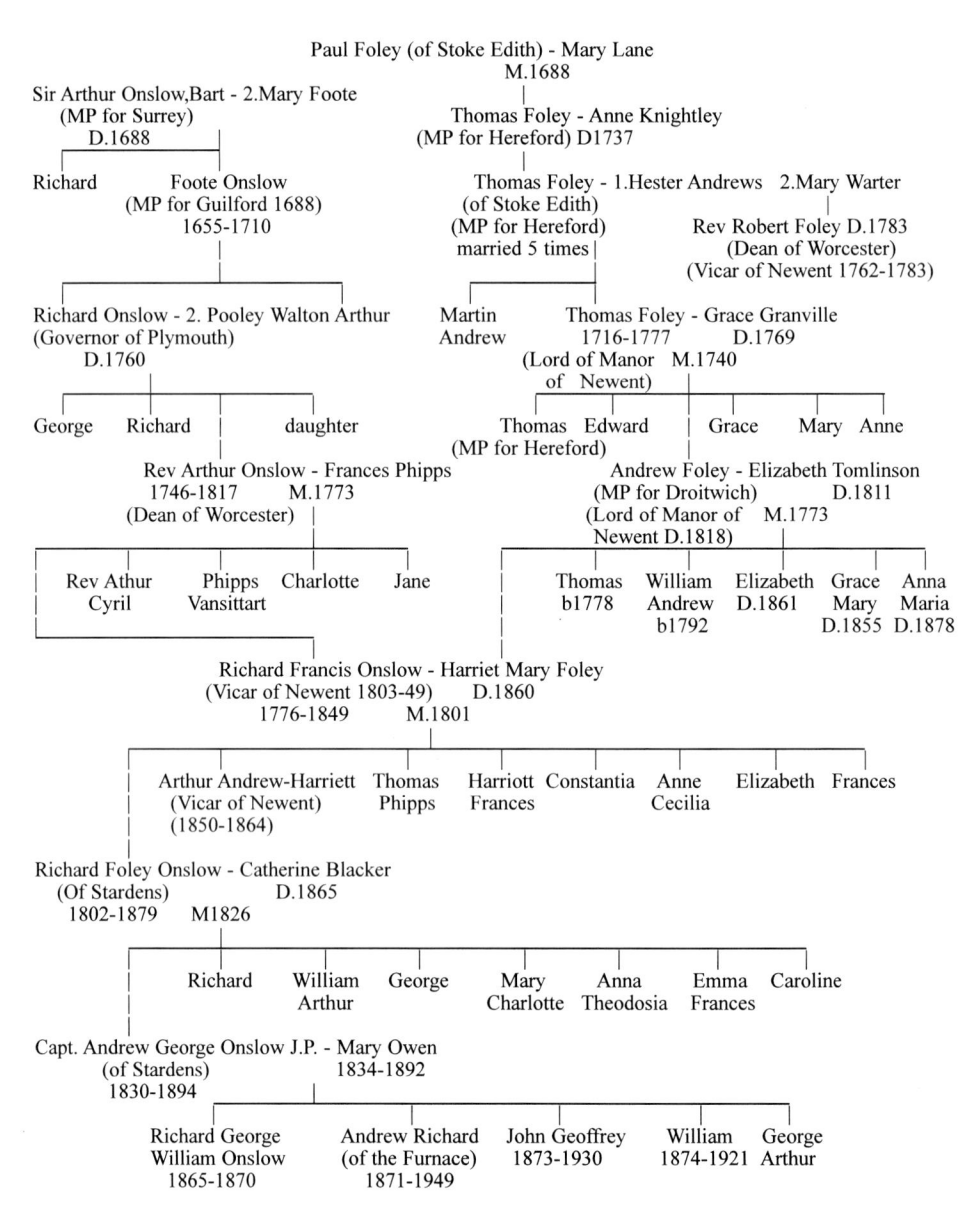

```
                         Paul Foley (of Stoke Edith) - Mary Lane
                                        M.1688
Sir Arthur Onslow,Bart - 2.Mary Foote      |
   (MP for Surrey)                   Thomas Foley - Anne Knightley
     D.1688                          (MP for Hereford) D1737
        |                                      |
Richard       Foote Onslow           Thomas Foley - 1.Hester Andrews  2.Mary Warter
              (MP for Guilford 1688)   (of Stoke Edith)                    |
                  1655-1710           (MP for Hereford)          Rev Robert Foley D.1783
                      |               married 5 times |           (Dean of Worcester)
                                                                (Vicar of Newent 1762-1783)
        |                                      |
Richard Onslow - 2. Pooley Walton Arthur    Martin      Thomas Foley - Grace Granville
(Governor of Plymouth)                      Andrew       1716-1777         D.1769
   D.1760                                              (Lord of Manor  M.1740
       |                                                 of  Newent)
                                                              |
George    Richard        daughter            Thomas   Edward        Grace    Mary  Anne
             |                                    (MP for Hereford)
          Rev Arthur Onslow - Frances Phipps        Andrew Foley - Elizabeth Tomlinson
             1746-1817        M.1773                (MP for Droitwich)      D.1811
          (Dean of Worcester) |                     (Lord of Manor of   M.1773
                                                      Newent D.1818)
                                                             |
  |         |         |         |              |         |          |        |       |
Rev Athur  Phipps   Charlotte  Jane          Thomas   William    Elizabeth Grace   Anna
  Cyril   Vansittart                         b1778    Andrew    D.1861    Mary    Maria
                                                       b1792             D.1855  D.1878
      |
         Richard Francis Onslow - Harriet Mary Foley
         (Vicar of Newent 1803-49)     D.1860
                 1776-1849         M.1801
                    |
  |        |               |           |         |          |         |         |
       Arthur Andrew-Harriett  Thomas    Harriott  Constantia  Anne    Elizabeth Frances
        (Vicar of Newent)     Phipps     Frances              Cecilia
         (1850-1864)
  |
Richard Foley Onslow - Catherine Blacker
  (Of Stardens)            D.1865
   1802-1879      M1826
       |
  |         |         |        |          |          |         |         |
         Richard    William  George     Mary       Anna      Emma    Caroline
                   Arthur                Charlotte Theodosia Frances
  |
Capt. Andrew George Onslow J.P. - Mary Owen
   (of Stardens)              1834-1892
    1830-1894
                    |
           |                |              |            |          |
       Richard George   Andrew Richard  John Geoffrey William   George
       William Onslow   (of the Furnace)  1873-1930    1874-1921 Arthur
         1865-1870        1871-1949

         Fig.31  Family tree showing the relationship of the Onslow
                 and Foley families and their connections with Newent
```

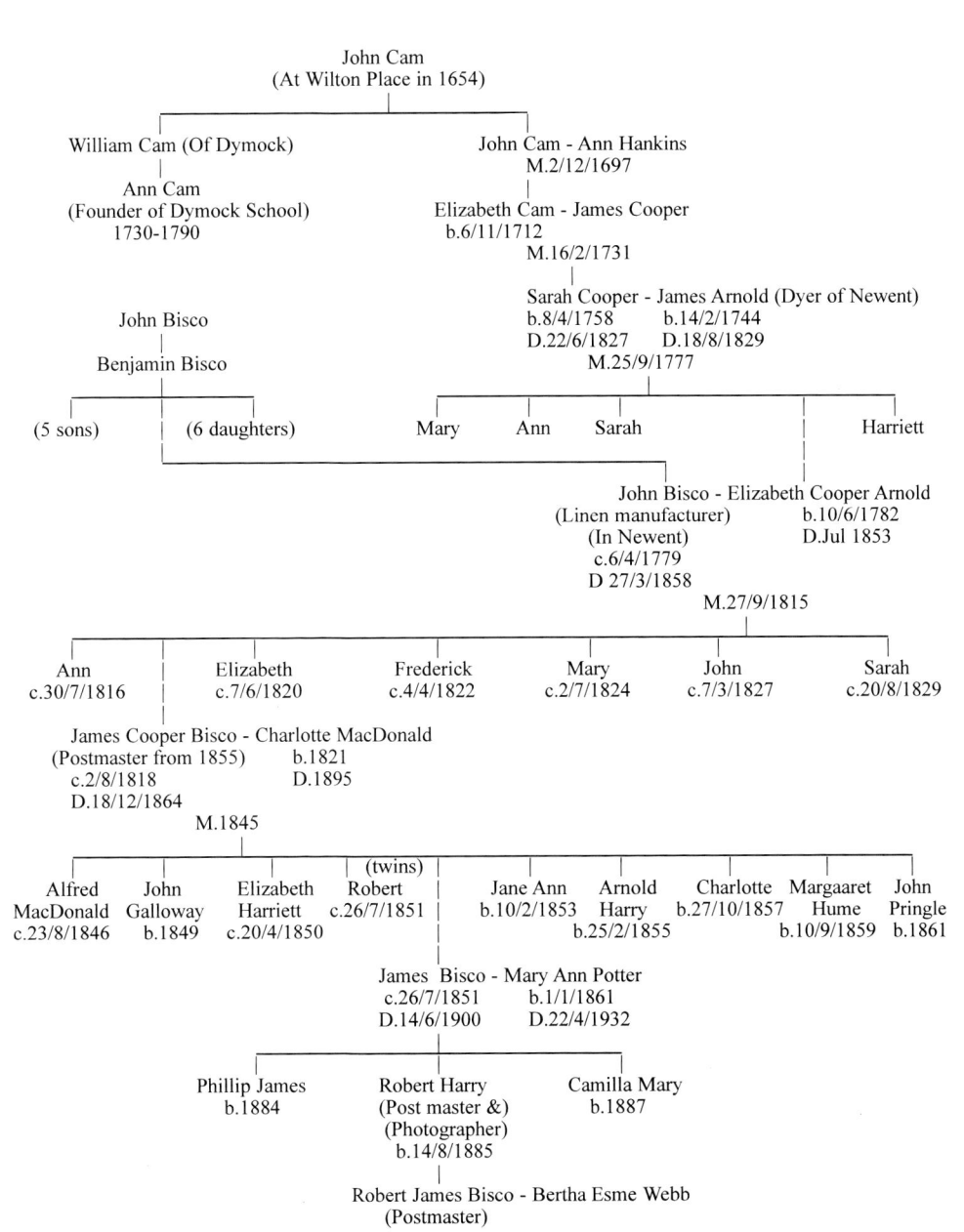

```
                                    John Cam
                            (At Wilton Place in 1654)
                                        |
        ┌───────────────────────────────┴───────────────────────────────┐
William Cam (Of Dymock)                                    John Cam - Ann Hankins
        |                                                      M.2/12/1697
    Ann Cam                                                         |
(Founder of Dymock School)                              Elizabeth Cam - James Cooper
    1730-1790                                                  b.6/11/1712
                                                               M.16/2/1731
                                                                    |
                                              Sarah Cooper - James Arnold (Dyer of Newent)
      John Bisco                                b.8/4/1758       b.14/2/1744
          |                                     D.22/6/1827      D.18/8/1829
     Benjamin Bisco                                   M.25/9/1777
          |
  ┌───────┴────────┐                       ┌───────┬───────┬────────────────┐
(5 sons)      (6 daughters)              Mary     Ann    Sarah           Harriett
                                                                            |
                                          John Bisco - Elizabeth Cooper Arnold
                                         (Linen manufacturer)    b.10/6/1782
                                            (In Newent)          D.Jul 1853
                                             c.6/4/1779
                                             D 27/3/1858
                                                        M.27/9/1815
     ┌────────┬──────────┬──────────┬──────────┬──────────┐
    Ann    Elizabeth  Frederick    Mary       John       Sarah
 c.30/7/1816 c.7/6/1820 c.4/4/1822 c.2/7/1824 c.7/3/1827 c.20/8/1829
     |
James Cooper Bisco - Charlotte MacDonald
(Postmaster from 1855)    b.1821
    c.2/8/1818            D.1895
    D.18/12/1864
            M.1845
     ┌──────┬──────────┬────────┬──────────┬────────┬──────────┬──────────┬────────┐
   Alfred   John    Elizabeth Robert  (twins) Jane Ann  Arnold  Charlotte Margaaret  John
 MacDonald Galloway  Harriett c.26/7/1851   b.10/2/1853 Harry  b.27/10/1857 Hume  Pringle
 c.23/8/1846 b.1849 c.20/4/1850                          b.25/2/1855        b.10/9/1859 b.1861
                                    |
                        James Bisco - Mary Ann Potter
                           c.26/7/1851    b.1/1/1861
                           D.14/6/1900    D.22/4/1932
                    ┌───────────┬──────────────┐
              Phillip James   Robert Harry   Camilla Mary
                b.1884       (Post master &)    b.1887
                              (Photographer)
                               b.14/8/1885
                                    |
                   Robert James Bisco - Bertha Esme Webb
                             (Postmaster)
```

Fig.32 Family tree of the Bisco family showing the relationship with Ann Cam of Dymock

References

1.	S Rudder	1779	History of Gloucestershire
2.	Anthony J Crump	1990	My ancestors came with the Conqueror
3.	Alfred S Ellis	1879	Transactions of the BGAS
4.	List of ministers		Newent Church
5.	Gloucestershire Subsidy Roll	1327	
6.	David Bick	1989	Crockett's Hole, The New Regard
7.	Frances Penney	1988	Churchyard Survey
8.	Nourse M.S.	c1720	GRO
9.	Bishop's Transcripts		GRO GDR/VI/164
10.	Parish Register		GRO P225 1/2
11.	Conder Document	1902	GRO D.412/Z3
12.	Dr K M Tomlinson	1995	The Edmonds Case
13.	David Bick	1992	Old Newent
14.	Gloucester Journal	1728	
15.	Gloucestershire Inquisitions Post Mortem	1236-1642	GRO ROL P3
16.	I E Gray, MBE,MA,FSA	1962	Newent Church Guide
17.	Michael Hooke	1999	The Oxenhall Anthology
18.	Daily Mail	1999	2nd February
19.	Newent Civic Society	2001	Newent Town Guide
20.	Foley Estate papers		Herefordshire Record Office
21.	Frances Penney	1988	St Marys Church Survey
22.	Visitation of Gloucestershire	1623	GRO
23.	Hereford Consistory Court		HDR 28 p283
24.	Mick Thurston	2001	A Brush With The Past
25.	Britton, Brayley & Brewer	1816	Beauties of England and Wales
26.	R E Bailey	2002	The History of the Bailey family
27.	Mrs D K Fallon	2001	Glos Fam. History Soc Mag Vol 90
28.	L Fullbrook-Leggatt	1952	Anglo-Saxon and Medieval Gloucester
29.	Tithe Assessment	1840	GRO D2710 ACC 4989
30.	Lists of male residents	1802-26	GRO D245 I/14-I/18
31.	Copy of Court Rolls	1396-1824	GRO D4277/1

32.	F J White	1953	The Hargreaves' Story
33.	Michael Hooke	2001	Private correspondence
34.	Survey of the Manor of Newent	1624	GRO Photocopy 914
35.	Will of John Nourse Morse	1830	GRO D1810/2
36.	J Douglas	1912	Historical Notes on Newent GRO PA225/2
37.	Janet Lane	2001	Company Information Sheet
38.	Jinny Marshall	2002	Notes on the Nourse family
39.	H F Cryer	2001	Private communication
40.	Eric Warde	2002	Notes on the Hengler family
41.	David Hales	2001	Private communication

6. War Prior to the 20th Century
Eric Warde

"The past is a foreign country, they do things differently there"
"The Go Between" published by L P Hartley 1999

While it is more than likely that "scraps" occurred both in and prior to the first millennium, little is known about Newent and war before the Norman invasion of England. Roman occupation of Town Farm, adjacent to today's Gloucester Road, is well established along with the earlier presence of Celts. How they both arrived is not known but mementos of their past have come to hand (chapter 1).

In the 10th century *"the Kingdom of Wessex gradually transformed itself, by conquest, into a kingdom of England"* (1). Whether Newent was involved in these struggles is unknown.

The Norman invasion of England in 1066 had a significant outcome on Newent, in particular the Church. The manner of the take-over is not on record except for the inclusion of Newent in the Botloe Hundred (2) and records from the Church of St Mary the Virgin, Newent's parish church (3). It is not known if the Normans took over the town without incident. Problems certainly arose in later years as a consequence of the assignment of Newent's church and priory to the Abbot and Convent of Cormeilles in Normandy by the conquerors at Hastings. This was later confirmed by Henry I, Henry II and Pope Alexander III (4). Henry I made the Church a cell of the prior and monks of Cormeilles but Edward III deprived Cormeilles of its authority over Newent, one of the consequences of his war with France.

Hockaday highlights the effect on St Mary's Church (3) of the Hundred Years War, started by Edward III in 1337 because of his claim to the French crown. It continued through the reigns of Richard II and the Lancastrian dynasty of Henry IV, V and VI until the forces of Henry VI were defeated at Castillion in 1453. However Calais was retained under successive English monarchs until 1558.

The Hundred Years War resulted in Edward III sequestering St Mary's Church and its assets. Hockaday lists instances throughout the reign of Edward III, *inter alia*, church appointments, the collection of tithes on his behalf and the appointment of his "favourites" to sinecures.

In 1415 the English army of Henry V engaged in a major battle with the French army at Agincourt. On Sunday 7th August Thomas Hooke and Sir Guy Whittington of Pauntley were with the King when they were attacked by a French scouting party. Together with a few others they succeeded in saving the

King and for his part Thomas was given Crookes Park Estate, near Newent where the family still reside (5). He was also given the King's sword. The legend is that Thomas Hooke held the sword to draw attention away from the King's disguise. The family has an ancient sword to commemorate the incident but the armourer at the Tower of London is doubtful that this is the original as it appears to be of a later date. Edward III had earlier appointed Robert Hoke as vicar of Newent, transferring him from Aldermaston (3).

The first war to go on record adjacent to Newent was the Battle of Tewkesbury, in May 1471, between the Houses of York and Lancaster. Newent is sufficiently close to Tewkesbury for its citizens to have probably had an unrecorded involvement.

The ascent of Henry VIII to the throne in 1509 was followed by a mooted further war with France. Consequently he launched an ambitious survey of both fiscal resources and armour availability in the spring of 1522. The town of Newent, listed under the Botloe Hundred, made an extensive survey and listed men, their wealth and their weapons, typically bows, arrows, gauntlets, swords, daggers, glaives, sailets, etc. (6).

Gloucestershire Military Survey 1522, Town of Newent

The Master of the College of the blessed Mary of Fotheringhay is Lord of vill and worth in temporalities £50 and in the rectory and other spiritualities, £34.

William Rudhale serjeant at law is steward.

Richard Crons	40s	£6 13s 8d	glaive [type of broadsword]
Thomas Dewcy	20s	£4	glaive, sword
John Keys		20s	
John Cuffe		£6 13s 4d	
Richard Clerk		£6 13s 4d	bow, arrows, sword & dagger
Walter Giles		£6 13s 4d	sword & dagger
Richard Wode		£40	sword
John Knollys sen		£3	glaive
John Knollys jun		20s	
John Pace		£4	glaive, sword, dagger
Thomas Beke	20s	20s	glaive
Alexander Hall		20s	glaive, dagger
Roger Hatton		40s	glaive
Thomas Beche		53s 4d	glaive, dagger
Thomas Clerk			bow and arrows
Richard Shawe			bow and arrows
Thomas Swayn			bow and arrows
William Pelley		26s 8d	

Further lists exist for the outlying tithings of Newent

In 1543 money was collected by the Church to fund the war with the Turks but donors are not listed (4). The culmination of this war was the destruction of the Muslim fleet at Lepanto in 1571 (7).

Some 65 years later, in 1608, with James I reigning, a further survey was implemented. Cash was not involved on this occasion but comment is made regarding the capabilities of the men listed and their station in life (8). The following is the list for Newent :-

Newent Burrowe
Wherof Sr Edward Winter Knight is Lord

Richard English, gent, 1.m
Arnolld Kyrke, gent. 1.m
John Williams als Baker, yeoman 3.p
Thomas Wall, yeoman 2.m
Thomas Addys, yeoman 2.m
John Wilse, yeoman 2.ca
Thomas Hill, yeoman 2.ca
Anthony Hill, wever 2.p
Thomas George, wever 2.m
Thomas Cottrell his servant 1.ca
Samuell Hope, husbandman 2.py
James Kynett, fletcher 3.py
John Lambe, yeoman 2.py
Robert Wilmot 2.m
John Pride, mercer 2.ca
Thomas Coninge, taylor 2.ca
Robert Upton, smith 3.p
John Upton his brother
Willm Monday, laborer 2.ca
Thomas Hill, wever 1.ca
Willm Quarrell, victualler 2.p
Willm Browninge, labourer 2.p
Raynold Williams, victualler 2.p
Willm Oliver, shoomaker 2.p
Thomas Oliver his son 1.ca
Richard Salaway, wever 1.ca
John Dobyns, jun, glover 2.ca
Thomas Hill, laborer 1.py
Willm Wolfe, sadler 2.ca

Thomas Jones, taylor 1.py
John Wheeler, carpenter 2.ca
Phillip Mayowe, couper 3.p
Roger Morgan, laborer 2.ca
Richard Cuffe, laborer 1.py
Richard Forty, laborer 1.ca
James Bower, carpenter 2.p
John Merricke his servant 1.py
Willm Coninge, taylor 2.ca
Daniell Drewe, taylor 2.m
James Hardwicke his servant 1.ca
John Readinge, milner 2.p
Edmond Sclicer, glover 2.ca
Walter Dowen, wever 2.py
John Hooper, wever 2.m
John Hewlet, laborer 2.p
Willm Pylmore, carpenter 3
John Yonge, jun, laborer 1.ca
John Danber, laborer 2.m
Anthony Band, smith 2.py
Ralph Carpenter, laborer 2.py
Thomas Watts, shoomaker 2.p
Willm Hayward, jun, taylor 2.ca
Thomas Warne, wever 1.m
Willm Reece, wever 2.ca
Allexander Mornington, milner
Robert Burton, brasier 2.p
Richard Elton, taylor 2.ca
Willm Greene, butcher 2.m

Arnold Crocket, tucker 1.m
Guy Bower, butcher 1.py
John Revell, mercer 2.y
Thomas Curtys, glover 3.py
Richard Clarke 1.p) shoomakers
Phillip Clarke 1.ca) servants to
              Willm Wathen
John Bullocke, husbandman 3.py
John Bower, butcher 1.ca
John White, butcher 1.ca
Willm Lingall, butcher
Guy Mayowe, husbandman 2.p
John Pickthorne, wyerdrawer 2.py
David Pritchard, laborer 2.ca
Guy Knowles, glover 2.py
Nicholas Bower, shoomaker 2.p
Ralph Batlyn, glover 2.py
Richard Halle, laborer 1.m
Roger Puckmore, wever 2.p
Thomas Osborne, laborer 2.py
Samuell Crocket, smith 1.ca
Willm Jenkins, haberdasher 1.m
John Hope, wever 1.ca) servants
Guy Hill, wever 1.ca) of Roger
John Wyet, wever 1.ca) Hill
Willm Lambe, glover 2.m
Richard Pryde, husbandman 3.py

Peter Tosier, butcher 2.m
John Cooke, jun, shoomaker 1.ca
Anthony Meeke, tucker 1.ca
Thomas Clarke, laborer 1.p
John Murell, laborer 1.py
Charles Guill'm, tannor 2.ca
Willm George, laborer 2.m
Willm Wilson, shoomaker 1.py
Willm Turbell, wever 2.m
John Lucker his servant 1.py
John Walle, jun, smith 1,ca
Willm Hayward, sen, taylor 2.ca
John Hartland his servant 1.ca
John Pytt, wever 1.m
Willm Powell his servant 1.ca
George Baker, sawier 3.py
Silvester Farre, shoomaker 3.py
Thomas Porter, laborer 1.py
John Walle, smith 1.m.tr
John Coxe 2.m.tr
Thomas Hill, mason 2.m.tr
Robert Hankins 2.p.tr
John Wyman 2.ca.tr
Thomas Longstaffe 2.p.tr

      Inhabytants chardged with the findinge of
        Armour not before mentioned

Thomas Walle aforesaid and Robert parsons have betwene them one musket fur'
John Astman the elder unable in body hath a musket fur'
Thomas Hill aforesaid yeom. John Drewe and William Hayward have betwene them one musket fur'
Raynolld Dobins gent hath one corslet fur'

      The numbers and letters after each name have the following meanings:-
1. = aged about 20 2. = aged about 40   3. = aged between 50 and 60
p. = of the tallest stature fit to make a pikeman
m. = of middle stature fit to make a musketeer
ca. = of lower stature fit to serve with a Calyver

py. = of the meanest stature fit for a pyoner, or of little other use
tr. = a trained soldier
sub. = a subsidy man
    There are other lists for the outlying tithings of Newent parish.

    Newent Church records for March 1613 also list an *"Assessment for armour"* carried out in 1613, some six years subsequent to the survey demanded by James I (3). The Newent vicar, Nathaniel Dod, is listed as having *"a Corset Furnished"*.

    The next, and final, English Civil War (1642-1648) arose from the actions of Charles I and Oliver Cromwell. One of the battles of this war was the Siege of Gloucester. Prince Rupert, a leading Royalist and nephew of Charles, not only had an outpost on May Hill but he also lodged in Newent. (9) The Royalist, Col Mynne, routed a force of Parliamentarians with a flank attack at Common Fields. Shot from cannon located adjacent to Conigree Court fell in the town. The Church spire was hit and residents were evacuated to high ground at Stardens. Col Mynne is said to have lodged at today's Black Dog Inn.(9)

    Between the Census returns of 1861 and 1891 (10) a Greenwich Pensioner, presumably the Naval equivalent of a Chelsea Pensioner, resided in Pool Hill. The 1861 return shows 53 year old Thomas Rodgers and his 39 year old wife, Elizabeth, both of Newent, who were born in Pauntley, as residing in Pool Hill. The exact address is difficult to establish, but they were interred in Pauntley Churchyard in February and March 1895. (11)

    The final event of the 19th century was the so-called Boer War. A magnificent stained glass window was installed in St Mary's Church by Andrew Knowles to commemorate the return of his son, Captain James Knowles, 15th Hussars, from the Boer War.

References

1)	Richard Fletcher Allen Lane	2002	Bloodfeud, Murder and Revenge in Anglo-Saxon England
2)	John Moore	1987	Domesday Book, Gloucesteshire
3)	Hockaday Abstracts, Gloucester Library		Vol 292/3
4)	Document reference HTE 212 Ibid		
5)	P Townsend	1969	Burkes Landed Gentry
6)	R W Hoyle	1993	The Military Survey of Gloucestershire
		1522	Bristol and Glos Arch Soc
7)	Tariq Ali, Verso	2002	The Clash of Fundamentalists
8)	John Smith	1980	Men and Armour for Gloucestershire in 1608
9)	Wyedean Tourist information Sheet No 23	1974	
10)	Census returns	GRO	
11)	Document P246 IN 1/6	GRO	

7. Newent in the Hockaday Abstracts
Eric Warde

Frank Step Hockaday (1855-1924) was a Lydney based antiquarian who started to research a history of the town in 1908. He discovered a dusty pile of church records in the Probate Office that caused him to learn Medieval Church Latin and embark on the task of examining similar Church Records across the whole of Gloucestershire. He prepared some 500 sets of abstracts, of which that for Newent is contained in volumes 292/293.

They are available in both the Gloucestershire Record Office (originals) and the Local Studies Section of the Brunswick Road Branch of the County Library Service (micro-film).

The following are brief notes in chronological order as they relate to Newent:-

1216   Henry III extends the lands of Newent Priory
1226   Henry grants Newent an annual fair
1253   Royal grant to the Abbot for a weekly Tuesday Market and a fair on the Feast Day of St Peter (June 29th) and the following two days
1283   Concern about oak trees at Killycote [Kilcot]
1297   Inquisition on lands of Robert Stallinge
1299   Roger called Goye instituted by the Bishop of Worcester
1301   Hugh de la Grave installed as Newent Priest by the Abbot of Cormeilles
1305   Writ to take proof of age of John - son and heir of Robert of Stallinge
1319   Royal charter to the Abbot for a weekly Friday market and a yearly market on the Feast of St Phillip and James (May 3) and two days after
1337   The Abbot ordered to pay Edward III 65d due on the Nativity of the Virgin last (September 8th) and 10 marks to William Trussel in part satisfaction of 1,000 granted by Edward for services on either side of the sea.
1338   The Prior paid 65d to Edward
1342   Appointment of Collectors of Arrears. Edward presents the church at Suckleye to Newent. [In 1341 the Register of Wulstan De Bransford, Bishop of Worcester refers to the King holding *"the temporalities of Newent Priory by reason of the war with France"*]
1343   Appointment of Walter Billyng to Newent Vicarage. Dues collectors appointed. Edward appoints Richard Batchelor to St Ethelbert's, Hereford on the demise of Roger of Hompton (war with France)
1344   Edward appoints inquisitors to establish the value of lands and benefices of the Priory of Newent. Benefices exchanged. Rent

	payments to Edward overdue due to the destruction of Cormeilles by the King's adversaries. Gifted Suckleye to Ralph of Brantyngham. [The Register of the Bishop of Worcester lists a writ summoning the Rector of Suckley *"to render 32 marks (£21-6s-8d) arrears of an annual pension of 4 marks (£2-13s-4d) which he unjustly detains*]
1345	Royal presentation of Newent to Reginald Mile due to the demise of Hugh de la Grave.
1347	Exchequer ordered to call Queen Isabel to explain why rents from Southampton are not paid. Edward does not intend to diminish future rents because of the war with France. Collectors of arrears of Priory appointed.
1349	John of Lye appointed to Lynton
1353	Edward presented Martelle [Martley], Diocese of Worcs., to Newent Priory.
1357	Edward presented Suckleye, Diocese of Worcs., to Newent Priory
1361	Inquisition into the execution of the will of Thomas of Bradestan
1363	Exchange Robert of Retford, Vicar of Newent, with John Lyleye, Rector of Utley (?)
1368	Conditional Royal Consent for John of Fever to cross to Calais
1370	Exchange of benefits - Reginald Mile to Newent/John Lilie to Lydyard Milicent. The Abbot of Cormeilles nominated John Faber, Prior of Newent as his attorney for one year. The King presented the Church of Marleleue to Newent.
1380	John Wynter, Parson of Lambourne, paid £4 to the King on the marriage of Robert, son and heir of William Wynter.
1382	John Devereux, King's Knight, petitioned for the grant of the Manor of Newent. Richard Fretk appointed to Suckilloy Church.
1385	The Manors/Priories of Fromton, Dorset and Newent, Glos, 350 marks overdue. Edward granted them to John together with place at Standard so that they may better maintain their rank
1390	Edward presents Michael Walden, Chaplain, to be Vicar of Newent, Diocese of Herefords.
1391	Edward gifts Marteley, Diocese of Worcs., to Newent
1393	Edward exchanges Michael Hooke, Vicar of Aldermaston, Diocese of Salisbury, with Reginald Clifton, Vicar of Newent.
1406	Dean of the Forest ordered to relax the sentence of suspension still in force against the Churches of Newent and Dymock
1431	Guy Dobyn pardoned for not appearing before the Justices of the Bench in connection with a debt of 40/- owed to Robert Cappes.

Similarly Richard Norman, gent and the Dean and Chaplaincy of Lichfield.
Richard Norman of Newent, pardoned for outlawry
Simon Preutout, citizen and Waxchandler of London, brother of the late John Preutout, citizen and Draper of London, pleaded that he had paid Robert Trees, citizen and Mercer of London, executor of John's will, 104/-. Accepted.

1434 Richard Norman, gent of Newent, was pardoned for problems arising from a debt of £29-6s-8d due to the Dean and Chapter of Lichfield.

1435 John Hoke replaced Robert Hooke as vicar of Newent.

1441 William Westbury, William Yelveston, Miles Soull, Robert Clynton and John Aberhare ordered to deliver Tilmere of Yartleton, in the Parish of Newent, Husbandman, to Hereford Gaol.

1445 A series of adultery/fornication trials run through until 1454 and very little else is reported. Verdicts vary from not guilty to whippings, fustigations and penances.
Phillip Staur and William of Aure accused John Parsons, of Newent, of breaking his word and committing perjury. The hearing was transferred to Taynton and then to Ross-on-Wye as Parsons complained it would not be safe for him to appear in Newent. The case was later transferred to Dene where it appears to have petered out. Concurrently Parsons was sued by John Smayer and again the case was discontinued.

1446 The executors of John Cowmeadowe, - John Bokland, Cowmeadowe's son and his relict, Joan - paid the fee to enable the will to be proved, by Joan some four months later.

1446-56 Records mostly adultery and related cases and testamentary pleas

1448 Sir Reginald Kawnot of Newent sued Robert Taylor of Oxenhall for breach of faith and perjury. The case was suspended.

1454 Richard Hardy and John Beche, churchwardens of Newent, sued Thomas Colwalle of Newent for subtraction of ecclesiastical rights. The parties agreed to arbitrate.

1456 John Baldwyne sued Richard Wallas Hille, John Walle, William Gunne of Upton and John Walden of Newent for perjury and breach of faith. Eventually they were ordered to come to an agreement.

1459 John Hoke, Perpetual Vicar of Newent, sued Henry Chue of Mitchel Dene and John Walker of Newent for unpaid tithes. The defendants failed to appear.

1468-1507 A number of adultery and probate cases recorded

1507	Alice Cam of Newent sued William Adus for failure to honour his contract to marry her. He agreed that he offered her marriage eight year ago but established that she had a prior contract with John Cole of Much Marcle. He later agreed to marry her within a fortnight after Easter under threat of ex-communication. A similar case between William Watts and Cecily Cowmeadow alleged a prior contract with Richard Pole.
1508	Roger Throw of Newent summoned due to his failure to attend church on Sundays and Feast Days. He confessed.
1509	Sir Roger Wattis, Chaplain of Newent, charged with intimacy with Joan, servant of William Hooper. Case dismissed.
1524	Master Thomas Byrde STB admitted as Perpetual Vicar of Newent by the Bishop of Hereford.
1526	John Dobyns of Newent, a student at Oxford, obtained a dismissory note from the Bishop of Hereford for all orders, major and minor, to be conferred on him by any Catholic Bishop provided no canonical impediments stood in the way.
1529	The Bishop of Hereford commanded the Vicar of Newent not to defer solemnization of marriage between Richard Carn of All Michael's, Worcs., (banns called twice), and Margery Bromwiche of Newent (banns called twice).
1537	Sir John Warde admitted as Perpetual Vicar of Newent due to the death of Thomas Byrde.
1538	Letters of administration for the will of Elen Dobyns granted to her lawful son, Guy.
1543	Names of Churchwardens and amounts collected for the war against the Turks, but no list of names.
1547	Master of the College of Fordinghaye, alias Fotheringhaye, Northants., appointed to the Lordship of the Manor of Newent, and the Rectory and Advowson of the Vicarage of Newent valued at two hundred, four score, five pounds, fourteen shillings, eleven pence, one half penny and one farthing (£285-14s-11.3/4d).
1547	Absolution of the will of Richard Hooke by his sons, Christopher and Guy.
1548	A note about Newent being a market town, visited by many people including youth, and the need to *"establish a teacher and erect a scole for the better and more Godlye bryngynge up of the same youthe"*. The churchwardens and other parishioners claimed that the vicar was not resident and further claimed that he had not distributed XLth pence

1762	Robert Foley DD, Trinity College, Cantab. Rector of Kingham, Oxon., valued at £17-11s-8d, seal value £200, requested a transfer to the Vicarage of Newent -£23/£250. This was granted and instituted on the presentation of Thomas Foley Esq of Stoke Edith.
1779	Certification to the Bishop of Gloucester that some of His Majesty's dissenting subjects; William Beale, John Prosser, William Morgan, Samuel Washburton. John Malvern and Thomas Wood wish to hold meetings for the worship of God in the dwelling house of Mary Ballinger. Registered.
1782	The Bishop of Gloucester sequestered tithes etc of the Vicarage of Newent that had been vacated by death and transferred them to Rowland Rogers, clerk and John Carless and William Hatton, churchwardens. John Foley MA instituted as vicar of Newent on the death of Robert Foley, presented by the Hon. Andrew Foley of Litttle Hatton, Oxon.
1792	Culver Street dissenters' house registered in the names of Richard Cue, Mickel Baldwin, - Langham, Danniel Baldwin, Benjamin Acton, George Jones and James Rosser.
1795	Some 30 years earlier Pickle Ash estate had been purchased to augment Minsterworth Vicarage. William Gyllet, clerk and vicar of Minsterworth petitioned, due to the poor condition of the buildings and the high cost of restoration to demolish the buildings. This was agreed.
1803	Richard Francis Onslow MA, Clerk instituted as vicar of Newent on the death of John Foley, presented by the Hon. Andrew Foley.
1804	Lambeth petitioned to allow Richard Francis Onslow to hold both Kidderminster (£30-15s-0d & £500), and Newent (£23 & £50) at the same time. Kidderminster is less than 30 miles from Newent.
1805	Petition of Hon. Andrew Foley accepted. A Dissenter's petition by Thomas Dayer, William Davis, George Bradley, William Garfield, I M Byron, R Connibere, Thomas Fearnley, and Samuel Jeffs to use a house, the property of Thomas Warne, for divine service was granted.
1808	A Dissenter's petition by James Brettell, William Gatfield, Charles Malvern, Elizabeth Warne, Sarah Peters, and Leda Hope to use Thomas Warne's house in Culver Street was granted. Richard Francis Onslow was licenced to be resident outside the Vicarage for two years as it is unfit for occupation and his chosen house is both more commodious for his family and more convenient for the performance of his duties as it is nearer the Church. (The Old Court).

1813	William Beale licensed as a curate
1816	Licence for Richard Francis Onslow to reside in the Court House was extended. It enjoys a common wall with the churchyard. Dissenters were allowed to use the house of William Nelms.
1817	Thomas Davis was appointed to Oxenhall, Pauntley and Upleadon.
1818	Consent for Richard Francis Onslow MA to live in the house belonging to Hon. Andrew Foley extended for three years. Richard Allen, a dissenting Minister from Gloucester, was allowed to use the house owned by Daniel Robins, cordwainer, for religious purposes.
1819	Thomas Davis, the vicar of Oxenhall, Pauntley and Upleadon lives in Newent. William Williams, dissenting Minister of Ryecroft, allowed to use the house occupied by Samuel Baldwin, woodcutter. John Williams of Ryecroft allowed to use the house of Samuel Reynolds, in Culver Street.
1820	The Methodist Minister from the Ledbury Circuit, Richard Allen, allowed to use the premises of John Davies at Bran Green. Dissenter William Nelmes, labourer, of Malswick, allowed to use a room in the possession of William Richardson. Dissenter Thomas Wood, labourer, of Bran Green, allowed to use his dwelling house.
1821	R F Onslow MA, Archdeacon of Worcs., and vicar of Newent, granted a further three years extension to reside at the Old Court.
1822	Thomas Davis still vicar at Oxenhall, Pauntley and Upleadon. William Beale, clerk and curate at Newent, granted a licence by Edward Thomas March Phillips, the Gloucester Diocese Chancellor, for marriages.
1824	R F Onslow's licence further extended. Dissenter George Jones, Minister of Gloucester, was granted a licence to use premises occupied by Benjamin Deakins. Also James Webb, labourer, allowed to use the house occupied by Benjamin Hodges, labourer. Also Robert Winfield, Minister of Gloucester, was licensed for a chapel, owned by James Webb of Malswick.
1827	R F Onslow's licence further extended. James Archibald licensed as a curate, £105
1828	Dissenter G H Roper Curzon granted a licence to use the house of Mary Drinkwater.

1829	Dissenter John Glass, Minister, granted a licence to use the house of John Tranter.
1830	R F Onslow's licence further extended.
1835	Dissenter Thomas Kington, of Castle Frome, Herefordshire, was granted a licence to use the Bran Green premises occupied by William Davis, and for the premises at Bottelloes Green occupied by John Layton.
1836	R F Onslow's licence further extended. Dissenter Thomas Kington licensed to use the premises of Richard Clwd at Kents Green and of William Peart at Kilcot.
1839-43	R F Onslow's licence extended annually.
1844	Dissenter John Hyett of the City of Gloucester, allowed to use the School Room, used by Abraham Lande, Teacher, and owned by William Nicholas, carpenter.
1845	R F Onslow's licence further extended. John James MA, appointed Stipendiary Curate, at £90 and to reside at the Glebe House.
1847	R F Onslow's licence further extended.
1848	Howard Lewis Parry BA, appointed Stipendiary Curate at £94-10s plus surplice £20 and to reside in the Glebe House. George Bowen Jones appointed Assistant Stipendiary Curate at £50 and to reside in any house in the Parish.
1850	Arhur Andrew Onslow BA, presented as vicar of Newent by Elizabeth Foley, spinster, of Newport House, Patroness. Howard Lewis Parry BA, to serve as curate at £125 plus surplice £20 George W Jones to serve as Stipendiary Curate at £80 and reside in the Parish.
1856	James Acton Butt BA appointed curate of Newent at £50 and to reside in the Parish. Charles Glynn MA, appointed Stipendiary Curate at £80 and surplice of £20, to reside in the Parish.
1858	Donald Stewart appointed curate.
1865	Patron Richard Foley Onslow presented Frederick Wood MA as vicar of Newent on the death of Arthur Andrew Onslow.
1877	Benjamin Ruck Keene, clerk and vicar of Newent, residing at Glebe House, absent due to illness.

8. The Doctors of Newent 1685-1912
Dr K M Tomlinson

In Medieval England the healing arts were concentrated in, and supervised by, the Church. At the Reformation, with the closing of the monasteries, clerics with some knowledge (be it only theoretical) were forced to practice their arts elsewhere. Problems arose in that gynaecological and surgical conditions were unsuitable for clerics, and physicians were unable to deal with such patients. It was therefore left to midwives and barber-surgeons to exercise their skills independently.

Away from main centres there was a shortage of doctors, so such work in the village or small town was left to folk healers with their wide knowledge of herbal medicines.

The first attempt at regulation of the profession came in 1518, when King Henry VIII founded the Royal College of Physicians, the object being to safeguard the status of Physicians in the City of London. It was further intended that the College should be a licensing and examining body. Apothecaries were legalized in 1643.

The licensing for Physicians in Tudor times was only available to graduates of Oxford or Cambridge, and consisted of an oral examination, conducted in Latin. All it achieved was to demonstrate that the candidate had knowledge of the ancient masters, and as such was considered fit to supervise surgeons and apothecaries, as well as oversee the quality of drugs supplied from the apothecary shops. It was not until the mid-19th century that an ordered pattern of science-orientated teaching was established.

The most important event in British medicine occurred in the Medical Act of 1858, which established the General Medical Council, to control admission to the Medical Register. The first official Medical Register was published in July 1859, featuring 15,000 names. The number subsequently rose to 23,000 in 1880, 50,000 in 1924, and 90,000 in 1958. The number of doctors on the register now (2001) stands at almost 200,000.

While basic details of those practicing in Newent since 1859 can readily be obtained from the official register, it has required a search of parish records and contemporary correspondence, a task which this author has endeavoured to do over the last fifty years, in order to glean more detailed information. The results of these searches are given chronologically.

| 1685 | John Billingsley | Clerk and Physician | Died |
| 1689 | Phillip Clarke | Barber Chirugeon | Married |

1725	William Price	Barber Surgeon	Buried
1728	John Cole	Surgeon	Died, aged 28
1744	John Barnes	Surgeon	Died
1745	John Bower	Surgeon	Buried
1745	William Wood, junr	Surgeon	
1767	Gilbert Jones	Apothecary	Buried
1776	James Richardson	Vide marble monument in the chancel of Newent Church inscribed :- *"In memory of James Richardson, late of this Town, Surgeon and Apothecary. His skill and judgement in his profession is established by a long series of extensive practise. His superior understanding and pleasant conversation greatly enhanced his society and friendship while his humane and liberal heart gained him universal esteem"*	
		Dr Richardson lived in Broad Street, now the site of Cost Cutter Store and, with his son, established the Spa and Pump Room at Hill Top, Newent.	
1792	Charles Aycrigg	Surgeon	
1815	George Hollister	Late Surgeon R.N.	Died 1861
1822	Dr Lovesay		
1840	Henry Vyner Ellis		
1857	Edmund Deane		
1859	William Douce Cattle	Late Surgeon, Turkish Cavalry Regt. Lived in the Red House, now Newent Post Office. In this year were also practising Drs Gabb, Ellis, Cooke, and Hollister.	
1867	Matthew Bass Smith	In 1873, as a result of *"infamous professional misconduct"* his name was erased from the medical register, but was restored in 1884.	
1870	John Rudge	Of Great Boulsdon Villa	
1872	James Cadle		
1872	James Hamilton Scott	Lived at The Villa, Newent, now Cleeve House	
1873	John Charles Cooke	Of the Porch House	Died

1874	William Norris Marshall	Died at the age of 74 at the Red House, now Newent Post Office, having practised medicine there for 38 years until his death in 1912.
1877	A note from the private diary of the Reverend Newbolt, Vicar of Dymock :-	

"Monday, April 16th. A sad accident today in the village. A Newent doctor was thrown from his horse in a state of drunkenness, and seriously hurt.

Tuesday April 17th. The poor man died today, never had been conscious"

His name is not known.

1881   Frank Smelt

It is unfortunate that contemporary records reveal few personal details of the various medical practitioners and their talents, but it can be observed from the above list that Newent was well served medically. Indeed, during some periods the number of medical men actually practising at any one time was disproportionately large for the size of the population.

One story that has emerged concerns Dr Hollister who lived for a time in the building that is now Lloyds Bank. During his life he was "badly done" by the lawyer Edmund Edmonds of the Pigeon House. When Dr Hollister died in 1861 (aged 72) according to his will he was to be buried in the Congregational Church burial ground in front of lawyer Edmonds' window, and a tomb erected so that when he looked through the window he would have a qualm of conscience for the injury he had done Dr Hollister. The very large memorial is still a striking feature of the grave yard.

Sources Parish Records
   Gloucester Journal
   Bigland's Monuments
   Maud Marshall's Diaries
   Miscellaneous contemporary correspondence

9. Law and Order

Transportees from Newent to Australia 1783-1842
Dr K M Tomlinson

Picture if you will the scene at one of the twice yearly held Assizes in Gloucester (either Lent or Summer) in the late 1700 s.

The verdict had been arrived at and those guilty led back into the court. The Judge in scarlet, flanked by the Javelin men, addresses each in turn and this was the awesome sentence :-

> *" It is therefore ordered and adjudged by this court that you be transported upon the seas to such a place as His Majesty, by advice from his Privy Council, I shall think fit to direct and appoint for the term of your natural life"*

The sentence could also be 7 years or 14 years depending on the offence, but in any case, however short, the shock of such a sentence was dreadful to the ears of the accused and his family waiting in the court. It must have sounded like a one way trip to the edge of the world; 15,000 miles over tempestuous and uncharted seas but, between 1783 and 1842, no less than 19 persons from Newent heard those very words addressed to them.

To understand the significance of this penalty of transportation it is necessary to know something about Crime and Punishment in the 18th and 19th centuries. Until the Restoration (1660) punishment in England was cut and dried. If guilty of a felony or treason the law directed death. Nothing else. This was not a manifestation of blood lust but there was really no alternative in law. The mode of death however was varied according to the type of crime.

For example the punishments prescribed for treason sought to combine the maximum of pain and ignominy first, hence the drawing of the person to the place of execution on a hurdle. Then followed the barbaric hanging, being cut down while alive to be disembowelled, castrated and then beheaded.

The period being dealt with, 1780-1842, produced a variety of punishments other than capital punishment e.g. fines, whipping, and the pillory, but due to the increasing lawlessness occasioned by the war, agricultural collapse and ruined harvest, there were on the statute book 223 offences punishable by death. These included murder, sheep or horse stealing, forgery etc. Having said this, of the 123 people hanged in Gloucestershire between 1786 and 1836 the majority were not for murder.

Reason slowly prevailed and fell back upon an alternative which had in fact been on the statute book since 1598. This was exile. This allowed that dangerous or incorrigible rogues could be sent to the galleys for life or transported to any place beyond the seas assigned for that purpose by the Privy Council.

Whilst originally this meant the East Indies or America, these areas became closed during and after the war of Independence in 1776 so an alternative had to be found in a hurry. Prisons such as they were, e.g. Westgate in Gloucester, were inadequate and filled to overflowing. The alternative devised by the Government was an institution known colloquially as "The Hulks".

An act was passed in 1780 whereby those sentenced to transportation could be *"kept at hard labour in raising sand, soil and gravel by cleaning the river Thames"*

To accommodate these prisoners, old ships were provided and anchored in the Thames near Woolwich. Prisoners so accommodated were taken in chains to their place of work and returned to the ship at night.

The number of felons was increased by the number of prisoners of war brought to this country; Danes, Swedes, Frenchmen, and Americans, until eventually there were no less than sixty hulks in service, some harbouring 1200 men aboard. Conditions aboard were harsh, insanitary and disease ridden. They were regarded as "floating tombs". There was a high mortality aboard, as high as one in three. The Gloucester Journal of Jan 22nd 1787 reported :-

"60 - 70 convicts have been sent within 3 months to the Thames from this county but only 20 remain alive"

These hulks were not cheap to run. When it was announced that Captain Cook had discovered Botany Bay in August 1786 the Cabinet quickly agreed that a penal colony be founded. Within a relatively short spell of time an expedition, known historically as "The Fleet", was constituted in order to populate the new colony.

This fleet set sail on Sunday May 13th 1787. The full story of its journey is well documented and is an epic of hardship and courage. It was quickly followed by others and for the purposes of this report it is suffice to say that until transportation ceased in 1886 no less than 137,368 males were embarked, of whom 2,382 died en route, while for females 25,351 embarked of whom 589 died. This made a grand total of 162,719 persons embarked of whom 2,971 died en route.

Local historians wishing to investigate the names of those condemned to transportation are fortunate that the law records for the period are, for the most part, complete, legible and accurate, but there are many sources which require to be examined. They are :- gaol registers, gaol books, penitentiary registers and registers of quarter sessions. From these sources we are able to obtain:-

a) Name, age, parish and occupation of the condemned
b) When and by whom the committal was made
c) Details of the offence with names of witnesses
d) Date of trial and sentence imposed
e) If the conviction was the first in the area (i.e Gloucestershire), and a physical description of the offender
f) Their ability to read and write noted
g) Their behaviour in court

From the above sources it was possible to establish that within the dates under review no less than nineteen persons resident in the Newent area were condemned to transportation. Their names, ages, offences, and sentence are tabulated below:-

Name	Age	Offence	Sentence
BARRETT, William	26	Burglary of clothes, com jewellery value £10	life
CLARKE, Charles	24	Stealing silver spoon and handkerchief (2nd offence)	10 yrs
CLIFFORD, Joseph	16	Stealing a pocket handkerchief (2nd offence)	7 yrs
DALBY, Joseph	35	Stealing bushel of wheat value £6	7 yrs
DAVIES, Thomas	60	Stealing sheets, blankets	14 yrs
DAVIS, Thomas	22	Breaking-in, stealing clothing (2nd offence)	life
GATFIELD, James	29	Stealing a "Severnline"	7 yrs
HILL, Thomas	21	Stealing £5, loaf, and flitch of bacon (2nd offence)	life
MAYO, William	20	Stealing a watch	life
MORGAN, James	22	Breaking-in, stealing silver spoons	life
PHILLIPS, John	37	Stealing 2 bushels of wheat (2nd offence)	7 yrs
PHILLIPS, Stephen	36	Stealing 1/8th peck of wheat (2nd offence)	7 yrs
PICKTHORNE, Wm	31	Breaking-in stealing two forks (2nd offence)	7 yrs
SELWYN, Henry	16	Stealing an ass, mare, & gelding (2nd offence)	7 yrs
TAYLOR, Thomas	20	Stealing a mare	life
THOMAS, James	23	Assault, robbery of hat & cotton handkerchief	life

THOMAS, George	22	Assault, robbery of hat & cotton handkerchief	life
PROBYN, William	22	Breaking-in stealing silver goods & clothing	life
PICKTHORNE, Hannah	28	Stealing sheets, clothing and silver	life

Thomas Davies, William Probyn, and Hannah Pickthorne all died en route. It should be noted that the previous offenders did not automatically incur the more severe sentence of "life" because the previous sentences in gaol were taken into consideration.

Few of those with shorter than life sentences returned to this country and many with life were eventually issued with "tickets of leave" for good behaviour and settled down in the country.

An insight to a transportee's view of his new life in a new country is perhaps best expressed by a short poem written by George Barrington who was sentenced in 1796 as a pickpocket. It was spoken as a prologue when an opera house was opened. It was entitled:-

<u>True Patriots All</u>

From distant climes o'er widespread seas we come
Though not with much eclat or beat of drum
We left our country for our country's good
And none will doubt but that our emigration
has proved most useful to the British nation

References
Registers of Quarter Sessions		GRO
Irene Wyatt	1947	BGAS Vol I Gloucestershire Records Series
Robert Hughes	1987	The Future Shore

Policing in Newent, Eric Warde

In 1839 Justices in Quarter Sessions were granted power to appoint paid police forces. The Gloucestershire Bench was among the first in the country to do so. Regrettably limited models existed. London's Metropolitan Police had been in existence for some ten years and the Irish Police Force was based on military lines. These were the sole UK Police Forces from which the way ahead could be evolved.

An Irish veteran, Anthony Thomas Lefroy was given the post of Gloucestershire's first Chief Constable. The Chief Constable's report for 1840 shows that five constables had been based at Newent. By 1851 a Sergeant and two constables were based at Newent with a further two constables at Dymock.

The purpose built Nicholson House became the Newent Police Station in 1889 and it also housed the Petty Session Court. It comprised cells, a general office, living accommodation for the sergeant and his family and the single officers.

In 1974, subsequent to the transfer of Newent from the Gloucester Division, Newent's Constabulary Section took up residence in an annex to the Holts Health Centre that had been built on the site of the home of the notorious Edmund Edmonds. Subsequently the Petty Sessional Court was transferred to Gloucester. Nicholson House became the headquarters for the 18 plus organization and, later, the Crime Museum.

In response to Home Office directions Gloucestershire's Constabulary was re-organized into fewer, but larger, divisions. Newent became part of the Cheltenham based Northern Division, and a further change in 1974 saw Newent included in the Western Division. This change did not last long for the 1982 re-organization brought about Newent's transfer to the Forest Sub-Division. Finally in 1998 Newent was once more transferred, this time to the Forest North Inspector Neighbourhood Area.

Over the years a number of characters have been stationed at Newent, one of whom was the late Stan Cross. He was the last Sergeant to serve at Nicholson House and was much liked by the residents. Another was Brian Calway who retired from the Gloucestershire Force with the rank of Chief Inspector, and later was elected as a County Councillor and a member of the Police Authority.

The late Liz Child, a cancer victim, had the honour of being the first female member of the Gloucestershire Constabulary to be appointed as Station Sergeant at Newent in the 1980s.

At one time Newent's Special Constabulary Force amounted to as many as fifty officers, with the late Inspector "Willy" Watson in charge. He was the proprietor of the town's ironmongery shop throughout the 1960s and 70s.

Reference
Geoff Sindrey & Ted Heath   A Forest Beat

10. Services
Derek Pearce

Water Supply

Before 1897 the town had no mains water supply and relied solely on shallow wells dug into the new red sandstone, a number of which still survive. It is fortunate that the town is situated over such a large area of this water retaining rock stratum.

In the Victorian era a custom built up of "taking the waters" at spa towns such as Malvern, Droitwitch, Bath and Cheltenham. Newent was no exception with a mineral spring east of the town. It is situated between Ell Brook and Hill Top about 800 m ENE of the church in the field at the base of a steep sandstone bank. A cottage was built by Dr Richardson and gardens laid out with an attendant to serve the waters. A footbridge was built over Ell Brook for the ease of travellers on the Gloucester to Newent road. The cottage had been abandoned by 1848 and demolished by 1922 (1)

The well is now capped over and the water fed into Ell Brook. Only the northern abutment of the footbridge is still visible.

In Rodmore Field on Nelfields Farm is a mineral spring said to be good for sore eyes.

After the drought of 1891 the City of Gloucester began a search for another source of water to supplement their existing overloaded supplies. A group of consultants, William Fox & Partners, were employed and ten possible schemes were considered (2). They finally decided to sink a trial borehole at Oxenhall a mile west of Newent (3). This 12" bore was started on 3rd January 1893 by the Aqueous Works and Diamond Rock Boring Co Ltd from London.

The Corporation stopped the boring at 290 ft being satisfied with the results, and taking the decision that there was an ample supply of pure water for the City of Gloucester. At this stage of the proceedings the Onslow Trustees became interested in the borehole in the hope that it would find coal (4). There was already an existing coal mine about a mile further west. They continued to a depth of 1,190 ft but found no coal. The bottom piece of the bore was sent to Gloucester Museum for preservation.

Although this borehole was never used for supply purposes the top can still be seen adjacent to the pumping station attendant's house.

Proposals were then put forward to Parliament for the sinking of a well and the construction of a permanent pumping station on the site. The water would be pumped up a 14" diameter main to a reservoir at Madam's Wood, Upleadon, and then gravitate to the City of Gloucester.

Fig.35 Newent Waterworks steam engine built in 1897 by Summers and Scott of Gloucester

Fig.36 Felling the Waterworks chimney in 1956

Fig. 37 Culver Street in 1909 showing a gas street lamp
(Photo R J Bisco)

The original proposals were for two tunnels to be excavated from the well, one in a westerly direction of approximately 1,000m and one in an easterly direction for approximately 500m. However these tunnels, or adits, did not need to be anywhere near this length to collect the required flow. The digging of the well commenced on 8th October 1894 with the first sod being turned by the Mayor of Gloucester. It was excavated to a depth of 170 ft by Ebeneezer Timmins & Co of Runcorn (5).

The two adits were driven at a depth of 145 ft. The western heading was 145 ft long, 5 ft high and 6 ft wide and proved to be unproductive. The other heading, driven in a north easterly direction, however, cut through several fissures in the sandstone and only needed to be cut 117 ft long. It is said that the water issuing from the rock was so great that when the workmen evacuated the well they left their tools behind in order to make a speedy retreat from the rising water, and that these tools are still where they were left.

The well was finally completed on 28th March. The yield was 36,000 gallons/hour with a daily minimum yield of 840,000 gallons.

The contract for the pumping engines finally went to the Gloucester firm of Summers and Scott, who constructed the steam engine shown in fig.35. Steam was obtained from three Cornish boilers each capable of supplying the pumps.

The reservoir at Madam's Wood was initially built to store 600,000 gallons but was increased to 1,850,000 gallons in 1901.

After the commissioning a standpipe was erected on the 14" main at the north end of Newent High Street for the use of the people of the town. The land on which the pumping station was built, and some of the land through which the 14" main was laid, was administered by the Onslow Trustees. This was a group of people charged with running the affairs of the estate under the terms of the will of Richard Foley Onslow dated 19th November 1870 for his grandson Andrew Richard Onslow.

An agreement was signed for the sale of the land to Gloucester Corporation, and for the necessary easements, for the sum of £100. In addition they negotiated a free water supply to 18 properties and farms on the estate. Because of the foresight of the trustees these properties received a free supply until 1986 when the agreement was terminated (5). A further eleven properties received a supply at a rate of one shilling per 1,000 gallons.

In 1909 plans were submitted to lay a mains supply into Newent Town and erect public standpipes for the residents. The contract was originally let to Mr William Westwood of Bromyard on 30th August 1909 but due to his failure to commence work on time it was transferred to Messrs Woodward & Co (Contractors) of Gloucester on 5th October (6).

The water rating area was defined by a line 10 chains either side of the mains. The last hydrant standpost was only removed in 1982 and is now preserved in the waterworks museum at Mythe Waterworks, Tewkesbury.

A stone drinking trough can be seen next to the Market House with the following inscription:-

"In grateful remembrance of Richard Foley Onslow of Stardens
1826-1879 and Andrew Knowles of Newent Court 1875-1909
      Go and do thou likewise
The memorial erected in grateful remembrance of much beneficial work in and for Newent by the above Richard Foley Onslow."

In December 1950 Ted Andrews took over as Station Superintendent, and in 1956 it was the turn of the Newent Pumping Station to be converted to electricity. The old steam pumps were shut off on 28th October 1956 by the shift operators, Gerald Gooch and Alfred Watkins, at 10 pm. It was estimated that these pumps had delivered 12 thousand million gallons of water since 1897(7).

The cost of the conversion work was £36,232 and it was estimated that the running costs would be reduced by 4d per 1000 gallons by electrification. During the work Mr Andrews kept a daily diary of the events. The 80 ft chimney was felled at 11-40 am on 1st November by chiselling away the brickwork on one side until it toppled. The top landed in the adjacent Ell Brook, where it can still be seen, and the weight of the falling masonry broke a 3" water main running across the site. (fig.36)

On the 3rd of May 1957 the staff at the station were engaged in installing a temporary submersible pump because of the shortage of water in Gloucester. Mr Andrews wrote :-

"Proceeded to lower the pump into the well (much panic from Gloucester). So many cars arrived from M.E.B. (Midlands Electricity Board) *that it looked very much like a race meeting".*

The following day work re-commenced at 6 am and after working all day the pump was started at 8-30 pm. Mr Andrews had obviously had a difficult time getting the pump working and wrote in his diary *"The end of a perfect day"* (8).

The station was re-opened on Monday 25th November 1957 by the Mayor of Gloucester, Gordon Payne O.B.E. J.P. There were about 70 people at the ceremony including Charles Ramstedt who helped assemble the original steam plant, and Fred Baldwin who had been an apprentice bricklayer on the construction of the building back in 1897. The former Station Superintendent for Newent and Ketford for 43 years, Stanley Reece, was also present (9).

Fig.38 Laying the water mains in Church Street in 1909
(Photo R J Bisco)

The two new pumps could pump 42,800 gallons/hour each and are driven by 125 H.P. electric motors. They are still in use today.

Because of the need to supply the rural areas with water Gloucester Corporation decided to construct three new reservoirs to be supplied by the newly modernized Ketford and Newent sources. All three were constructed at the same altitude of 96.01 m A.O.D. and sited at Glasshouse, Pfera Hall, and Gospel Oak. They were completed in 1959. Pfera Hall has a capacity of 1,136 cubic metres (250,000 gallons) whilst the other two are twice as big. They are of reinforced concrete construction and covered with earth. Upleadon reservoir has now been abandoned (10).

In 1987 two large barrel mains were laid in the lawn of Newent Pumping Station to increase the chlorine contact time and improve disinfection. The original cast iron water mains in the Town were concrete lined in the early 1990's to improve water quality.

Newent's water supply was the responsibility of Gloucester Corporation until 1967 when North West Gloucestershire Water Board was set up. It was then taken over by Severn Trent Water Authority in 1975, which became a private company in 1989 (5).

Sewerage

Because of the large number of shallow wells in the area it was considered more important to construct a proper sewage disposal scheme before a piped water supply. A report on the proposed sewerage of Newent was submitted to the Sanitary Committee by Mr T Curley in 1866 (11). Until then each house had its own "privie" or earth closet, which was little more than a hole in the ground. Mr Curley observed that *"the Workhouse is in a very deplorable condition for the want of sewerage. The stench about the place is terrific"*.

A plan of the sewers dated 1874 indicates that the recommendations of the 1866 report had been largely completed by then. This included a sewage treatment works on the north side of Cleeve Lane, opposite the present works. This was in fact no more than two settling tanks, the solid matter having to be removed manually, and the water overflowing into the brook.

By 1930 the Newent Rural District Council (12) records show there were two sewage treatment works at this time; the Cleeve Lane works serving most of the town, and a small works by the railway station receiving sewage from 34 properties and the schools in Station Road and Ross Road. This latter works has since been closed down and the flow diverted to Cleeve Lane.

In 1943 the Cleeve Lane works was extended to meet the additional flow from the prisoner of war camp, by the addition of an upward flow sedimentation tank of 8,400 gallons capacity. It then consisted of two sedimentation tanks, a rectangular bacteria bed with perforated trough distribution, and a humus pit.

On 30th November 1953 Newent RDC approved a scheme to build a new sewage works at a cost of £27,000 but by 1959 it had still not been started, allegedly because local farmers were unwilling to have the works on their land. The original Cleeve Lane works was by now grossly overloaded due to the increased population and water usage. It was described as *"the whole thing being totally inadequate and ineffective"*.

The new works was finally built by 1965 on the opposite side of Cleeve Lane to the original works. The two sedimentation tanks, two bacteria beds, two humus tanks and two storm tanks are still in use, now alongside the newer treatment plant. The eight sludge drying beds are still present but are no longer used. It was designed by A H S Waters and Partners, and built by Messrs George Law Ltd. The design allowed for a dry weather flow of 127,000 gallons/day and a peak flow of 381,000 gallons/day. The final cost was £105,000.

On the 4th December 1970 a report was submitted on the enlarging of the works, involving the purchase of additional land south and east of the works. By 1972 the proposed extensions were complete at a cost of £200,000. This involved a new sedimentation tank, two bacteria beds, one new humus tank, a sludge holding tank, and a sludge pressing plant. The sewerage system was also extended to the Pool Hill, Upleadon, and Highleadon areas.

In 1974 the sewers and the sewage treatment works were transferred to the newly formed Severn Trent Water Authority when the government reorganized water services. The Water Authority was required to allow the Local Authority, the Forest of Dean District Council, to act as its agents to maintain the sewers, but in the 1990s this responsibility was being taken over by the newly privatised Severn Trent Water Ltd.

Electricity

Although Ledbury had an electric supply in 1914 and Much Marcle in 1928, Newent was not connected until the early 1930s. On Monday 21st January 1929 a parish meeting was called in the Court House *"For the purpose of considering the desirability of obtaining a supply of electric current for lighting and other purposes in the Parish of Newent"*.

Initially the Gloucester Corporation considered supplying Newent and the Electricity Commission had ruled in their favour over the West Gloucestershire Company. But the proposals were not economic. Despite this the Gloucester Corporation objected to The Shropshire, Worcestershire and Staffordshire Electric Power Company submitting a proposal. After some discussion the Gloucester Corporation withdrew at the end of March and the Shropshire, Worcestershire and Staffordshire Electric Power Company submitted their plans to supply Newent on 19th May 1930. They stated that supplies should be available by the winter (13).

The streets initially supplied were :- New Street (High St), Lewall Street, Broad Street, Ross Road, Bridge Street (Dymock Road), Culver Street (200 yds), Bury Bar Lane (150 yds), and Gloucester Street (180 yds) (14). St Mary's Church was first lit by electricity in 1931.

In the winter the quarterly charges were set at 12/6d per Kw/hr for the first 15 units and 10d for anything over. In the summer quarters the charges were 8/4d per Kw/hr for the first 10 units and 10d for anything over. In addition there was a quarterly service charge of 2/6d per room wired, plus 1.5d per unit.

Telephone

Gloucester City had its first telephone in 1887 when the Gloucester Telephone Company was formed. This became the Western Counties and South Wales Company, which was in turn absorbed by the United Telephone Company in 1892. By 1912 the General Post Office had taken over (15).

In 1900 there were 257 exchange lines in Gloucester but it was a few years before Newent was connected. Number 1 was of course the Post Office, run by the Bisco family, and number 2 was the local doctor. The George Hotel was advertising its telephone number as Newent 3 in 1910 (16), and in 1923 the first manual exchange was installed in the Post Office which was run by three generations of the Bisco family between 1855 and 1983.

By 1927 there were 17 private residences connected and 32 numbers (17). The first available automatic exchange was opened in Gloucester in 1927 and in 1960 Gloucester became the 12th exchange in the country to introduce subscriber trunk dialling (15). The present Telephone Exchange is off Holts Road.

Gas Supply

The Parish Council first discussed the provision of street lighting in 1850 and the following year set up a small committee to look into the project, under the chairmanship of Edmund Edmonds. The Newent Gas Light and Coke Company was set up in 1850 with Edmonds being a major shareholder. It was a non-statutory company and therefore did not require an Act of Parliament. Land was purchased in Watery Lane, opposite the present recreation ground, where Squire Onslow had kept his kennel of hounds, and the gas works was active by 1851. By the end of the year there were 20 gas lamps in operation.

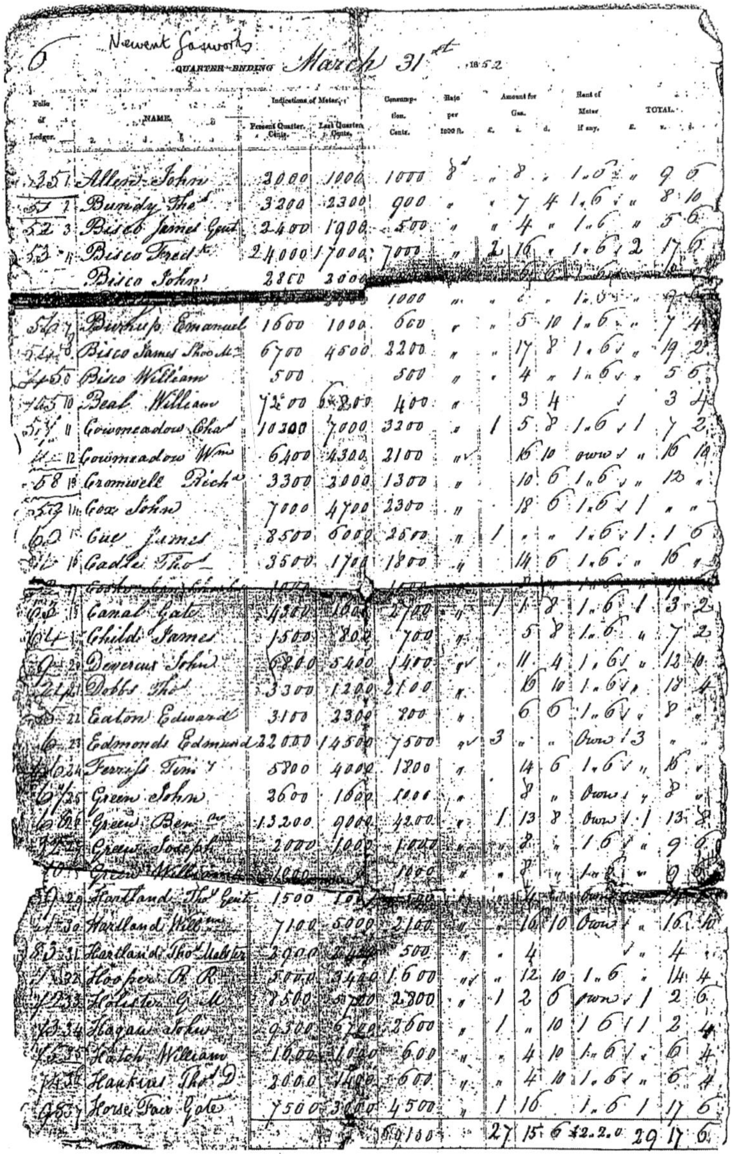

Fig.39 A page of the accounts of the Newent Gas Light and Coke Co Ltd for the March quarter of 1852. In some cases they are incorrect.

The gas was charged at 8/- per 1,000 cubic feet with an additional charge of 1/6d for the meter, unless the customer had his own. Fig.39 shows a page of the company accounts for the March quarter of 1852 (although some of the mathematics leave something to be desired).

In Victorian times gas was mainly used for lighting and in 1869 the Parish Council again discussed the provision of street lamps. On 27th August 1869 they entered into a contract with the Newent Gas Light and Coke Company for the supply of 24 lamps at a cost of £60 a year. The lamps to operate from dusk until 1-00 a.m. from 1st September until 1st May *"Except three nights before and three nights after the full of the moon during the period, and on each of the said excepted nights as shall be cloudy"*

The contract was signed by Edmund Edmonds on behalf of the company. The Town Lighting Inspectors were Frank Chadley and Frederick Bisco. Early photographs of the the Town show most of the lamps were attached to buildings with only a small number free standing (18).

In 1892 the undertaking became a limited company and in 1893 they applied for a Board of Trade order to purchase an adjacent area of land from John Hatton so they could enlarge the works (19). The original working capital of the company was £4000 and this order extended it by a further £2000. The order specified that the minimum pressure in the mains should be 0.6 inches water gauge from midnight to sunset, and 0.8 inches water gauge from sunset to midnight (20). This was to cope with the additional demand for lighting. These pressures were well below the minimum of 2 inches water gauge specified in the 20th century, although in reality pressures would normally have been much higher. The pressure would have been governed by the size and weight of the gas holder. Initially there was only one gas holder with a second one of similar size being added when the works was enlarged in the 1890s. The two holders had a capacity of 9,000 cubic feet. The maximum price of gas in 1893 was 5/10d per 1,000 cu ft.

By 1896 the lighting rate was 6d in the pound to raise the cost of £65 p.a.. The following year this had risen to £73 (21).

In 1900 a dividend of 2.5% was paid on a capital of £2,800. In addition the Company had a £1,000 loan at 4%. The annual production of gas was 4 million cu ft. By this time the number of customers had risen to 170, of whom 50 had pre-payment meters and 56 had stoves, and there were 32 public lamps. The price of gas had reduced to 5/3d per 1,000 cu ft. The chairman and engineer of the company was William North, the manager was T C Severs, and the secretary was William Phillips.

By 1914 the number of customers had risen to 200 and they used 385 tons of coal to produce the gas which was distributed around the town by 2.5 miles of main. Mr I Vickers had taken over as manager.

In 1938 the Engineer and Manager made a return for the Gas Times Register stating the annual production was 6.5 million cu ft of 500 Btu gas and that the Company had 202 customers. The gas price was 5/10d per 1,000 cu ft, exactly the same as it had been 45 years earlier.

In 1945 the Company had 4 miles of mostly 4 inch diameter lead jointed cast iron main supplying the following streets :- New St, High St, Ross Road, Gloucester St, Lewall St, Broad St, Church St, Bridge St, Watery Lane, and Culver St (22). Only the southern end of Culver St had a section of 3 inch main. The capacity of the works was 80,000 cu ft/day delivered at a pressure of 6 inches water gauge, which meant there was considerable scope for additional load. The gas was charged at a flat rate of 6/4d per 1,000 cu ft although it was possible to negotiate a lower rate by special contract (22).

In 1940 the company was re-constituted and in 1945 Norman Somerville was still the secretary and manager, when there were 230 customers. In 1949 when the company was nationalized 10.69 million cubic feet of 420 Btu Tully gas was produced by the works. It was owned at this time by T.W.Little & Sons Ltd who also owned Mitcheldean Gas Works. The engineer was F G Little and the manager E H England.

When the company was nationalized on May 1st 1949 it became part of the South Western Gas Board. In 1950 the works was under the control of the former Ross-on-Wye engineer and manager A C Willsmere. The production had risen to 11.5 million cu ft of Tully gas and the price to 7/2d per 1,000 cu ft (23). The works was closed down in 1955/6 and Newent was fed via a high pressure main from Gloucester. One of the gas holders and the retort house were demolished and the remaining building fronting Watery Lane was converted into a private house. Mr G A Lusted, a former naval man, was the manager for a time after World War II and lived in the converted buildings.

With increasing demand on the system the remaining two lift gas holder was insufficient to provide enough pressure. A governor station was installed from the high pressure main and a compressor and two high pressure receivers built to allow the stored gas in the holder to be used at times of high demand. One of the receivers was later removed (24).

The town was converted to natural gas in the early 1970s at a cost of £45.9 per customer (25), and is now fed via a high pressure main and governor station in Watery Lane, off the main from Gloucester to Ross-on-Wye. The surviving gas holder was demolished and all that remains on the gasworks site is a small kiosk, and the converted offices.

Post

Before the advent of the postage stamp, mail was paid for by the recipient. If they did not pay the fee the item was publicly displayed. In 1770 the Post messenger was drowned in the floods between Gloucester and Newent and the Town was partly cut off (26). It was not until 1840 that the "Penny Black" was issued for pre-paid delivery.

In the 1820s letters were carried by horse mail which left Newent for Gloucester each morning at 8-00 am, returning at 4-00 pm. This system was used until 1854, by which time the mail coach had taken over. The Postmaster in 1822 was Thomas Hartle (27). He is still listed as Postmaster in the 1851 census at the age of 89, being assisted by his daughter Jane.

Coaches to Gloucester left the George Inn at 7-30 am each morning. There were also coaches to Ross-on-Wye and Hereford. Each coach had a name; the "Rising Sun", the "Champion", and the "Veteran". From 1844 there was also a coach service called the "Alert" from Ledbury to Gloucester, calling at Newent every Monday, Wednesday, and Saturday at 9-00 am and returning at 6-00 pm. This system continued until the opening of the railway in 1885.

Mr James Cooper Bisco took over the post office on 4th February 1855 and was the first of a long line of the Bisco family who ran the service for over 100 years. Before becoming postmaster Mr Bisco was a cordwainer. The Bisco family were originally Huguenots who settled in Devon, then moved up to Stroud and finally to Newent in the 18th century. The name was originally spelt "Bischof". The first post office was at No.8, Church Street where the present charity shop is.

James Bisco married Charlotte MacDonald from Edinburgh, and when James died in 1864 she took over. In 1880 their son James and his wife Mary Ann continued the business. When James died in 1900, Mary Ann moved to Broad Street next to the United Reformed Church (presently a disused garage), with her son Robert Harry. Before her marriage Mary Ann had been a ladies maid to Lady Camilla Somers at Cliffords Mesne. Robert became a keen amateur photographer and captured many local scenes before the first World War.

In 1918 the family moved to the Red House, opposite the church, the site of the present post office. It is called the "Red House" because it was at one time covered with virginia creeper which gave it the distinctive colour in the autumn.

Robert Harry succeeded as postmaster in 1932. He retired in 1955 and has son Robert James took over as the last in the family line. The tradition ended in 1983 when he too retired (28). The present postmaster is Robin Vizor.

Between the two World Wars the mail was taken from the post office to Newent railway station on a flat bed trolley. The engine driver would sound his whistle once as he was arriving at the station, and this would be the signal for Robert Harry to send the mail. He gave two hoots when he was at the station and three hoots when he was due to depart. This was just enough time to get from the post office to the station and load the mail.

A typical working day for a postman in the 1930s was to deliver mail to Highleadon, Upleadon, and Pool Hill and then return the same way collecting from the letter boxes. He would stop at Eden's Hill, Upleadon for a rest then continue to Highleadon and back to Newent. He was paid 12/6d per week with an extra 2/6d if he used his own bicycle.

At Brand Green there was a farmer who was noted for his home made cider. It was known locally as the "Welcome Inn" because anyone was welcome especially the postman. On one occasion a postman who had called at the farm was late returning and gave the excuse that his bicycle wheel was buckled. Postmaster Robert Harry Bisco was not fooled and replied "Its not your wheel that's "buckled", its you!"

There were 13 regular staff employed after World War II and this was increased by a further dozen at Christmas to cope with the seasonal load. The Memorial Hall was used for the extra sorting and three vans were used for the parcel delivery.

References

1. L Richardson (HMSO) 1930   Wells and Springs of Gloucesteshire
2. William Fox   1891   Report on the best means of increasing the water supply of the City of Gloucester
3. Act of Parliament (58 Vict ch xci)   1895
4. L Richardson & R Austin   1912   Water supply of the City of Gloucester (Proceedings of the Cotteswold Naturalists Field Club vol XVII Pt 3)
5. D A Pearce   1988   History of Water Supply in Gloucestershire
6. Severn Trent Water Ltd record plans   Tewkesbury Water Museum
7. Gloucester Citizen newspaper report   1956
8. Mr Andrew's diary   Accidentally destroyed in 1994
9. Gloucester Citizen newspaper report   1957
10. North West Gloucestershire Water Board, Engineering 100 booklet   1967
11. T Curley   1866   Report on the proposed sewerage of Newent
12. Newent Rural District Council Minutes
13. Gloucester Citizen   1930   GRO D7206/1/3
14. Shropshire, Worcestershire, and Staffordshire Electric Power Company special order 1930   GRO Q/Rum 666
15. A Dodd   1987   History of the Telephone Service in Gloucester   GRO ROL G3
16. T Ward   1994   Around Newent
17. Kelly's Directory   1927
18. Newent Gas Light and Coke Co Contract   GRO P225 LW 1/1   1869
19. Gas Orders Confirmation (No 2) Act   1893
20. Newent Gas Order   GRO Q/Rum 506 & Q/Rum 510 1893
21. Newent Lighting Rate Books   GRO DA30 513   1896/7
22. G Payne   1945 Gloucestershire, a Survey
23. Gas World Year Book   1950
24. South Western Gas Board plan   CO/169/B   1964
25. C Elliot   1980   History of Natural Gas Conversion in Great Britain
26. Beale Correspondence   1752-1805   National Register of Archives
27. Kelly's Directory   1822
28. Bob Bisco   2001   Private communication

11. Education
Kathleen Setters

There was of course no such thing as a state system of education in this country until the beginning of the 19th century. Those who had the means paid for their children to be taught at home, or in small schools, usually run by private individuals, often under the aegis of the Church. It was thought unnecessary, even wrong, to educate the poor, who might become discontented with their lot if they knew better ! In addition children from a young age were needed as labour on the land and in cottage industries.

Education for the poor was mainly in the hands of the Church and charitable individuals, who set out to give instruction in religion and reading, possibly also in writing and arithmetic, and in practical skills like spinning, sewing, gardening and ploughing.

Rudder (1) mentions a Charity School in Newent in 1779 but does not say where it was sited or under whose direction. This may have been the school mentioned by Martha Roberts (nee Herbert) in her Victorian Diary when she talks about her grandparents :-

"Now this grandmother of mine [Ann Herbert, nee Stockley] *was a gifted woman and must have come from good stock, for though born early in the 1700's, yet she was educated herself and determined that her children should be. (in those far-off days, only the better-class could read and write) and so her sons were sent to Newent Grammar School, the head-master, the Rev Theophilus Beale being also Vicar of Newent. To the Vicar's wife her daughters went for so many hours daily, going into the boy's school for arithmetic and some other things, and here they obtained a good sound education which lifted them far above those less fortunate than themselves and made them appear prodigies of learning to most people, even when I was a Girl."*

(Note; Theophilus Beale was not vicar of Newent)

Unregulated teachers and teaching may often have left much to be desired; Schoolmistress Haynes, who may have taught in this school, was of a doubtful reputation according to those responsible for the relief of the poor in 1785, who noted *"Perhaps the less said of her and her daughter the better"* (2).

It is possible that in Newent a "Town School" may once have existed in the Chantry Chapel (dedicated to St James and St Ann) in St Mary's Churchyard, as chantry priests often ran schools as a sideline. There are references to a "Dame" school kept in *"a very old building"* in the churchyard; this building was knocked down in 1810 and the material used to repair the almshouses. We know that on 3rd September 1726 Ann Knowles, a widow, was buried, who was said to have taught school in this town for 46 years (3).

For a few pennies a week families who did not qualify for charity schooling would send their little sons to Dame schools like the one run by Mary Nicholls, the widow of a carpenter in Newent.

For the really poor, that is those in the Workhouse, there was tuition in reading, writing and catechism, and the girls were also taught to spin, sew or knit. In October 1772 the Vestry in Newent ordered *"that for the better encouragement of a spirit of industry among the lower classes of people in this Parish all persons not chargeable to the Parish shall be indulged in having their children taught at the Workhouse to spin, knit and read at the expense of the Parish"*. It is interesting to note that reading was considered the most important subject for children to learn. To accommodate the pupils the Vestry decided, in April 1773, that *"a room over the Mill House and stable at the Workhouse be put in order for a schoolroom"*

Gentlemen sent their sons to be educated at boarding schools. There was a school in Newent for which an advertisement in December 1788 said *"Young gentlemen boarded and educated in Classics, writing the various hands, accounts, the mathematics, etc by Rev W Beale and assistants"*. The fees were *"thirteen guineas a year and one guinea entrance, washing included"*. The school evidently flourished and in 1798 Mr Beale announced that the school *"will be opened on Tuesday the 24th July when the early attendance of the young gentlemen is requested"* (4).

Poor children were set to work at an early age and premiums were paid to masters to persuade them to take poor children as apprentices, to be taught a trade. In 1652 in Newent, Walter Nourse left *"forty shillings yearly to apprentice two poor children in husbandry"*. William Rogers left a *"rent charge of £3 on lands in Kilcot to apprentice a poor boy to the handicraft trade"*; and Timothy Nourse left £10 a year to enable five poor children to be apprenticed. A few children only were helped in this way. The majority of pauper apprentices were not so lucky and in May 1788, for example, 22 children over the age of seven years were allocated to their masters by ballot. This was necessary because masters were unwilling to take small children who had to be fed and clothed while they were taught a trade

Among the orders for apprentices in the Vestry minutes book there is a very surprising one. In February 1773 the Vestry ordered that *"the youngest daughter of John Farley, cooper, be put in the Blue Coat School"* at a cost of two shillings a week. No reason is given for this action, which gave a rare opportunity of education to a girl (5).

Gentlemen were able to contract out of taking apprentices, on payment of £5-5s-0d to the Parish, but in November 1799 it was determined *"that the former resolution be declared null and void and that gentlemen be put on a footing with the tradesmen and farmers of the Parish"*.

The building in Broad Street which now houses Lloyds Bank was the boys' school kept, in 1830, by Mr Beale who was the Curate of Newent and Vicar of Dymock. William Baron, who was the Parish Clerk and died in 1907 aged 86, said that he went to school at a house kept by Mr Cooper; the house, called the Poplars, faced the garden between High House and Cook's Bakery.

By the beginning of the 19th century the Industrial Revolution was beginning to alter the pattern of work, as the coming of machinery meant that workers had to exercise intelligence and judgement. The ruling classes, whose concern had been to maintain a subservient lower class as cheap labour, began to realize that the workers needed some form of education for the sake of industrial efficiency, and also to ensure that they made wise use of the powers their growing economic importance gave them. In addition the wholesale drift from poor agricultural areas into towns and the large increase in the national population weakened the parochial system, where the Church largely controlled educational provision, and to fill this "urban gap" the idea that the state should help to educate children began to grow.

There was opposition to grants from the rates for the purpose, partly because it would undermine the Church's near monopoly of education. New academies, founded and funded by mill and factory owners, many of whom were dissenters, vied with the schools run by the established church. The controversy between secular and religious teaching delayed the establishment of a national system of education for at least 50 years.

The Factory Acts of the first half of the 19th century exposed the terrible conditions of child workers. Hours of work were reduced and instruction in the three R's and religion was made mandatory. In 1833 the Government voted £20,000 for building schools. In 1842 and 1845 Acts were passed to encourage the endowment of sites for schools. These schools were established through the charity and good works of the well off, who were concerned to ensure that the poor were taught the principles and beliefs approved by them. From 1864 schools receiving state aid were made subject to a "payment by results" system designed to make education either cheaper or more efficient.

In Newent the first important step towards elementary education was taken by two local benefactors. On April 18th 1848 Miss Elizabeth Foley and Richard Foley Onslow Esq gave to the Vicar and Churchwardens of the Parish of Newent a piece of land at Picklenash to be used *"as and for a school............*

and for the residence of the schoolmaster and schoolmistress of the said school....... in furtherance of the ends and designs of the incorporated National Society for promoting the Education of the Poor in the principles of the Established Church". The Minister was to be the chairman responsible for the management and the members of the committee were local gentlemen who gave at least 20 shillings for the school's support. There was provision for the appointment of a Committee of Ladies (being members of the Church of England) to assist in *"the visitation and management of the girls and infants schools"* and for inspection by the inspectors who were appointed by an Order in Council of 1840. The school functioned as three separate departments - boys, girls and infants - each in the charge of a master or mistress.

Pupils were charged a penny a week for their education, and teachers were paid according to the number of children who attended, and the numbers who passed the basic examinations in the three R's.

Joseph Wilkes, headmaster in 1845, recorded *"83 boys present today".* There was a wide age range. He had the assistance of a pupil teacher, Thomas Addis. The committee controlling the school had decided to adopt the system whereby older and brighter children were to oversee some of the classes and impart some instruction to them, i.e. act as "monitors". For this they were paid a few coppers a week. Some monitors went on to become pupil teachers, and in this role they became members of the school staff, in fact "apprentices" to the schoolmaster who gave them formal instruction during a period of the day set aside for the purpose. At the end of four years they could take an examination to qualify them as certificated teachers.

A fascinating glimpse into day to day life at Picklenash is provided by the log books which the headteachers maintained (6). The 1863 log opens with the entry : *"March 2 : Tom Trouncer came to school to say that his brother James had gone off to Hereford in a boat without his mother's knowledge. March 9 : Trouncer returned safe from his voyage".* (The Gloucestershire and Herefordshire Canal had been completed in 1845).

Other interesting entries are :-
March 31 Charlie Davis kept in all the dinner time (2 hours) for refusing to sing
April 14 Seven boys called to account for going into the girls school during the dinner time.
Oct 2 Desks well cleared out to make room for the boys at the Night School

1864 *Feb 25 C Jenkins, J Wood and G Whittaker to pay 2.5d for window*
July 7 A lesson in drilling

Oct 20 F Baron requested to leave the school and to be admitted again only by leave from Revds F Harrison or M B H Burland. Reasons - non-compliance with the school rules. Defiance of all orders. His evil influence on the school generally.

***1865** Jan 25 to Feb 6 : No school on account of the depth of snow.*

***1866** Jan 26 Notice given that school will meet every Saturday morning to make out for lost week* (Jan 1-8, owing to measles).
March 21 Day of Humiliation on account of cattle plague - Boys to church - Weekly examination in the afternoon.

***1869** March 22 Boys informed of holidays next week and asked to put off potato planting till then.*
June 7 All latecomers to suffer punishment in proportion to the distance they have to come.

***1871** June 16 Sent after Burges. Word brought that he will come when he has new shoes.*
June 30 William sent word to say that his Master, Mr Farmer, would give him leave to attend examination next Thursday. Is to come to the Master's House on Monday, Tuesday, and Wednesday evenings to look up his work (left three months). On Thursday sent after Job Jaques. Word brought back that he is cherry minding, but will come to school next week.

***1872** March 19 First Class can now work examples in the Metric System of weights and Measures, and have a fair knowledge of the proposed Decimal Coinage. A chart of the Metric System hangs on the walls of the school-room.*
May 6 Pupil Teacher Jefferies called suddenly away, and his class taken by one of the elder boys in the school
November 7 On Monday saw one of the 1st Class boys (Frank Hawkins) smoking - took him to task about it shewing him the folly of such bad habits - and wrote to his parents concerning it saying that if he persisted in the habit I should be compelled (as an example to the school) to strike my pen through his name.

***1874** April 17 A lavatory has this week been erected for the boys. It will be a great convenience to the school*

Fig.40 Pupils at the High Street Private School c1920

Fig.41 Mrs J Perillo (née Orme) and her school class, c1928
(photo Mrs Perillo)

September 25 This being Newent Onion Fair secular instruction was commenced at 9 and the school dismissed at one o'clock

November 27 Geo Thos & Jno Preece have been sent after most days this week, & the message returned was "wanted to mind the house & to nurse the children"

1875 *March 12 On Tuesday and today detected three or four boys copying from one another's slates during the Arithmetic lesson - gave them a severe caution*

1877 *July 6 School fees raised to twopence in each school for each child.*

A successful private school was established in the Porch House, Church Street, Newent, by the Rev Dr Joseph White. The date of its opening is unknown, but maps of the town from the second half of the 19th century show a school at the rear of the Porch House. The 1881 census described it as a Grammar School with Dr White as Headmaster and his sister Emma as assistant, his aunt as "manageress", Frederick Lawley as assistant teacher and three women as domestic servants. Sixteen names were listed as scholar/teachers, most of them teenagers, but one J. James was aged 23. He may have been one of the occasional mature students whom Dr White prepared for the priesthood. There were no Newent children among the scholars, the majority coming from distant places - London, Yorkshire and Wales, with only five locals, from Gloucester, Ledbury and Mitcheldean. There is no record of how long the school continued but in its day it must have enjoyed status.

A "Commission on Unemployment in Agriculture" was carried out between 1867 and 1868, and in Volume XVII Dr James Fraser reported on the Newent Poor Law Union. He said the *"educational condition of the labouring classes appears to me to be low. There are large areas nearly destitute of school, or only provided with inefficient ones"*. But in spite of this efficient schools prospered, for example Mr Osmond Ricardo of Bromsberrow *"who will tolerate no frivolous excuses for irregularities finds no difficulty in filling his rooms with a crowd of eager and punctual scholars"*.

"The incumbent of Upleadon has a fairly efficient school under Government inspection taught by a mistress only, finds he cannot retain his bigger boys there; they are drawn off by the superior attractions of Mr Ricardo's school at Pauntley"

In 1886 John Shambrook published "Life and Labours of John Hall". *"Mr Hall arrived in Gorsley on 21 January 1831. The next day he opened the day school and at once a goodly number of scholars, some of them being young men and maidens from 16 to 20 years of age."*

Other establishments came and went as Picklenash School continued, with additional buildings to accommodate the growing population. In the 19th century state schools were set up at Cliffords Mesne (1863), Gorsley (1877), Oxenhall (1883), Pauntley (1870), and Upleadon. Some pupils would have transferred between them if a new school opened in a more convenient place.

Fig.42 Picklenash School, Group V 1926 (photo Terry Jackson)

Mrs Jane Orme Perillo taught at a private school, set up in 1928, in a first floor room in a building behind The Poplars in High Street (fig.41). The school was owned and run by Miss Beeby, and most of the pupils came from the Dymock area, some by horse and trap. There were approximately 24 children between 8 and 14 years, to whom Mrs Perillo (then Miss Orme) the only teacher, taught all subjects (7).

In the 1960s Dr Tomlinson, a local general practitioner with a surgery at the Porch House, opposite St Mary's Church, opened a small preparatory school, called the Porch House School. This was inspected by the authorities, and officially registered under the Child Minder's Act. It was a non profit making venture, all the costs being equally shared by the parents of the participating children. It proved to be a happy and scholastically successful experiment, with two successive groups of seven and six pupils and four part-time teachers, including a Mademoiselle for French. It closed when the second group reached the necessary age for entry into further schooling (8).

Fig. 43 Picklenash School, Standard 3, 1929 (photo Terry Jackson)

Picklenash School continued as two schools, one for boys and one for girls, each under its own headteacher, until 1926. In that year a new headmaster was appointed, and given charge over both boys and girls in one school. In 1949, owing to reorganization of local schools, Picklenash received senior pupils from a number of neighbouring village schools, and new buildings were erected to accommodate them. At this time there were some 500 children in attendance, aged from five to fifteen years. In 1952 Picklenash School assumed its present status of a Primary school for children from five to eleven years. More senior pupils transferred to Newent School, which had been founded in

1925 as a co-educational Grammar School and then became a bilateral Grammar-Modern School having nearly 650 pupils. It was housed in the buildings on the north side of Ross Road which subsequently became the Community Centre.

Mr Richard Stokes was appointed headmaster of Picklenash in 1952, and he and his wife came to live in Drumlanrig, Ross Road, the school house. Mrs Mary Stokes, his widow, remembers that Picklenash was a very happy school, although the buildings were not in a very good state; there were coke stoves and old double desks. There were huts which had to be used for the seniors, and a huge playing field. Pupils could have free piano lessons, after school, taught by Mrs Gibbs, and Mrs Wilkinson taught violin. Mr Stokes bought a lot of percussion instruments and the school put on shows. There was a hall which had to serve as assembly hall, canteen and theatre for both Picklenash and the bi-lateral school. Mr Peacock, head of the bi-lateral school, put on Gilbert and Sullivan operas. He had a good music staff (7).

At one time eleven year old pupils from Picklenash used to go on a Mediterranean cruise at a reasonable cost, but when this became too expensive Mr Stokes arranged school visits to Rhos-on-Sea in Wales.

When the sharing of the bi-lateral school's swimming pool became impossible Mr Stokes put forward the idea of Picklenash having its own pool. The County Education Department would not give the idea any backing, but the parents formed a committee, chaired by Mr Tom Clark from Gorsley, and raised the money by holding fetes, supper dances etc. Finally the parents helped to build the new pool (7).

Picklenash Primary School split in the mid 1960s into Glebe Infants School and Picklenash Junior School sharing the same site. The Early Years building was constructed on the edge of the Picklenash playing field under a joint effort from both schools. In 2001 the Newent Opportunity Group constructed an extension to the Early Years building using the Bradfords Lane entrance, and in 2002 Picklenash School was redeveloped to accommodate more permanent classrooms.

The two sections of the bi-lateral school came together in 1965 in a new purpose-built school in Watery Lane.

A newly-built County Junior School was opened by HRH the Duke of Gloucester on 24th April 1985, and the original old buildings were sold and converted into residential dwellings. The new school accommodated 280 pupils.

References
1. S Rudder   1779   History of Goucestershire
2. List of the Poor   1785-90   GRO D1791/6
3. Parish Register   GRO
4. Gloucester Journal   1798
5. Vestry Minutes   1773   GRO
6. Picklenash School Logbooks
7. Information from :-   Mrs J Perillo
                         Mrs K Clarke
                         Miss S Parry
                         Len Millar
                         Mr J Thomas
8. Mrs C Tomlinson   2002   Private communication

12. Relief of the Poor 1768-1918
Frances Penney

In medieval times the relief of the poor was undertaken by the Church but, with the dissolution of the monasteries (1536-39), this duty eventually fell on the parish. In 1572 the office of Overseer of the Poor was created.

The Poor Law Act of 1601 made each Parish officially responsible for its poor. The aged and sick were to be relieved and provided, if necessary, with cottages; pauper children were to be apprenticed and the able poor set *"on work"*. The money for this purpose was raised by the Poor Rate and expended by the Overseer of the Poor, acting on the instructions of the Vestry, the local government authority of the 18th and 19th centuries.

An Act of 1662, usually known as the Act of Settlement, empowered the Parish authorities to remove a stranger unless he rented a tenement worth £10 a year, a rent far beyond the means of any labourer.

A poor man could enter the Parish on a temporary basis provided he had a certificate from his own parish to say he would be taken back should he be in need. In October 1772 Newent Vestry resolved *"That every person residing in this Parish that are not parishioners shall have immediate notice that unless they produce certificates of their settlements they shall be removed within one month from the date hereof"*. In 1781 it was agreed that the Workhouse Master *"Shall have twenty pounds to remove all paupers that do not belong to the Parish of Newent"*.

A woman acquired settlement in her husband's parish and a child in its father's, except in the case of an illegitimate child who became a charge on its mother's. In May 1790 the Vestry meeting ordered *"that Mr Godsell is desired to visit Richard Phillip's house on Bottley Green to see who the woman is that is there with big belly"*. His report *"It's Sarah Hall, a Parishioner"*, confirmed that the expected baby would belong to the Parish of Newent.

Paupers received in-relief, in the Workhouse, and out-relief, in their own homes. The amounts varied from three pence to 2/6d a week, paid in the Vestry after morning service, but such relief was given only after investigation into the condition and behaviour of the applicant. There is even a note on 27th January 1791 that no relief would be given to anyone who kept a dog.

Payments were made to the sick but in 1769 it was ordered *"that to prevent fraud for the future no person shall be allowed pay on plea of illness unless that sickness is first certified to the Parish under the hand of the Parish Apothecary"*.

In 1774 there seems to be the beginnings of preventative medicine when in April it was resolved, by a majority vote, that the poor should be inoculated against smallpox at the Parish expense, at the rate of one guinea for every five persons. By 1779 the Vestry was looking for the *"Doctors that does it cheapest"*.

The authorities also had to provide clothes for the poor, sometimes for children who were said to be naked or almost naked. The minutes book contains many entries such as *"Thos Newton shall have a pair of shoes"* or *"Bob Collier shall have a flannel wascoat"* . One girl was to have *"a petty coat of strong warm flannel"*. It was ordered in November 1768 that *"Jane Halliday shall have a pair of second hand stays, gown, and handkerchief upon her quitting the Workhouse and going to service"*.

Money to provide the clothing came partly from the Poor Rate and partly from Charities. That of Timothy Nourse provided clothing for three old men and widows, and that of Lucy Stokes was used *"to find two grey gowns faced with black for two poor widows of good reputation"*. In 1772 timber on the Poor Land was sold by auction for the sum of £10-15s-0d and the money spent on clothing for poor boys and girls.

Attempts were made to find work for the able poor. In 1785 the Vestry resolved that *"the Overseer do buy all the shoes for the Parish use of those shoemakers that will constantly employ Stephen Lightfoot and William Partridge"*.

In 1798 a Steward was employed, at an annual salary of £25, to supervise the work of the poor. He had to make a list of those able to work and what they could do. They were to start at 6-00 am from Lady Day to Michaelmas and at 7-00 am from Michaelmas to Lady Day or *"as soon as they can see to work"*. Children were included in the list and many were considered capable of working, like Richard Haines who, at the age of seven, was to spin.

In 1816 the Vestry noticed the distress of the poor whose difficulty in finding work was increased by competition from men discharged from the Army and Navy at the ending of the Napoleonic wars. It was decided that the principal inhabitants should give the unemployed work at the rate *"not less than one shilling per day nor exceeding 1s-6d per day"* . Each man seeking work carried a recommendation signed by the Guardian of the Poor *"Please to find employment for the bearer of this note for the space of six days from the date thereof"*.

The winter of 1799-1800 was severe and in January 1800 a shop was set up *"for the relief of the Poor during the present inclement season"*. Financed by private subscription and a sixpenny rate, it would provide soup *"a more cheap, more palatable, more wholesome and more nutritious diet than bread"*, every Tuesday and Thursday *"from half past ten o'clock till two"*. The soup cost one penny a quart, large measure (whatever it cost to make) and the poor were provided with tickets to be exchanged at the shop only for food which also included rice, potatoes and white herrings at reduced prices. In that way the authorities said a poor man *"will eat the real mixture he pays for, he will make sixpence go as far as a shilling and he cannot spend his money in an alehouse"*.

Further help was given in May 1800 when seed potatoes, purchased for £5, were given to the poor who had gardens, while it was also agreed that *"mixed corn and other provisions be sold to the poor at a reduced price"*.

These were all official actions but there were private acts of charity. In June 1810 Mr Hankins, from the Scarr, found that small shops sold *"the worst flour at the highest prices to the poor"* so he bought good wheat flour at his own expense and sold it to them at market price.

A small note book covering the period 1785-9 contains the names of all the poor in the town and surrounding tythings. The candid comments make interesting reading. Also included are lists of those receiving relief at specific times. The first group *"received at the Church upon St Thomas and Good Friday"*. The second list gives the names, and number of children, of the poor receiving amounts of 6d, 9d,12d or, rarely, 18d a week during the hard frost of January 1789, the coldest January for 80 years.

Boulsdon

Anne Matthews	-	W. 2 children very poor and almost naked, her husband probably not dead, nor of this parish
John Coller	-	3 or 4 young children, honest poor, careful, hard working, rapidly declining
J S Clutterbuck	-	Does not want. The wife a most sad infamous jade and maintains at home two children by another man, though near twenty years old each. He has now a wife and eleven children
- Williams	-	Husband ran away and pretended to be dead. In great distress. Husband since brought back. Since committed to gaol for not finding security for a bastard child sworn to him. At liberty now.

Kilcot

Wm Philips	-	3 children at home - sickly - had ague all the summer, now a cottage of their own.
Wm Morgan	-	6 ch at home. Very poor - a thief - ran away to avoid being committed to gaol.
John Merrick	-	3 ch. all young - broken farmer miserably poor, removed to a house of Hill's next Mrs Thackwells.

Thos Predeth	-	One child at home - drunken dog. Has spent a great deal of money very foolishly.
Widow Baxter	-	As vile a woman as any in the Parish. She is a thief herself. By her persuasions her husband who was honestly inclined took to sheep stealing and was hanged in 1784. She has since lived with one Dobbs a horse stealer and has sold all her goods to supply him with money. She has one child which she has sent to John Merrick's of Kilcot - gone off and taken her child with her.
Joseph Fogg	-	2 in family - no bed - no clothes scarcely - husband ill - lazy
J Markey	-	Widower. Since married again - very wicked daughter

Town

G Vaughan	-	2 or 3 children at home. The house and children always kept neat and clean.
Fr Russell	-	1 child - the man but sickly - the woman dirty, honest, obliging - drunken - lives in Almshouse.
Thos Higgs	-	sick, lazy, 3 C. Wife works hard and would do well but for her idle rib. Eldest daughter will soon be ruined if not put out, Husband dead
Jos Taylor	-	Has one child - bad breed - married into almost as bad - a son of the devil's daughter.
Esther Pugh	-	Foolish - single woman
Wm Jones	-	A shoemaker - lazy - no family - now almost incapable of work - dd [dead?]
Anne Matthews	-	Widow lives with Jo Palmer, they have helped to ruin each other - since separated.
Wm Joyner	-	A weaver, lives at the Berrow - seems half crack'd.
Wm Partridge	-	A Cobler - large family - one child burnt to death lately. Wife sometimes mad.
Eliz Trap	-	A clumsy saucy lazy jade, fit only for a cart mare to go in the shafts.
Sar. Pitt	-	A widow - husband killed by a tree falling on him
Mary Price	-	Her husband ran away - left her. One child - poor and naked.
Wid Dee	-	Husband transported - a lazy boy at home, that ought to be out - poor. Woman very wicked. [last three words added later]

Wm Holder	-	.... work at the stocking trade
Jenny Holiday	-	Half fool, half mad and poor and would spend whenever she had.
Mary Wheeler	-	Widow - mother to Taylor the butcher's wife - a shame she should have assistance from the Parish.
John Farley	-	A cooper - loves drink
Taylor Billingham	-	Diligent, poor and strives to maintain his family
Thos Napper	-	5 children, wretchedly poor, industrious, wants his rent to be paid September 1786
Bragget Jn	-	If not sent to sea soon will undoubtedly make his exit at the gallows. Tho' scarcely 17 he is a notorious thief and has been once whipp'd at the castle, Gloucester.
Michael Harris	-	By his own consent he would be drunk every morning by breakfast, a sad quarrelsome rascal, his wife is civil, sober and industrious.
School Mistress Haynes	-	Perhaps the less said of her and her daughter the better, the husband profligate and idle.
Billy Prichard	-	A dish turner
Jno Jones Jn	-	Son of Jones of Keels - shall have nothing - undutiful to the father.
Wm Merrick	-	Self and Wife - great lubberly Dr [daughter] at home.
Powell Reuben	-	Coleford Street, a rascal
Stone Jno Sn	-	A nailer - lazy and poor

Compton

Wm Beard	-	Has a large family, almost naked and owes his misfortunes principally to his having been bound for another person who was insolvent. He did rent Waterdines formerly. It would be true charity to relieve this miserable wretch. - has 5 children at home and another child now dead.
Js Peters	-	A carpenter and wheelwright, 6 children at home - industrious and poor from the accounts of Herbert and Astman. Ye family bred up the wife. A rank Methodist.
Thos Morgan	-	Bran Green. Does not want, house burnt down since, does not want
Thos Philips	-	At the 3 Ashes, poor
Jno Uzell	-	In Town - a rogue

William Hooper was appointed Master, at a yearly salary of £10, to direct the work; to teach the children to read, write, and say their catechism; to teach the girls to spin, sew, or knit; to read prayers to them every night; to keep a day book showing the expenses of the house, the state of the sick and poor and an account of the work done.

The Vestry next considered the food to be provided for the inmates. *"Breakfast shall be milk or onion porridge, broth or suchlike, in quantity proportionate to the age. Dinner with hot meat shall be every Sunday, Tuesday, and Thursday with garden stuff and a pudding on Sunday, and the other days rice, milk toast and Tudor hasty pudding, broth, bread and cheese and the like. Their supper shall be constantly bread and cheese, meat broth or the like".*

The drink provided was *"good wholesome cider or perry, or beer at the rate of 3 bushels of malt to the hogshead of 110 gallons".* One hour was allowed for dinner *"always ready at one o'clock"* and half an hour for breakfast and supper at a time *"to be determined at the discretion of the Master according to the different seasons of the year".*

Admission to the Workhouse, on Mondays only, was granted on an order from a Churchwarden, Overseer or Inspector. A pauper brought all his goods which were held as a security for the cost of *"maintaining and burying him"* ; if he left the Workhouse any unappropriated goods were returned to him. No children were to be admitted without their parents, and no wife without her husband.

Those who were able worked, and diligent workers were allowed one penny in every shilling they earned. Money earned outside the house to be given to the Master and work could only be undertaken with the Master's permission.

The work of the inmates seems to have been mainly spinning, both flax and wool, some of which was supplied by a James Bamford of Gloucester in 1771, together with a man to instruct the workers for two months. Later in 1786, Martha Stephens was appointed *"to conduct the spinning work"* and allowed a proportion of the money earned by each wheel. It was noted that six pence a day could be earned spinning woollen yarn.

The men could take outside work and in August 1772 some were given leave to go out to harvest work and hop pulling. They also collected wood for the Workhouse fires and gathered *"stone for the benefit of the highways".*

Mr Hooper issued an ultimatum to the Governors in June 1773; he would leave *"unless the salary be increased to £20 per annum".* The Governors were of the opinion that *"a proper Master may be got at much less expense"* so they accepted his resignation and advertised the vacancy in the Gloucester Journal. Edward Godsell was appointed in August 1773 at a salary of £15 a year, from which he allowed the parish *"three pounds a year during the time he keeps his grandchild in the house"*. This was about the amount it cost to maintain each inmate

The Parish apothecary was appointed to attend the sick in the Workhouse and, in July 1772, it was decided that the sick *"shall be allowed something extraordinary as wine panada or tarts at the discretion of the inspectors"*. Panada was made from bread cooked in a liquid, presumably wine in this case, until soft then flavoured with spices and sugar.

Attention was paid to the welfare of child inmates, as for example in July 1785, when three women were deputed to look after several children each *"to wash and comb and clean them every day and keep their clothes mended"*.

As well as housing, feeding and clothing the paupers, giving them medical attention and finding them work, the Governors made provision for their spiritual well-being. In March 1772 they ordered *"that each child shall be allowed one hour every morning and one hour every evening to be instructed in the reading of their catechism"*. They also ordered that *" one common prayer book and one Bible be immediately bought for the use of this workhouse and that the whole family be called together at nine o'clock every morning and at six o'clock every evening and the common prayer read by Mr Hooper or by Thomas Holliday, every person absenting him or herself, if able to attend, shall go without a meal of victual."*

Accommodation was provided for some in the Almshouses established in 1639 for the *"habitation, relief, better settling and nursing"* of the poor. But the families could be turned out if children were *"kept at home in idleness and laziness"*; this meant that the children, from the age of seven years, had to be sent as apprentices to Masters chosen by the Vestry.

The second volume of the Vestry minutes (1820-1836) makes little mention of the relief of the poor or the workhouse. But in 1832 there is a record of the sale of *"One rood and sixteen perches of land, part of the workhouse garden"* to the Herefordshire and Gloucestershire Canal Company for £49. This sale confirms the position of the 1768 workhouse and proves it was the property of the parish of Newent.

With the passing of the Poor Law Act of 1834 neighbouring parishes were banded together to form Unions, with a Board of Guardians responsible for levying the money to run the workhouse and allow payments to the poor.

The first meeting of the Newent Union Board was held at the George Hotel on 15th September 1835, following the order and directions of the Poor Law Commissioners, and attended by seven ex-officio Guardians and representatives of fourteen of the eighteen parishes who made up the Union.

These were Newent, Bromsberrow, Dymock, Kempley, Oxenhall, Taynton, Highleadon, Hartpury, Upleadon, Tibberton, Corse, Aston Ingham, Redmarley D'Abitot, and Staunton. Absentees were from Preston, Pauntley, Rudford, and Linton.

It was agreed that the parishes should be grouped in four districts, each with a paid Relieving Officer, and that the officer of District number one, Newent, should be Governor of the Workhouse at Newent, with his wife as matron, for a salary of £75 a year. The Workhouse was to be valued *"for the purpose of renting"* and consideration was given to repairs and alterations to several workhouses, though only that at Redmarley is named. The valuation was undertaken on behalf of the Parish of Newent, showing the workhouse valued at £1,200, with a rental of £70 a year. By agreement with the parish this valuation was later reduced to *"£1,000 for value as purchase"* and £55 a year for rental. It was also agreed that repairs would be an Establishment Charge i.e. the responsibility of the Union. The question of who paid for what cropped up again over the question of insurance. Should it be the Union or the Parish of Newent, to which the property belonged and in which the freehold was vested? Back came the answer from the Poor Law Commissioners that it was an *"Establishment charge and each Parish must bear its proportion"*.

The Poor Law Commissioners set the rules and regulations and settled any difficulties that were referred to them. They approved the alteration and enlargement of the Workhouse that was to be carried out in 1836 and, in 1845, agreed to the building of a house for the reception of vagabonds at a cost of £90.

It appears from the minutes that, in some cases, Parishes used to running their own affairs resented handing over their authority and money to the central Union. In February 1836 the Churchwardens and Overseers of the Poor from Preston were summoned before two J.P.s for disobeying an order of the Guardians to pay *"the levy for their proportion of Union expenses"*. By 1844 things were running more smoothly and the accounts for each quarter show in great detail the amounts expended on the paupers in the Workhouse for food, fuel and clothing; on out-relief in money and kind; and in expenses to the Building Fund. These accounts also show the amounts spent on each parish and the levy paid by them. At the end of each quarter each parish is shown an amount owed to them or by them to balance the accounts.

The Workhouse admitted paupers from all the parishes in the Union, as the very first Admission Register in 1835 shows. The new inmates came from Aston Ingham, Linton, Dymock and Pauntley.

The census return of 1851 gives information about the Workhouse. In residence were: the Master (Hugh Finegan, born in Ireland), the Matron (Ann

Finegan, born in York), the Schoolmistress (Sarah Williams, born in Whitchurch, Herefordshire) and the Porter (James Watkins, born in Dymock), together with 12 men aged between 20 and 76, 18 women aged between 22 and 77, and 39 children. These were aged between three weeks and 15 years of whom six boys and nine girls were orphans. The majority of the inmates were born within the Union but some were from farther away; Horsham, Hereford, South Wales, High Wycombe and Monmouth.

The minutes for 1857 show tenders that were accepted for contracts to supply food, cleaning materials and clothing for the inmates. Tea, sugar, rice, oatmeal, cheese, salt, vinegar, arrowroot and treacle were listed together with best yellow soap, candles and starch, to be supplied by Elizabeth Moores. Richard Moody supplied good beef, mutton and suet; John Preedy good bacon and E. Pocock good strong beer at 1/- a gallon.

J.C. Biscoe tendered to supply shoes which *"are home manufactured goods and I can warrant the work to be firm"*. He wisely sent samples for inspection.

There was a garden at the workhouse which provided vegetables and pigs were reared for meat.

In November 1845 the Newent Workhouse was in a better position than those in other parts of the country. A letter from the Poor Law Commissioners said that, owing to the failure of the potato crop, workhouses would not be able to supply *"this article prescribed by the dietary"*. The Guardians replied that the crop here was good and that anyone who wished to know about *"the preservation of potatoes and the process of extracting farina"* from them should apply to the master. *"The medical officers say it is equally as wholesome and nutritious as that in the shops and the workhouse will sell it at a rate not exceeding three pence a pound"*.

There were, of course, problems with inmates. In 1844 the Guardians ordered James Keil to be returned to the care of *"some decent person"* in his own parish of Hartpury because he was annoying other inmates by *"screaming and making hideous noises"*.

There was serious trouble in 1845. Elizabeth Blackwell's arm was broken in a scuffle with the Master, Mr Stone. He went to investigate a disturbance in the women's room and found her complaining about the food. She swore continuously and called him a c——d old b———-d. When ordered out she kicked his shins, he boxed her ears, took hold of her shoulders and arms and they scuffled. She said the potatoes, cooked in their jackets, were dirty and had slugs in them and the *"soup stunk like pigswash"*. His reply was that the potatoes may have been dirty but *"nothing to hurt"* and the soup, which he had eaten *"was as good as usual"*.

The medical officer, Mr Cooke, who set the broken bone, said it was very small *"no larger than that of a child of 6 or 7 years"* and a little violence would have broken it. Although Blackwell was known as a bad character, often punished for disorderly conduct, the Master was reprimanded as he should not have struck her.

Nevertheless the Guardians had to report the incident to the Commissioners who wrote directly to the Master saying the violence was unnecessarily great and, unless he could give a further explanation, he would be dismissed. The Guardians' reply pleaded provocation by the woman and stressed that he had given nine years of honest and trustworthy service, treating the poor with great humanity.

These recommendations were strong enough to persuade the Commissioners to let the Master remain in office, but he must be *"more cautious and circumspect in future in your behaviour in dealing with such cases"*. In his letter of thanks to the Guardians the Master promised to *"show gratitude by diligently and honestly attending to your interests"*.

In 1851 an inmate, Jane Manning, declared that she was pregnant by James Watkins, the Workhouse porter. He denied any connection with her and, as she was known to be a bad character and somewhat idiotic, the truth of her statement was doubted. Two weeks later she admitted that her mother had told her to name the porter, but that she could not say whose child it was until after it was born. The porter who had stayed away, protesting his innocence, was told he could resume his duties.

Sarah Jeynes was also brought before the Guardians *"in a condition likely to add to the population of the country"*, but there are no further details.

Another disorderly inmate was Elizabeth Morgan of Aston Ingham; her punishment was to be given only bread and water every alternate day for a week.

In 1870 several men and one woman were arrested because they had deserted their children, leaving them a charge on the Union. The schoolmistress resigned when asked to explain why several children were dirty. The Matron was ordered to keep the children in her care clean.

William Hodges took beer into the workhouse, for which action he was taken before the Justices and given 14 days hard labour.

Two children absconded by climbing the fence in the yard and remained at liberty for some time. When reprimanded for not going after them the Master said he had not been told what to do. According to the Poor Law Board, to whom the Master was referred, children over 14, wearing clothes belonging to the workhouse, should have been taken before a J.P. to be dealt with according to the law. The Master was not empowered to capture those under 14 unless they were wearing workhouse clothes.

There was always a school in the workhouse but in September 1870 Lady Beauchamp offered to maintain and educate two girls for two years in her Industrial School. The Guardians allowed £5 to provide the necessary outfit for the girls.

The medical needs of the poor were considered at the first meeting in 1838 and medical officers appointed. By 1845 the doctors were George Hollister, John Cooke and Thomas Hooper. They all reported successfully vaccinating the children of the parishes in the Union, 91 under one year and 234 about one year old, in the year ended 29th September 1845. The Poor Law Commissioners to whom this was reported replied that this was good but that the number of those under one year vaccinated fell short of the number of births in the year.

Under the Compulsory Vaccination Act of 1867 parents who did not take their children to be vaccinated could be prosecuted. Yet on one occasion in 1870 Mr Cattle, then Medical Officer, failed to attend leaving parents to wait for five hours. He was severely reprimanded. He was also guilty of not going to visit a sick child who died on the way home from the surgery to which his mother was forced to take him.

Mr Cooke, asked to explain why he had not attended a woman who died of a haemorrhage after giving birth to twins, said he had no order to go so would not have been paid for the visit.

A formal notice sent to workhouses in 1871 said that the attention of the Local Government Board had been drawn to accounts of accidents occurring through the absence of proper regulation for the bathing of inmates. In future these rules should be applied :- Every inmate should be bathed on admission, after a prescribed examination. After that, bathing would be once a month unless the medical officer prescribed otherwise. The officer in charge should check the temperature of the water, not higher than 98 degrees Fahrenheit, and some paid officer or servant appointed by the Guardians should oversee the arrangement. This entailed issuing the key to the hot tap and collecting it afterwards. A schoolmaster should always be present when a child was bathed and *"any marks, bruises, wounds, sores, or local pain"* should be reported to the Master or Matron. A separate towel should be provided for every inmate, and towels should be washed before being used again.

Casual paupers who were housed for one night had to earn their bed and food. Men could work breaking stones (for the repair of roads), not less than 1.5 cwt or more than 4 cwt; or pick oakum (one pound of unbeaten or two pounds of beaten); or do three hours work in digging or pumping or cutting wood, or grinding corn. Those who stayed more than one night had to work, for each entire day they were there, breaking 7 cwt of stones (not less than 5 or more than 12); pick 4 pounds unbeaten or 8 pounds beaten oakum; or do 9 hours digging, pumping, cutting wood or grinding corn.

Women had to pick half a pound of unbeaten or one pound of beaten oakum; or do three hours work in washing or scrubbing and cleaning. The amount of oakum was quadrupled for each full day and nine hours work of washing, or cleaning or needlework had to be worked.

It is not clear if that amount of work was demanded of regular inmates but the regulations of 1871 state that those who discharge themselves may be detained for periods from 24 to 72 hours. Punishments for those who abscond, or escape from, or leave the Workhouse or wilfully give a false name or make a false statement for the purpose of obtaining relief may, on conviction, be sentenced as an *"idle or disorderly person"* with imprisonment in the house of correction with hard labour.

The same punishment befell anyone who destroyed his own clothes or damaged any of the property of the Guardians. In addition he could be sentenced as *"a rogue and a vagabond".*

How different from the kinder and more humane treatment in the old workhouse in the 18th century.

Severe weather in December 1870 and January 1871 made it necessary to make payments to able-bodied men, particularly watermen and woodcutters. With the approval of the Poor Law Board 31 men with wives and children received relief of 1/- to 2/- a week and loaves of bread (from two to seven according to need). Later, in August 1871, the Guardians were told that the amount of relief per head in this Union, calculated on the population, was much higher than in this and adjoining counties.

In December 1871 a committee appointed to look into the workings of the Union found the current system of administration was defective. The Guardians considered several cases of out-relief given to men with five, seven or eight children. It was felt that not enough attention had been given to circumstances - whether there were relatives who could help - or to the character and habits of the applicant.

A plea was made for Guardians from all the parishes to attend more regularly as they would have better information in these cases.

There was also a nuisance removal committee who reported that inferior cottages should be improved and sanitary nuisances abated. It was suggested that wages should be adjusted so that the poor could live without parish relief, and that superfluous public houses should be suppressed, the lowest estimate being one half of them.

In the minute books there are meticulously kept accounts for each quarter of the year and in 1878 a booklet, setting out all details of the administration of the Union for the half year ended 25th March, was printed by A Clarke of the Express office (now Gooch's Sports Shop).

In addition to the Board of Guardians, the Overseers of the Poor and the Collectors of Rates, there was the Rural Sanitary Authority, headed by the Medical Officer of Health (with a salary of £20 a year) and a Sanitary Inspector; a Union Assessment Committee (to set the rates); a visiting Committee; and a School Attendance Committee.

The Relieving Officers for each district attended weekly at certain places in the parishes to distribute and receive applications for relief. The Medical Officers set times and places for vaccinations and were paid 1/6 to 3/- a head according to the distance they had to travel. Registration Officers for births, marriages and deaths attended in the individual parishes.

During the half year Newent Parish spent £334-8s-7d on paupers in the workhouse and £1,461-0s-11d on out-relief. Income came from parish rates, the sale of rags and bones, from the Local Government Board and from profits on the pig account, the stone account, baking and the garden.

At that time (1878) Newent had a population of 3168, there were 11 men, 11 women and 13 children under 16 in the workhouse and 57 men, 101 women and 50 children receiving out-relief.

By May 1918 there were only 20 inmates, costing 14/- a week each, in the workhouse. The Local Government Board suggested it should be closed. The Guardians considered increasing the numbers by taking in mental defectives, but the premises were said not to be suitable. The other option was to board the inmates in other workhouses. Gloucester, Ross and Upton-on-Severn had no spare accommodation but Tewkesbury offered to help at 10/- a week for fit paupers and 12/6 for those who were sick.

This was accepted in September and a month's notice given to the Medical Officer, the Chaplain, Nurse and Cook. The Rev. W.H.Conner replied that *"the closure is not unwelcome and the grave want of consideration which the Governors have shown to my feelings and convictions .... have made tenure of the office irksome to me. I would have resigned long ago if it hadn't been for the spiritual interests of the inmates".* The inmates were sent to Tewkesbury by ambulance and cars, and with them went a pantechnicon containing bedsteads, linen, clothing and provisions.

The following year the disposal of part of the premises was discussed, with some rooms kept in use as offices and a boardroom for the Guardians. The approval of the Ministry of Health was sought and gained provided the price was *"consistent with a proper valuation"*. An auction in March 1920 produced no offers and it was hoped to sell by private treaty. In July 1920 Miss Hutchinson asked if the newly formed Women's Institute could use a room (formerly the men's dormitory) for their meetings. Her request was granted at a rent of 1/- a year.

By 1921 the yearly charges on the property were heavy and as a sale was still not forthcoming, permission was sought to let the part the Guardians had authority to sell. Gloucestershire County Council wanted to establish a Secondary School in Newent and the Guardians approached the Education Committee with a view to letting as the property might not be suitable for purchase.

At a special meeting in October 1921 Mr Chew proposed that, as there was a need for a Secondary School for pupils whose parents could not afford to pay fees and train fares to Gloucester, the Guardians *"should hand over free of all cost all the premises now owned by the Board to the Gloucestershire Education Committee"*.

The Ministry of Health, whose approval was needed, replied that all the Guardians must receive 14 days notice of a formal resolution to authorize the sale to *"Gloucestershire County Council of the whole block of buildings known as Newent Workhouse, with the land attached thereto, for the nominal consideration of £1"*

In January 1922 Mr Chew saw the plans for a school of 150 pupils which was to be established in the near future. Although the purchase was sanctioned in May 1922 it was not until September 1923 that all matters were settled, including altering the conveyance to make clear that, if the premises were not used as a school, they were to be handed back to the Guardians. The County Council took possession on 1st January 1924.

By the Local Government Act of 1929 responsibility for the relief of the poor was transferred from the Board of Guardians to the County Council.

Sources

Newent Vestry Minutes	GRO P225 VE2/1	1768 -1818
	GRO P225 VE2/2	1819 -1830
Board of Guardians minutes	GRO G/NE 8a	1835 -1923
Booklet	GRO P11	1878
Rules of Bathing	GRO D 2391	
Admissions Register	GRO G/NE 60/1	
List of the Poor	GRO D1791/6	

13. Industries
David Bick

The industrial history of any district is greatly influenced by its geology which determines the extent of its mineral wealth. Nearly all parishes were at least to some degree endowed, if only with such prosaic resources as clay, gravel or stone. But Newent had more than most; it had reserves of coal and iron ores, although never enough to rival its neighbour, the Forest of Dean. Even so, in antiquity and again in more recent times, such dreams did not seem altogether out of the question.

But in addition the wide range of strata including the Permian, the Old Red Sandstone and the Silurian rocks around May Hill and Gorsley gave rise to a number of lesser industries, all of which sadly, are no more. There were of course, other activities independent of mineral resources, such as corn milling, brass-working and clock-making, perhaps more trade or craft than industry, which also deserve a mention.

Iron mining and smelting

"I confess that these old metallurgical processes have a peculiar charm for me.... something which has done good service in its day has gone forever"
John Percy, Iron and Steel, p 326

This industry is very ancient, and almost certainly pre-Roman. It arose because of extensive, if on the whole low-grade, amounts of iron ore were deposited just above the Coal Measures where they outcrop north of Kilcot as far as Castle Tump. Such ores could be quarried opencast, often leaving little or no evidence behind. But an indication of the amount raised may be gathered from the vast heaps of partially smelted cinders still surviving locally in the 17th and 18th centuries (1). Some at least dated back to the Romans, for in 1779 Rudder, the county historian, recorded how in re-working the tips for their residual iron content, *"the workmen found several coins of Julius Caesar, Nerva, Vespasian etc, and some pieces of fine Roman pottery, now all dispersed and destroyed"*.

Rudder's testimony has been amply confirmed in recent years. Traces of much Roman activity including iron-smelting was found during construction of Newent's Business Park in 1992/3. A few years previously, similar evidence was found in ploughed fields east of Moat Farm where the soil is almost black, the whole site extending to over 100 acres. There were also extensive operations in parts of Taynton and Tibberton, where field names such as Middle Cinders, Cinders East and Lower Cinders are reminders of a forgotten past (2).

The industry, as well as coal mining, was alive at the time of the Conquest, and both were active in 1172 (3). But our main evidence dates from the first half of the 17th century. From this time, the huge quantities of cinders which had accumulated over a wide area from the Forest of Dean northwards, began to be re-smelted together with iron ore proper, using the newly introduced charcoal-fired blast furnaces. A dozen or so operations of this kind had been established in or near Dean when a local man, Francis Finch, converted an old mill just to the north of Newent, for the purpose. It was variously known as Elmbridge, Oxenhall or Newent Furnace, and operated almost continuously during the winter (for reasons explained shortly) from about 1639 to 1751.

Most of the forest iron went *up river* by boats to forges beyond Worcester, and Newent was well placed for such markets because of lower transport costs. Some at least of Finch's ore came from Oxenhall just east of Holder's Lane as it approaches Four Oaks, and many years ago, the late Mr Hough who lived in a cottage there showed me a splendid lump of "kidney ore" which very probably had come from the workings. In the Woodward Collection at Cambridge a specimen of Newent ore, collected some three centuries ago, can still be seen. (Drawer B.7.1)

By 1660, Finch had sold his interests to Thomas Foley, an ironmaster from Stourbridge. Foley, his sons and partners, soon gained almost a monopoly of the iron trade in the region, and we are fortunate that many of their business accounts survive in great detail. Annual production of pig-iron was around 400-500 tons, which was mainly carted via Forge Lane, Upleadon, to Ashleworth for shipment via the Severn. However, some artefacts such as firebacks for decorating and protecting the back of inglenook fireplaces, were cast at the works, of which a dozen or more survive locally (4). They were crude in form and long out of fashion elsewhere, being simply made by pouring the molten metal into a rectangular mould into which a few stamps had been usually impressed giving a date and initial letters, often those of the owner, factor or moulder. More sophisticated firebacks displaying Coats of Arms, lions and unicorns etc could be made from a single wooden pattern, and in quantity. But the interesting thing about the homespun Newent examples is that no two were ever the same, they were all one-offs and unique, and nowadays greatly prized.

The Newent ironworks employed some hundreds of people, but mainly on contract, and wages were often supplemented by other work. Farmers and carriers commonly filled this role. The main demand for labour was not at the furnace itself, but in supplying and carting the cinders, iron ore and especially charcoal. The latter amounted easily to the heaviest overhead, but its production gave great employment in woods and coppices for miles around, some being as far away as Dean. The round and level platforms about 20 ft diameter with a very black soil, are common features in woodland still to be found if you keep your eyes open. As to cinder consumption, this probably amounted to some 100,000 tons during the lifetime of the furnace.

Fig.44 A fireback cast at Newent Ironworks in 1655

Furnaces needed a strong blast of air to gain the high temperatures required for smelting. Waterwheels were the usual source of power for operating the bellows, which resembled the ordinary domestic variety, but on a very much larger scale. Running continuously, such wheels had a prodigious thirst, which in the Newent area could only be quenched by building large reservoirs, and even then, production of iron was limited to the wintertime with its heavier rainfall. Shutting down and re-starting the furnace was attended by such heavy expense that a reliable water supply was an absolute priority.

Fig. 45 A fireback almost certainly cast at Newent Ironworks in 1671

In total, four big ponds and a number of smaller ones totalling many acres were eventually constructed, of which only one, Furnace Pond near the old canal at Oxenhall, still retains its sheet of water. About half a mile from the furnace, it dates from its very beginnings and was fed by a long leat or watercourse which skirted round the south side of the church to tap the upper reaches of Ell Brook somewhere near Hill House. (Interestingly enough, long after the works closed, a short-lived branch of the Hereford & Gloucester Canal took a parallel course in 1796 to Hill House Colliery).

But more reservoirs were soon needed. As well as a number of small ponds, three large ones were eventually constructed (see fig.46) on Gorsley Common, which was then a wild and barren tract of some 400 acres, and very different to the patchwork of smallholdings and other desirable properties we know today. One dated from 1666 and cost some £64, being followed by another at nearly double the sum in 1694/5. These were heavy outlays, in addition to continual overheads such as payments to landlords for watercourse rents, and wayleaves for carrying cinders and other materials. The biggest pond, No.1 on the plan, (grid reference 681257) was just below Linton Hall, and was not drained until 1860.

As an archaeological testimony of these ancient waterworks, even after two and a half centuries and generations of intensive agriculture, a surprising amount remains to reward the explorer. Fortunately, nearly all the sites are accessible by public footpaths as indicated on Ordnance maps.

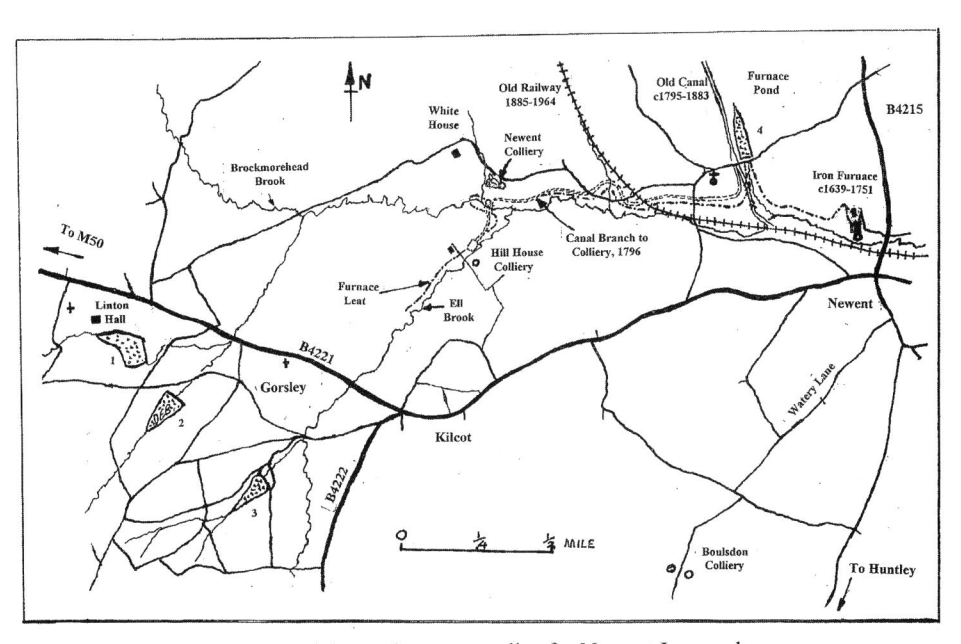

Fig.46 Coalpits, and water supplies for Newent Ironworks

In addition to Furnace Pond, a well known haven of wildlife, the earthen dams of the other three big ponds also survive, though long forgotten and lost beneath hedgerows, trees and scrub. Dams 2 (683255) and 3 (687250) have long since been breached by floods, but that of Gorsley Pool, No.1, is still intact and so is its sluice-chamber, of masonry construction easily visible at the base of the dam and the size of a small room. It is well worthy of conservation. Traces of the leat can also be distinguished in a field just south of the Brockmorehead Brook and close to the route of the ill-fated canal colliery branch of 1796. It again appears as a shallow shelf curving round in a field a few yards north of Whitehouse Lane, at grid reference 705266. Just to the east are remnants of a masonry aqueduct where it crossed a stream, but beyond here all has succumbed to the plough.

Newent Furnace closed down for reasons that are not very clear, but it appears that cinders and local ores were running out. Charcoal was probably not a problem as woods were continually cut down by rotation, and need be no more destroyed than harvesting destroys a cornfield. The huge charcoal store and the blowing house still survive in Furnace Lane, and are listed buildings. The whole story of the ironworks deserves a book in itself, but more details are available in *The Mines of Newent and Ross* (1).

Coal Mining

Coal seams which outcropped at the surface must have been known from earliest times. The main working areas were around Boulsdon, and in a narrow band from behind Kilcot as far north as Castle Tump. Surprisingly, it appears that these two areas, small as they are, have different origins in geological time, and are quite distinct (6).

Geological difficulties rendered these coal ventures more or less doomed from the start, but great were the efforts over the centuries to turn them to account, and it is a pity that so few records have survived. The seams were up to 8 ft thick but badly faulted and where overlaid by the water-bearing New Red Sandstone, a further hazard arose. The latter however, did not apply to the Great Boulsdon operations, which tottered on with sundry intermissions at least from 1608 for the next two centuries. In 1807 the pits were described as *in their infant state* but in fact were now in mortal decline. A very heavy roof consumed huge quantities of pit-props to keep the workings open, and probably no more than a handful of men were ever engaged at a time. In the latter years John Nourse Morse of Southerns was much involved but the division of the ground under several different owners was another difficulty. He died in 1830, aged 90, after which his large estates in and around Newent were sold by auction.

Fig.47 Newent Colliery in 1879.
The grassgrown tip still survives in Whitehouse Lane

The low ground between the B4221 road at Kilcot and Whitehouse Lane was also intensively worked, with as many as half a dozen shafts in a single field. In the 1700s the construction of the Hereford and Gloucester Canal brought new hopes, and the company actually opened pits between Lower House and Hill House on its own account, with a branch from its main line at Oxenhall. But it carried little traffic and soon closed. The painful fact soon dawned, that instead of aiding the coalfield, the canal was bringing in better coal from the Midlands. The market for the Newent coal was very local, and mainly for lime-burning and brick-making. A coal owner from Somerset, Richard Perkins, took over the pits for a while in conjunction with John Moggridge of Boyce Court, but about 1800 they closed. The Kilcot collieries later revived, and we learn something of the workforce from the Census Returns of 1841; the venture did not last long afterwards.

Address	Name	Occupation	Age
Kilcot	William Perkes	Engineer	20
	Robert Rudge	Coal Miner	20
	William Predett	Coal Miner	40
Near Lower House	John Weale	Coal Miner	35
	Elizabeth Weale	-	40
Colliery Cottage	Joseph George	Coal Merchant	40
Collier's Cabin	John Day	Coal Miner	50
	Henry Portlock	Coal Miner	15

The Weales had seven children between one month and 15 years, several apparently also being miners

The final revival came in the 1870s, but only on a very small scale. The most determined attempt came in 1876 when the Newent Colliery Co. sank a shaft 448 ft deep just south of the lane east of White House on part of the Onslow Estate. The venture was launched by a shadowy figure named William Aston and most of the capital came from the Stourbridge-Birmingham area. A nominal capital of £7,000 soon proved quite insufficient, and a new concern, the Newent Coal and Iron Co. took over a year later. But by this time the shaft, sunk through treacherous beds of the New Red Sandstone, had encountered excessive inflows of water at times amounting to 1,000 gallons per minute. This required the heavy cost of installing and working a powerful underground steam pump (which is probably still in situ), but at last all appeared well when a 7 ft seam of coal was struck in July 1879. Great were the jubilations, with a free dinner for the men at the George Hotel, Newent; but they were premature. The coal soon petered out and with other heavy burdens, a year later the company had no option but to wind up. This however, incensed the Onslow Trustees, to whom rents were outstanding; they thereupon distrained and put up the whole plant for auction over the heads of the company. The sale, by Bruton Knowles & Co, took place in November 1880.

Now, all that remains of the enterprise is a nicely wooded hillock, the old waste tip, as a fitting memorial to the coal mining past of Newent. An intriguing question is how hard-headed industrialists were ever persuaded literally to sink their money in a pit on an estate where the geology was so very unfavourable, and where worthwhile reserves of coal had never been proven.

There was however, a final attempt to re-open Newent Colliery about 1924, by a mushroom company with the grandiose title The British Mines Debenture Corporation. Blatant lies as to the history and prospects of the area were told in a promotional leaflet entitled *A Coal Romance,* and published by Leonard Hays and Co. of Gloucester, but fortunately for any gullible investors, the enterprise never left the ground (7). Many further details of local adventures for coal can be found in *The Mines of Newent and Ross* (1).

Stone and Lime

Within a few miles of the town nearly every geological formation from the Jurassic to the Silurian makes its presence felt, each having its own contribution in building and limestone. The following table illustrates some of the products which gave the buildings in the locality their particular character, as for instance, the lovely honey-coloured Gorsley stone, so reminiscent of the Cotswolds, but much older geologically and a sandstone rather than a limestone.

Geological Period	Parish (examples)	Products	Colour of stone (examples)
Jurassic (lower Lias)	Ashleworth Highnam, Corse	Limestone, lime flagstones, bricks	Cream, grey/blue *Rudford Church*
Trias (New Red Sandstone)	Corse, Upleadon, Tibberton, Newent, Redmarley Pauntley, Newent	Bricks, pottery, Iron-ore Silver Sand	Grey/white, *Corse Church* Grey Orange, *Redmarley Church* Red/brown, *Newent Furnace Charcoal Store*
Carboniferous (coal measures)	Newent Oxenhall, Dymock	Coal, iron-ore bricks	No examples
Devonian (Old Red Sandstone) Silurian	Dymock Kempley, Linton Newent, Taynton Longhope	Bricks, flagstones roofing slates Limestone, lime, iron-ore, bricks tiles	Grey/red brown, *Longhope Church* Cream/orange, *Picklenash Old School* Red/brown, *Cottages on May Hill*

Building stone was last worked at the parish quarry in Quarry Lane, until 1941, when the war took away the labour. Since then, Gorsley stone for making repairs or extensions has been at a premium, with artificial stone often used in its place and with generally unhappy result, for the two are incompatible and do not weather in the same way. The parish quarry is now designated as of Special Scientific Interest, being at the junction of the Old Red and Silurian formations.

Just to the north and tucked out of sight was Green's Quarry, a larger working with beds of blueish limestone much used for lime-burning. The lime was valued as first-rate for agricultural improvement even 200 years ago. The whole area was then one wild and more or less uninhabited common, and there was talk of a branch to the canal at Oxenhall, but it came to nothing. The building stone was being sold at one shilling per ton, or around £30 in today's money (8). The limekilns were at the quarry, and over a period of time more and bigger ones were added, making six in total, the last being the largest within many miles (9). When I came to Newent 30 years ago they were all there, though in ruins, but sadly this unique battery has not been spared, all except one or two kilns having succumbed to make way for a new dwelling.

There was also a quarry just across the main road opposite Quarry Lane, but it is now filled in and gone without trace. The biggest of all, now badly overgrown and nearly inaccessible, was in the wood north of Pound Farm and next to the M50 motorway, The remnants of two limekilns still survive. Another quarry for Gorsley stone was at the cross-roads in Clifford's Mesne, where a red-bricked house now stands. It was once very deep and the stone went to Newent station by traction engine.

The Old and New Red Sandstones of the district were generally too soft for building, although Redmarley Church is mainly of the latter, in a buff colour, the old quarry being a few hundred yards to the south-east. Some of the red beds also served for roofing tiles and flags. Better for the purpose were the blue-grey Lias flagstones from the Corse Lawn area, and they can still be found in many old houses, cellars and out-buildings. Rudford Church is built of similar material, but the stone is now very badly weathered.

Brickworks and Potteries

Nearly all the various geological formations around Newent had clays suitable for brickmaking, but it is said that the first bricks came from Gloucester, mainly for the tops of chimneys. The first house made wholly of brick still survives in Broad Street, the ground floor being a butcher's shop. Its high wall bordering Court Lane is a later addition, but at the rear the original brickwork is still visible. For many new dwellings, bricks were often fired on the spot to save the cost of carriage. The Foley partnership accounts reveal the scale of production on their lands when we read of stocks at Gorsley and Shaw Common in 1752, as follows: Bricks, 78,000; Tiles, 28,000. There was also a big works at Moat Farm, near St Anthony's Cross going in 1744, where *Plain tiles, cress, gutters, hipps, squares, wire-brick stock and common bricks* were advertised in the Gloucester Journal.

In the 1890s one George Ballinger established a brick and tile works using beds of both red and blue clay at Clifford's Mesne, an unlikely location bearing in mind its isolation. But like another venture, the Newent Brick and Pipeworks at Aylescroft Farm, it lasted a number of years. Just beyond the parish, the Taynton Brick and Tileworks on the way to Huntley deserves a mention because of its range and diversity of products, including garden ornaments and glazed vases and tobacco jars. Such items are worth looking out for; many of the old bricks and tiles bore the maker's name, and are also worth collecting as examples of bygone local industries (8)(10).

Corn and other Mills

According to the Domesday Survey of 1086/7, Newent had three mills. We cannot be sure of their locations except to say that they may well have endured in use for centuries, along with various others which arose in the meantime.

A list of the known sites is given below, as well as a few details as far as space permits. Mostly however, they are long forgotten, with often barely a stone remaining to remind us where one generation after another of millers lived, worked and died. Generally, the mill house and the mill were one, a mixed blessing due to the dust, noise and vibration inseparable from working conditions.

(Further information is given in "The Mills of Gloucestershire", Mills & Riemer, 1989)

Note: an asterisk denotes that buildings survive. A cross denotes that some or all of the millrace exists.

On the Ell Brook

Hill House Mill (grid reference 698263?) This was a former grist mill demolished before 1780 (11)

Crookes Mill+ (706265) Demolished before 1900, traces remain.

Furnace Mill (719265) The ironworks later occupied the site.

Cleeve Mill*+ (732262) Operating until the 1950s, much of the machinery survives, including an iron waterwheel visible from the road. The site is reputedly Saxon.

Okle Pitcher Mill* (737259) Alongside the canal and later, the railway, this historic name has recently been replaced by a concocted title "Oakelbrook Mill".

Brass Mill*+ (742256) This was once called Okeley Mill. In 1646 it had lately been converted into a brass hammer-mill; hence its present name.

Malswick Mill*+ (756247) The house and mill are separate, close to the B4215 road.

On the Watery Lane Brook

Common Fields Mill (715253?) This must have stood opposite Bradford's Lane. The mill race is shown on old Ordnance maps running ENE from Common Fields House, and a breached earthen dam upstream was presumably a millpond. Below the mill site, the stream down Watery Lane was culverted and lost to view within living memory.

On Peacock's Brook

Boulsdon Mill+ (714245) In a valley east of Great Boulsdon, all that remains is a well defined millrace and a nearby ground called "Mill Field" on the tithe map.

Tannery Mill (721257) This was demolished in recent years to make way for a new development, but some of the old tannery buildings have been sympathetically converted.

Mill+ (name unknown) (727262) Near a footbridge, some masonrywork still survives in the bed of the brook which was diverted to form a millrace.

Fig. 48. Lancaster Sawmills, Newent c1960. Next to bandsaw is Jimmy Addis (sawyer) & Jimmy Dee (in cap, the saw doctor). Right is Victor Champkin.

Sawmills

Ladder and Fencing Industries (Newent) Ltd in Horsefair Lane owes its origins to the late Herbert Lancaster who lived at Shirley House, Newent. Not a local man, he began before the First World War and established a fine reputation using home grown timber, making everything from lock-gates to blocks and tackle for the Mayflower sailing ship. The GWR put in a private siding to the works, and a steam traction-engine hauled the timber before a French Latil tractor replaced it in the 1930s. In 1930, Jimmy Dee of Newent started there at 14 years old (7 am - 6 pm) and never lost a day's work in nearly 40 years. Lancaster gave employment to 60 or 70 people and was much respected, Lancaster Terrace being named after him. Later, the firm passed through several hands, including Price, Walker & Co. of Gloucester.

Cider and Perry

Gloucestershire was long famous for its cider, and perry made from the Taynton Quash pear which was said to equal champagne. Orchards were everywhere, but most have been grubbed up. The old Perry-pear trees were all tall and stately, and lived much longer than cider-apple trees. You can still see them opposite the Kilcot Inn, at Malswick by the roadside, and in many other places (13).

In addition two hundred years ago the district was world-famous for the wonderful Styre apple, which had been found growing wild in a hedge. Its cider was like nectar, the best matured varieties would sell for the incredible price of £21 per barrel of 52.5 gallons, or about £10-£15 per bottle at today's prices. In those days, Dymock alone was making over 100,000 gallons of perry and cider every year. Sadly, the Styre apple eventually died out, presumably due to disease, and hardly a Quash tree remains (14).

One of the growers was John Nourse Morse who lived at Southerns in Southend Lane. He paid his men in bronze tokens redeemable in Newent, and preferably at his own general stores. He owned much of the town and a colliery at Boulsdon as well, and died in 1830 at the ripe old age of 90. Practically every farm had its own cider mill, and some still remain, long disused in their original buildings. They now fetch a fortune as garden ornaments, but hopefully one or two may yet return to their proper use.

Newent cider regained the limelight in a somewhat dubious fashion just after the second world war when a plausible rogue named Frank White, alias Eustace Hamilton Ian Stewart-Hargreaves, bought Stardens (see chapter 5).

"Loveliest of trees, the cherry now
Is hung with bloom along the bough,
And stands about the woodland ride
Wearing white for Eastertide."

Housman's well known stanza reminds us of another local product. Eric Freeman's pickers, and men with muzzle-loaders were up at 4 am to save the 5 or 6 ton crop from the birds. Who would suppose that the Supermarket car park by the Memorial Hall was where it all took place.

Nowadays, Newent is still an apple-growing area, and there was also a hop industry, about which little is known. Two old hop-kilns at Durbridge Mill are a legacy of this forgotten chapter, and there was a hop-yard at Sandyways, north of the town.

Fig.49 The face of a Newent Clock by T Bradley, 1820

Miscellany

Newent had a number of other industries, including a tannery in Culver Street and a gasworks in Watery Lane opposite the Recreation Ground; the offices still survive as a brick dwelling close to the road. There were maltings in Culver Street next to Barclays Bank and at the Malt House in High Street; both buildings remain, though used for other purposes.

Flax was grown in the district, and it was suggested that daffodil fields owe their origins to commerce, the plants being used to prepare a dye. There was also weaving, and the Biscos, a well known Newent family came long ago as Huguenots in connection with the trade. The town also supported craftsmen such as Thomas Bradley who made watches and clocks for many years prior to 1849 (15). Not long ago I came across a grandfather clock with a 12 inch painted face marked *T. Bradley, Newent* and inscribed on the back *October 20, 1820.* Long may it remain in the district.

Around 1910 a bicycle called the Ellbrook after the nearby stream was made over a blacksmith's shop in Wharf Pitch (near the fire-station) but no survivors are known (16). More forgotten ventures might be mentioned, but space forbids.

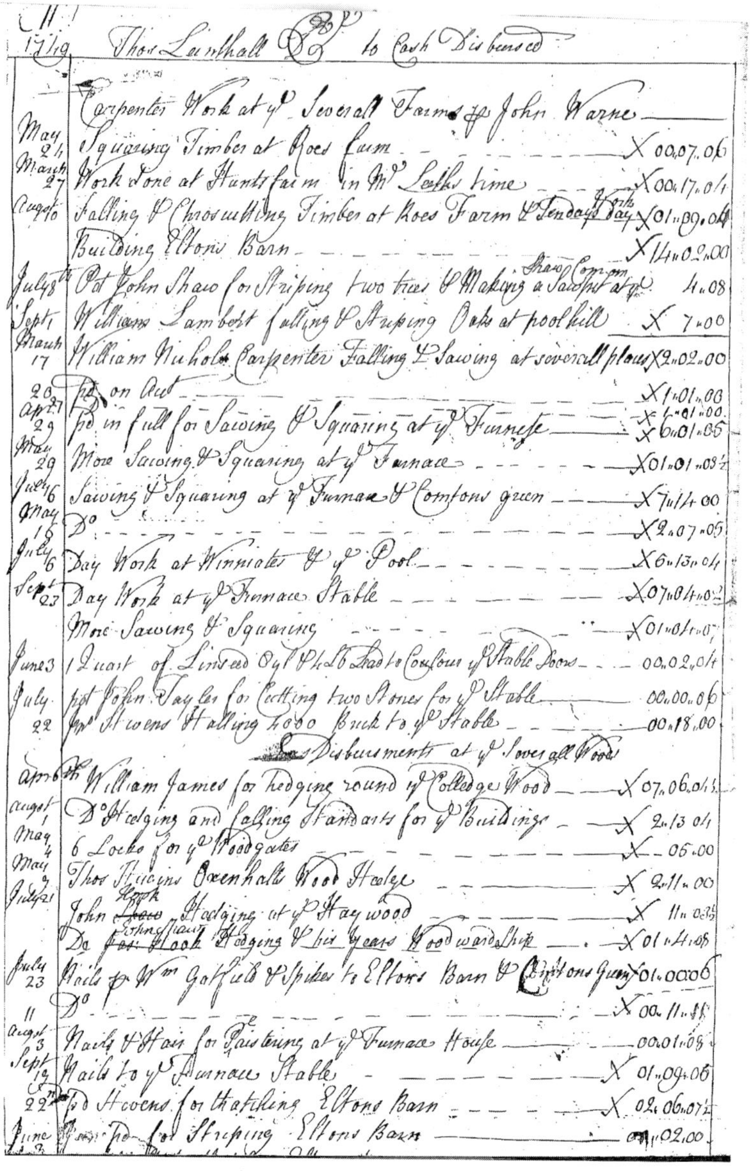

1749	Thos Lunthall Dr to Cash Disbursed	
	Carpenter Work at ye Severall Farms ꝑ John Warne	
May 24	Squaring Timber at Roes Farm	X 00.07.06
March 27	Work done at Hunts farm in Mr Leths time	X 00.17.04
Augst 10	Falling & Chrosscutting Timber at Roes Farm & Tenday Oaks	X 01.09.04
	Building Eltons Barn	X 14.02.00
July 18	Pd John Shaw for Striping two trees & Making a Sawpit at ye Sharp Compn	4.08
Sept	William Lambert falling & Striping Oaks at poolhill	X 7.00
March 17	William Nichols Carpenter Falling & Sawing at severall plans	X 2.02.00
20	pd on Acct	X 1.01.00
Apr 27		X 1.01.00
May 29	Do in full for Sawing & Squaring at ye Furnace	X 6.01.05
May 29	More Sawing & Squaring at ye Furnace	X 01.01.03
July 16	Sawing & Squaring at ye Furnace & Comptons green	X 7.14.00
May 18	Do	X 2.07.05
July 6	Day Work at Winniates & ye Pool	X 6.13.04
Sept 23	Day Work at ye Furnace Stable	X 07.04.02
	More Sawing & Squaring	X 01.01.0
June 3	1 Quart of Linseed Oyl & Lb Lead to Couleur of Stable Doors	00.02.04
July	pd John Tayler for Cutting two Stones for ye Stable	00.00.06
22	Mr Stevens Falling 1000 Brick to ye Stable	00.18.00
	Disbursments at ye Soverall Wood	
April 6	William James for hedging round ye Colledge Wood	X 07.06.04
Augst 1	Do Hedging and falling Standarts for ye Buildings	X 2.13.04
May 4	6 Locks for ye Wood gates	X .05.00
May 3	Thos Higgins Oxenhall Wood Heleye	X 2.11.00
July 21	John Hugh Hedging at ye Haywood	X 11.0
	John Shaw for Hook Hedging & his years Woodwardship	X 01.14.08
July 23	Nails ꝑ Wm Gotfield & Spikes to Eltons Barn & Comptons Green	X 01.00.06
11	Do	X 00.11.11
Augst 3	Nails & Hair for Paistering at ye Furnace House	00.01.08
Sept	Nails to ye Furnace Stable	X 01.09.06
22	Do Stevens for thatching Eltons Barn	X 02.06.07
June 13	Do Do for Striping Eltons Barn	02.00

Fig.50 A page from the Newent Ironworks Accounts of 1749
(transcribed on the next page)

1749	Thomas Leinthall to Cash Disbursed	
	Carpenter work at ye severall farms of John Warne	
May 24	Squaring timber at Roes Farm	00-07-06
March 27	Work done at Hunts Farm in Mr Leiths time	00-17-04
Augst 10	Falling & chroscutting timber at Roes Farm & ten days dayworks	01-09-04
	Building Eltons Barn	14-02-00
July 8th	Pd John Shaw for striping two trees & making a sawpit at Shaw Common	4-08
Sept 1	William Lambert falling & striping oaks at Poolhill	7-00
March 17	William Nichols carpenter falling & sawing at severall places	2-02-00
20	Pd on Acct	1-01-00
Apr 27	D "	1-01-00
29	Pd in full for sawing & squaring at ye Furnese	6-01-05
May 29	More sawing & squaring at ye Furnace	01-10-8.5
Jul 16	Sawing & squaring at ye Furnace & Comtons Green	7-14-00
May 16	Do "	2-07-05
July 6	Day work at Winniates & ye Pool	6-13-04
Sept 23	Day work at ye Furnace Stable	07-04-02
	More sawing & squaring	01-04-07
June 3	1 quart of Linseed Oyl pt L6 lead to coulour ye stable doors	00-02-04
July 22	Pd John Tayler for cutting two stones for ye stable	00-00-06
	Jno Stevens halling 4000 brick to ye stable	00-18-00
	Disbursments at ye severall woods	
Apr 6	William James for hedging round ye Colledge Wood	07-06-04
Augst 1	Do hedging and falling standarts for ye buildings	2-13-04
May 4	6 locks for ye Woodgates	05-00
May 9	Thos Hugins Oxenhalls Wood Hedge	2-11-00
July 21	John Hook hedging at ye Haywood	11-03
	Do John Shaw hedging at his years woodwardship	1-4-08
July 23	Nails per Wm Gatfield & spikes to Eltons Barn & Comtons Green	01-00-06
11	Do	00-11-11
August 3	Nails & hair for plaistering at ye Furnace House	00-01-08
Sept 19	Nails to ye Furnace stable	01-09-06
22 nd	Pd Stevens for thatching Eltons Barn	02-06-7.5
June 3	Pd for striping Eltons Barn	0?-02-00

Fig.51 Transcription of page of Furnace Accounts 1749
(Note:- Thomas Leinthall was Steward/Manager to Thos Foley)

References
1. David Bick   1987   The Mines of Newent and Ross
2. Don Sherratt   1998   Newent's Roman Past
3. Dugdale   1846   Monasticon Anglicanum,
                                     Vol VI, Pt 2, 1075-7
4. I am indebted to Van Goulding for certain information from this source
5. David Bick   1985   Period Homes, Sept p 21-4
6. Brit Geol Survey   1989   Geology of the Country
                                     around Tewkesbury
7. GRO D 3398, PRO, BT 31/28518
8. David Bick   1992   Old Newent and District
9. David Bick   1984   Limekilns on the Glos-Heref. Border,
                                     Ind. Arch. Review
10. Don Sherratt   2000   Taynton's Industrial Past
11. GRO, D 1882
12. GRO, D 22 T 10
13. L C Luckwell &   1963   Perry Pears, Univ. Bristol
    A Pollard
14. Marshall   1796   The Rural Economy of Gloucestershire,
                                     Vol 2
15. Graham Dowdler   1984   Gloucestershire Watchmakers
16. Information from the late Mr Jenkins of Lancaster Terrace

14. The Newent Glasshouse and Potteries
Don Sherratt

The origins of the Newent Glasshouse go back to the glass making industry that operated at the furthermost corner of the parish over four centuries ago. It is one of only a small number of glass making areas in Britain that were started up in the late 16th century by immigrant glass workers. The site covers parts of the Newent and Taynton parishes and earlier researchers have referred to it as "The Newent Glasshouse". Most of the hamlet lies within the Taynton parish boundaries but the main glassworking area was just over the border in the parish of Newent.

Fig. 52 Sign outside the Glasshouse Inn, Taynton. A reminder of the glass industry that operated in the locality in the late 16th to early 17th centuries.

One of the earliest references to the Glasshouse is for the year 1598, when Sir Jeremy Bowes obtained letters patent which said: *"In Gloucestershire one Houx a Frenchman hath built a glasshouse and furnace and doth make great quantities of glass"*. In 1591 Queen Elizabeth I had granted Bowes a twelve year monopoly over the British glass industry and he was attempting to squash any illegal competition. Most of the families who settled at the foot of Yartleton Hill (May Hill) and began making glass were Protestants of French and Flemish origin, known as Huguenots.

In the 16th century Europe was in great turmoil with the people suffering repression and religious persecution. Thousands of the families fled their country with many settling in Britain and among them were highly skilled glass workers. Some of these immigrant glass makers are known to have come from

Normandy and Lorraine between 1567 and 1572 and perhaps escaped just in time, for in 1572 twenty thousand French Protestants were massacred at what became known as The Massacre of St Bartholomew's.

The history of some of the Huguenot glassmaking families who came to England and eventually settled in the Newent area can be traced back to 1473 when they lived in the Darney area of Lorraine. Lorraine at that time was an independent border state between France and Germany and came under the jurisdiction of the Dukes of Lorraine. Some of the more prominent families were named Thysac, Hennezel, Thietry and Houx. There are many different spellings of these names in old records such as in the case of Tysac, Thisac, Thysac, Thise, and Tixot but they are all known to be of the same family line.

Glassmaking at that time was a highly respected profession and the glassmakers had many special privileges. Many of them were the elite of society being of noble rank equivalent to the status of a knight. One of their homes was a very imposing building built by Nicolas de Thysac in about the middle of the 16th century known as the Chateau of Lichecourt and it was the seat of the Thysac and the Hennezel families for several generations. In England things were entirely different, with workers regarded as among the lowest classes, many lived in utter squalor. These differences were eventually to lead to great friction.

The special skills of glassmaking were passed from father to son and were a highly guarded secret; everyone involved had to swear never to divulge them. Ceremonies of "The swearing of the Glassmakers Oath" were held annually and had to be taken by any newcomers joining the profession. Intermarriage between the glassmaker families was commonplace, particularly amongst the Tysacs and the Hennezels, perhaps because of the need to keep the secrets within the family.

The Tysacs seem to have been of a rather hot blooded nature for the history of their family records several murders. They lived in a very turbulent period of history when it was up to every man to defend himself. Being nobles they were allowed to carry swords and these were often used as a way to settle old scores or even petty quarrels. In October 1579 Christophe de Thysac killed his cousin Balthazar de Hennezel during a family argument and so he had to flee to England where he is believed to have died in about 1595. It seems that religious persecution and the odd murder were not the only reason why the Lorraine glassmakers left for England. Taxation became penal and this coupled with over production of their glasswares led to a severe decline in their industry.

On arriving in England some of the immigrants set up business in London in the parish of St. Olaves and operated a glasshouse there known as the

Crutched Friars Glasshouse. Among those glass workers were the Houxs and Thisacs (Tysacks), an exception among them was Henry Bridgman who was a native Englishman, with relatives in the Newent and Gloucester area. Whilst at St. Olaves the Bridgmans produced a son; the local church register there records that Henry, the son of Henry Bridgman glassmaker, was christened on 23rd March 1594.

Although skilled men in their own right they came under the influence of a master Venetian glassmaker named Jacopo Verzelini and together they began to produce glass superior to the out-dated and inferior British products. Trouble flared as the old established glassmakers began to lose trade to these newcomers. In order to protect their livelihoods the locals accused the foreigners of destroying the forests through using the vast quantities of timber required to fire their kilns. The trouble makers were able to get the local iron workers on their side as they also needed the timber to make the charcoal for their furnaces. Threats were made to burn down the Frenchmen's homes and even death threats were made, one glasshouse together with its kilns and equipment was completely destroyed by fire. As a result many of them left London in 1576 and moved to Buckholt in the forests of Hampshire, to Staffordshire and the Weald of Sussex. In about the year 1590 they moved on again, to St. Weonards, Herefordshire and into Gloucestershire; settling in Woodchester and the Taynton/Newent border, on wooded land below May Hill.

Fig.53 Site of one of the glass kilns with Clifford Manor in the distance. It would no doubt have been woodland when the glassmakers settled there in the 1590s.

Evidence concerning some of these early settlers can be found in the 16th/17th century Bishops Transcripts and other ecclesiastical and estate records for Newent.

1598 14th July	Baptized - *Daughter of Mr Bridgman of the Glasshouse* Buried - *Anne Bridgman daughter of Mr Bridgman of the Glasshouse*
October 1599	Baptized - *Tysack Abram Sonne of a Frenchman of the Glasshouse*
1599	Baptized - *John Pylme sonne of Jasper Pylme a Frenchman of the Glasshouse*
Feb 24th 1601	Baptized - *Margaret daughter of Anthony Voyden glass founder*
1603	Baptized - *Thomas son of Anthony of the Glasshouse* (probably referring to the same Anthony Voyden)
1607	Abraham Liscourt paid £10 rent to Sir John Wintour for land on the Manor of Yartleton (May Hill)
1608	In the Consistory Court, Magdalene Liscourt (alias Tysack) accused J Hook of Taynton of defamation of character. (He had gone around saying that she wasn't what she should be)
1617	Buried - *Magdalene, wife of Abraham Liscourt*
1634	The will of John Bulnoys (glassmaker) was proved and part of the will says *"I give and bequeath unto John Bulnoys my eldest son all my moulds and tools for making glass whatsoever"*
1638	Married - *John Gulney aged 23 years to Alice Powell of Newent*

The earliest written evidence of glass workers at the Newent Glasshouse is in 1598; it is very probable that they arrived at an earlier date. Much reliance is put on church records, yet it could well have taken a considerable time for these foreigners to get integrated into the local society and church life. Some records may have been made at other local churches where the records for that period are incomplete, such as Taynton where in 1606 it was reported that the records were *"ill penned and carelessly kept"*. Coins of many reigns including those of Mary Tudor 1553-1554, Philip and Mary 1554-1558, Elizabeth I 1558-1603, James I 1603-1625 and Charles I 1625-1649 have been recovered from the Glasshouse site.

What brought these foreigners to this part of Gloucestershire is not known for certain but the Bridgmans could well be the link. Henry Bridgman was a member of the glassmaking colony at St. Olaves and it is highly probable that he was related to the Bridgmans who were living in the vicinity of the glasshouse site. John Brayne, a close relative of the Bridgmans, lived at the Moat, Newent. In his will of 1599 he bequeathed some of his belongings, including several animals, to his cousin Bridget Bridgman of the Glasshouse. No doubt Henry would have told his colleagues about the plentiful supply of timber and suitable sand to be found there. John Lowe, the present owner of the site (Moses Meadow), says that when ploughing the field isolated seams of silver sand can be seen. He believes that at one time a sand pit had been in the field and was later filled in with pottery debris. Much of the area at that time would have been common land and could have been claimed by simply building a house upon it; this method of obtaining land on May Hill was rife two and a half centuries later!

From old records it appears that some of the settlers changed their names after leaving their homeland. Abraham Liscourt is believed to have been Abraham Tysack and it seems that he took his alias from the name of his ancestral home; the Chateau of Lichecourt. The reasons may never be known, but he may well have feared reprisals for breaking the glassmakers oath or perhaps to shake off the slur on the family name after Christopher Tysack (who was probably his father) killed Balthasar Henezell in 1579. Magdalene Liscourt died in 1617 and it appears that Abraham then moved to Newcastle-on-Tyne and set up a glass industry there encouraged by Sir Robert Mansell who, at that time, had considerable control over the glass making industry. It is recorded that Abraham's daughter, Ann, married at Newcastle in 1619. It is known that other members of the colony moved to Lye and Kingswinford, Staffordshire in the early 1600's. It is intriguing that in 1612 the Tysack name appears in the church register at Kingswinford when the son of Paul and Bridget Tysack was baptized. Bridget is thought to have been the daughter of Henry and Bridget Bridgman of the Newent Glasshouse. Abraham Liscourt claimed that he and Paul Tysack invented the revolutionary method of using coal instead of wood in glassmaking, therefore it is highly probable that Paul worked at the Newent Glasshouse at one time and that is where he met his future wife Bridget.

Glass making in the sixteenth century was an industrial process filled with great secrecy. In Venice death contracts were taken out on anyone who stole their formulae, nevertheless the secrets did get out and were brought to Britain. The main ingredient of glass is sand but an essential ingredient is potash. Ash produced from the plant glasswort, after it had been dried and burnt, was the preferred source, but potash from burnt bracken could also be used. The formula was about 60 parts sand to 40 potash. Other ingredients could be added to produce different types of glass. Most of the glass found at the Glasshouse site is of a pale green colour, this being caused by iron residues in the sand.

To make glass, a container known as a "pot" or "kettle" is heated inside a kiln or furnace until it reaches a white heat. The ingredients known as the frit are then added; a temperature of between 1300 and 1500 degrees Celsius is required to reduce the frit to a semi-liquid, suitable for forming into glassware. A major problem would have been to produce a pot that would withstand the great heat without shattering. Some of the best sources of clay in Britain suitable for this purpose were at Stourbridge, Staffordshire and in Yorkshire.

Fig.54 Some of the many glass fragments from Moses Meadow

Base of a glass linen smoother

Making these pots was a long and laborious process taking several weeks of painstaking work; a shattered pot would be a major disaster. From the pieces found at the glasshouse it is estimated that these pots would have been approximately 24" high, 18" diameter and would have held about 150 lbs of glass.

Glass making may have taken place at a number of different sites as several concentrations of glass shards have been found. One site that has been positively identified, probably the major one, was in a field shown on the 1840 Tithe Map as Moses Meadow. It is within the Newent boundary at the junction of Judges Lane and the road to Clifford's Mesne. When this field is ploughed dark areas are exposed that show where the glass making site and some later pottery sites were situated. It is in this area that most glass fragments were found but, due to many years of agricultural cultivation, fragments were of small size.

Some trial holes were dug in early 1998 when glassmaking debris was found to a depth of approximately 18 inches. These consisted of pieces of glass, "pot" fragments, cinders and brick. A layer of stone was encountered at that depth, possibly being the floor of the kiln or the working area.

Quantities of glass have also been found in the gardens of Clifford Manor and fragments can be found scattered in local fields. Mr Oliver Watkins, aged 97 of May Hill, said that glass was also made in a field to the left of the road to Clifford's Mesne, opposite Moses Meadow. The Tithe Map of 1840 shows "Old Quarry and Glasshouse" at a position a short distance from the present Glasshouse Inn. Adjoining it is a field called Abraham's Patch, this name may well have been carried down from the days of the original glass founders, perhaps after Tysack Abram or Abraham Liscourt. Several cottages dating to the 15th or 16th centuries still stand nearby to this day, such as Monks Spout Cottage and Tudor Cottage. Several cottages once stood on land at the junction of Judges Lane and the road from Taynton and adjacent to Glasshouse Green; the area is now a landscaped garden. Those old dwellings may well have housed some of the early settlers.

Fig.55 Part of pot/crucible from Moses Meadow. Pale green glass is still adhering to the bottom and side

Open top type pot/crucible similar to the sort used at Newent Glass-house in the 16th & 17th centuries

In 1968 Gloucester City Museum investigated the Glasshouse site when they collected many fragments of glass by field walking; these are now stored at Brunswick Road, Gloucester. Despite this, some of the distinctive light green glass can still be found in the plough soil. Some of the fragments are said to be of beakers, goblets, wine glasses, bottles and window glass. A few decorated pieces have also been recovered together with various glass rods and tubes, the most complete article being a linen smoother. Glass slag and parts of the crucibles (pots), where the glass had fused to the sides have also been found. No complete items in Glasshouse green glass from this site are known to exist today. A resident of May Hill has a tankard in pale blue glass that is believed to have been made at the Newent Glasshouse.

Whilst metal detecting in Moses Meadow between 1996 and 2001, a number of interesting discoveries were made. Coins covering several reigns, from as early as Edward IV (1461-1470) were recovered also buttons, buckles and other items spanning a period of 400 years. An interesting object unearthed from the site was a 17th century silver bodkin with the owner's initials "I.A." engraved on it. In addition to their domestic use bodkins were also worn in the hair by women of that period as a popular item of fashion. From the small hole at the blunt end would be suspended a drop pearl attached by a silver wire. Part of an old Pedlars song of 1677 called "The Triumphant Widow" went :-

"Silver bodkins for your hair. Bobs which maidens love to wear"

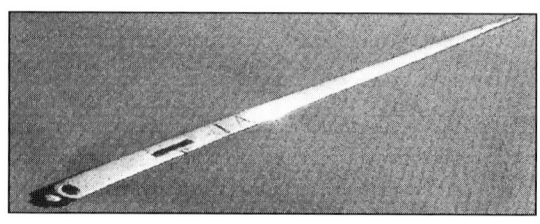

Fig.56 17th century silver bodkin from Moses Meadow. Engraved I.A.

The protests concerning the depletion of the forests which began in London as a localized dispute in the late 1500's gradually spread throughout the entire country. In 1615 under the orders of James I the use of timber for glass making was prohibited. This did not appear to cause the immediate closure of Newent Glasshouse for it continued for at least another 23 years, no doubt using coal that could be obtained from the Forest of Dean or even from Newent. It is believed that by 1638 the Huguenot glass makers had all moved away. No doubt they realized that their future lay in the area where the essential clay was at hand and where there was also an abundance of good quality cheap coal. Paul and

Bridget Tysack are the first names to appear there and are believed to have been the founders of the extensive and important glass making industry that developed in Stourbridge. Eventually large glassmaking companies became established there such as Brierley Glass, Stewart Crystal and Royal Doulton Glass; most of them are still operating there to this day.

The old traditions live on, in the form of Cowdy's Glassworks in Culver Street, Newent.

Fig.57 (above) James I shilling 1604/5 found in Moses Meadow
(below) Charles I halfcrown 1635/6 found in Moses Meadow

The Pottery making period from c1640 to 1750

After the glassmakers moved away, Moses Meadow and the adjoining field called Hilly Ground became occupied by families of potters. It is recorded that in 1640 widow Davis paid £1 per year to rent the Glasshouse, no doubt that was the turning point at which glass making ceased and pottery production began. In addition to the many glass fragments found at the kiln site in Moses Meadow pottery shards are in abundance. It is highly probable that widow

Davis or her family began making pottery at the Glasshouse site on a small scale, supplying the needs of the surrounding villages. A few years later the names of several potters by the name of Davis appear in old Newent records. Although it has not yet been proved, it is highly probable that they were the same family line.

Fig.58 Rims of plates and dishes giving some indication of the style of decoration. (found on Hilly Field)

As the business developed, other potters moved to the site, mainly onto Hilly Field. Later this land belonged to the Foley family. From the estate map of 1775 it can be seen that a small hamlet once occupied this field. A road passed through it running in an east to west direction with cottages and gardens on either side. A number of furnace sites can be identified close to this old road indicating that the potters operated as separate groups. The original glasshouse building was demolished sometime prior to 1707.

From time immemorial Moses Meadow and the adjoining Hilly Field were divided by a stream that emanates from springs on May Hill and joins the Taynton Brook midway between Home Farm and the Black House Farm. In the 1960's this stream was diverted through pipes and part of the field was bulldozed in order to fill in the redundant stream bed; this caused the two fields to be merged into one. At the same time the hollow-way formed by the old road was also filled in.

Fig.59 Pot rims showing finger mouldings.
Under magnification finger prints can still be seen.

Large quantities of pottery shards can still be seen in the plough soil today many of them being rims, handles and bases. The main products produced there were plates, dishes, jugs, chamber pots and a wide range of storage pots. As can be seen from the shards collected, many items had been decorated with a white slip in a very distinctive pattern. Many of the pots were glazed on the interior, some having a finger moulded decoration round the outer edge of the rim; in some cases the potter's finger prints can still be seen. Most of the undecorated material is of a dull red appearance although there is a quantity of hard grey pottery; some of it possibly created through over firing.

From the quantity and diversity of the objects found in Moses Meadow and the adjoining field it can be concluded that a considerable number of people lived there, no doubt with large families but occupying perhaps only six dwellings as can be seen on a map of the 18th century. Over 250 buttons, 25 buckles, 40 coins and other objects of every day life have been unearthed using metal detectors.

From Newent parish records it can be seen that John Davis was a potter at the Glasshouse in 1676 and that he died in 1710. In his will he is described as a yeoman, and part of his will says *"my son John shall have the use of the workhouse and kiln belonging to the house I live in until my grandson Robert reaches the age of 17"*. William Jones is mentioned in 1682 and his death is recorded in 1711. There is also a record of a John and Robert Davis living there between 1705 and 1711, and a George Warren, who died in 1728. Henry Davis died in 1750 and is described as a potter living in a cottage in the tithing of Cugley, the same tithing as the Glasshouse.

Today only one building is visible in the field, the owner believes that at one time it had been inhabited. In later years it had been used as a cattle shed but is now a ruin. A map of 1811 shows several buildings still standing on Moses Meadow and Hilly Field but by 1838 all traces of the old hamlet and the glasshouse buildings had disappeared., the Tithe Map of that date shows the site as open fields. From the evidence found the site appears to have been finally abandoned sometime between 1807 and 1838.

Fig.60 A pot identified as Newent Glasshouse pottery
(By courtesy of Gloucester City Museum and Art Gallery)

Fig.61 A dish identified as
Newent Glasshouse pottery (Courtesy of Gloucester
City Museum and Art Gallery)

References
Don Tyzack Glass, Tools and Tyzacks
Alan Vince Newent Glasshouse (Occasional Paper No.7)
Seaby The Standard Catalogue of British Coins

15. Religion
D A Pearce

The earliest record of the town is in the Domesday Survey of 1086 and it would be expected that a Saxon church of some description would have existed, although there is no evidence remaining of the actual building.

However there are several pieces of evidence which point towards the existence of a Saxon church on the site of the present parish church. In 1912 excavations on the north side of the church, for a new vestry, unearthed a stone tablet about 8" by 6.5" by 1" thick buried at a depth of 5 feet. It is carved on both sides and bears the name "EDRED" on one side. In the 1950s G. Zarnecki put forward the view that the tablet dated from the late 10th or early 11th century (1). However further research by R M Bradfield (2) suggests it may be as early as the 8th century. Perhaps Edred was the head of a small monastic community. A replica of the stone is displayed in the Lady Chapel.

In the entrance to the church, beneath the tower are two large grave slabs which R M Bradfield attributes, from the carvings, to be 7th century Celtic origin. Four other sculpted fragments, replicas of which are on show in the church, were found in the south wall during work on one of the windows in the 1880s.

Also in the entrance is part of a 9th century Saxon cross shaft which was found in the churchyard in 1907, during levelling. These relics indicate that an Anglo-Saxon place of worship existed on the site well before the Norman conquest.

After 1066 the Manor of Newent was granted to William Fitz Osbern. His son Roger gave it to the Benedictine Abbey of St Mary at Cormeilles in Normandy, and they established a small priory on the site of the present Old Court.

It is said that the only canonized saint to visit Newent was Saint Cantalupe, Bishop of Hereford, in the 11th century when he came to collect tithes from the Priory.

In all probability a Norman church was built by the Abbey but no remains are visible in the present building. The oldest parts which can be seen are the 13th century arcade between the chancel and the Lady Chapel, and the 14th century tower and Lady Chapel (3).

In 1242 Pope Alexander III issued a Bull confirming various donations in Normandy and England to the Priory of Newent (5) which had originally been granted in 1168. King Henry II (1154-1189) confirmed the grant of the Manor of Newent to receive lands and income *"as they ever held them in the reign of King Henry, my granfather, and particularly all the manor of Newent, with all*

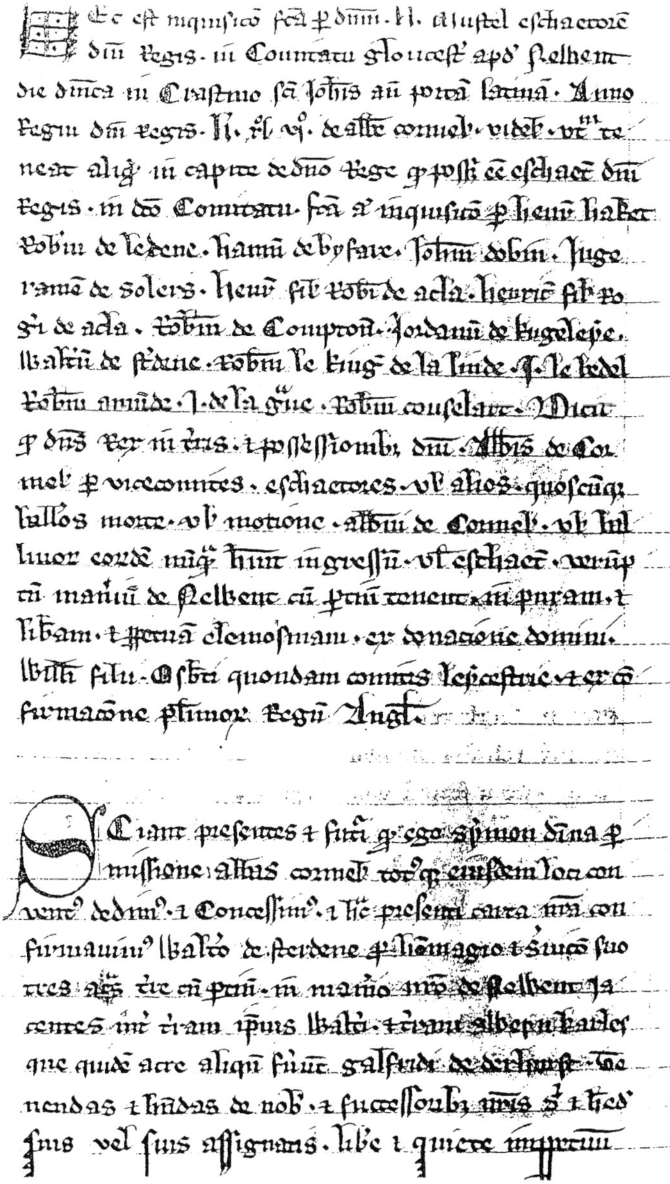

Fig.62 Part of the Latin Cartulary of Newent Priory, 1242

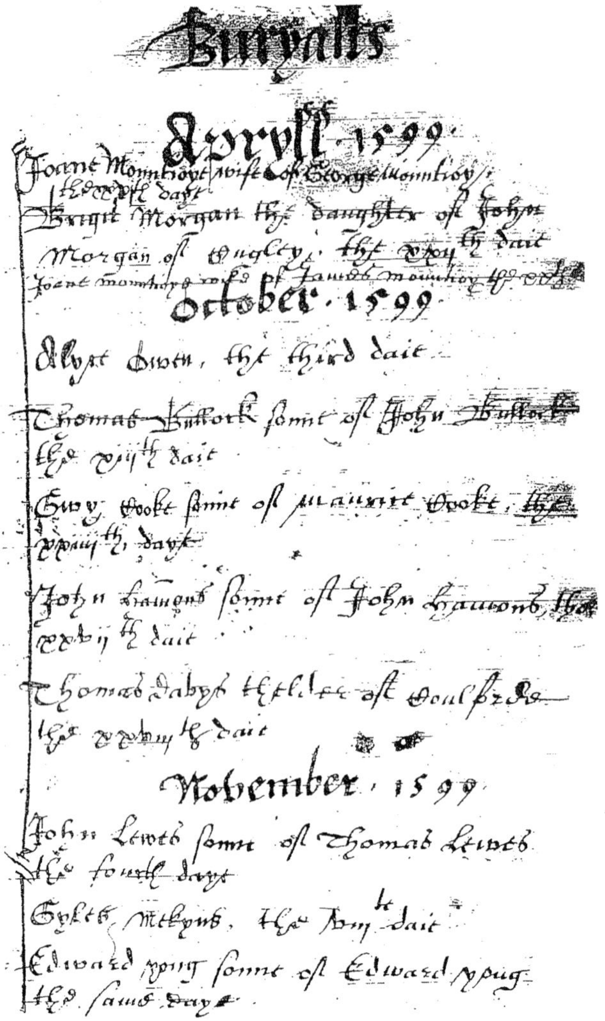

Fig.63 A copy of the early Bishop's Transcripts of Newent from the reign of Queen Elizabeth I (Courtesy of Glos Record Office). The first section reads:-
Buryalls
Apryll 1599
Joane Mountjoye wife of George Mountjoye the 26th daye
Brigit Morgan the daughter of John Morgan of Cugley the 22nd daie
Joane Mountjoye wife of James Mountjoye the 20th daie

its appurtenances; to wit, five hides of land, and the church, with all the tythes, oblations, meadows, mills, and the woods of Iarclesdune, and of Tedeswude, Compton, Lind, Eacle, and Meleswiche, with the mill and meadows; and Onghelie, with all the new ploughed grounds belonging to Newent and Stanling; Buledune, with its chapel".

The list continues with various land and rents in other parts of the County and elsewhere. In the document of Pope Alexander III some of the place names are spelt differently i.e. Cumpton, Linde, Eclam, Meleswit, Ligesley and Bolesdon.

In 1370 the Abbot of Cormeilles nominated John Faber, the Prior of Newent, as his attorney for one year (24). The priory was eventually dissolved by Henry VIII.

According to Walter Nourse (4) the nave of the Church was originally 18ft longer than at present, at the western end. The east window fell in on July 15th 1651 just after the wedding of William Lightfoote and Jane Kerry. It is said that William and Jane were found alone together during their courtship. Jane was angry at being discovered and declared that if she ever did marry Lightfoote the Church would fall on their heads. Many thought that the window collapse was a warning from God not to tell lies. It was rebuilt by a local builder, Fernando Grimes, but it was again destroyed in a storm in 1788. It was then filled in with stone until 1881 when the present Gothic window was constructed.

Much repair work and alteration has been carried out on the church over the years. On February 18th 1661 *"there was a very high wind which blew down the steeple".* Perhaps it had been weakened by a cannon shot which hit it during the civil war in 1644. The top section was replaced in 1872 but it was again damaged by lightning in 1934. It was partly rebuilt once again in 1972 after a considerable fund raising effort which included an 18 mile sponsored walk organized by the Newent Round Table.

On the night of Sunday 18th January 1674 the original nave collapsed due to a heavy weight of snow. Fortunately the church was empty at the time and thereafter for many years an annual sermon of thanksgiving was preached. The timbers had been damaged by water due to the lead being removed from the roof during the civil war. A Newent carpenter, Edward Taylor, who had worked with Sir Christopher Wren, rebuilt it without central pillars, using oak from Lea Bailey Wood in the Forest of Dean donated by King Charles II. Some of the stone was dug out of Culver Street. On the eastern gable end above the present ceiling is an inscription :-

"Francis Jones of Hasfield and James Hill of Cheltenham masons were ye head workmen in rebuilding this church. The first stones in ye foundations by them were laid July 31st Anno Dom = 1675

Edward Taylor of ys towne carpenter, was ye contriver and head workman in building this roofe of ye church Anno Dom 1679."

Edward Taylor died in 1721 at the age of 87. Mr Greenbank of Worcester was the plumber who leaded the roof (4).

Considerable argument took place about where people should sit in the rebuilt church. It went on for over two years between Walter Nourse, Mr Rogers, Timothy Nourse, and Mr Skynner. They even tried to get the Bishop to mediate. In those days private pews were common practice. In 1834 when Edward Bower's house in Church Street was put up for sale it was offered with a private pew in the church

Under the arches between the chancel and the Lady Chapel is an alabaster tomb of a knight and his lady (Fig.66) which has been dated between 1370 and 1385 and may be one of the Grandison family (5).

The Chantry certificates of 1584 show that there was a separate chapel in the churchyard dedicated to St James and St Anne in the reign of King Henry VI. It is likely that this later became the town Dame School which was demolished in 1810. When the building was demolished it was occupied by John Dee and his wife. The materials were used for the repair of the Almshouses and the churchwardens had *"to allow two guineas a year towards finding a residence for John Dee and his wife, the late occupants of the said house"* (18).

The organ was built by Thomas Warn of Newent in 1737 and has been moved several times. It replaced the Church Band and so annoyed Mr William Green who had played the bass viol, that he left to become a dissenter. There is a tombstone in the Churchyard recording *"Robert Warn, organist of this Church died July 1770"*. There was some dissatisfaction with one organist because on 14th November 1813 a Vestry meeting (18) was held for *"the purpose of taking into consideration the sense of the Parish relative to the competency of Mr Cope the organist whether or not it be the voice of the Parish that he should continue organist or not"*. It was ordered *"that this meeting be adjourned until Sunday 28th November, Mr Cope demanding a meeting of the Parishioners in general to know their sentiments whether he is to continue or not"*. There is no record of the next meeting but a memorial high on the south wall of the Church records *"Henry Hayward, 23 years organist of this Church died January 1st 1837, aged 47 years"*. He must have been appointed in December 1813 after the dismissal of Mr Cope. The organist was paid £40 a year in 1814 and £2-2s-0d was paid *"to the boy Hayward* [the organist's son] *for blowing the organ"* in 1820 (17). At various times during the 18th and 19th centuries there were galleries around the chancel. In November 1776 there was a dispute between Miss Goodman and

Fig.64 St Mary's Parish Church dating from the 13th century

Mr Chinn regarding a seat in his gallery and as a result she postponed her wedding *"tho' she is violently in love, she had rather give up her husband than her dignity"*(19). At this time the Vestry could not agree about permission to build another gallery. All the galleries have now gone, the last being finally removed in 1912 during another period of restoration. Public subscriptions raised £1,369-13s-9d for the work and a list of over 200 people who gave donations was published. They even collected money from people skating on Newent Lake in the winter (22).

The Vestry minutes show that in March 1812 the church pinnacles were repaired at a cost of £60-14s-0d and the following year £28-10s-3.5d was paid for painting the Church (17). The inside walls were plastered at this time but this was removed in the Victorian era.

Although interment was allowed in the church it was decreed in April 1786 that *"No person be buried in the Vestry or Chancel till they have paid twenty shillings over and above the present time which said twenty shillings shall be lay'd out in repairing the pavement of the Church"*. In 1819 this fee was increased to five guineas and a certificate had to be given that the corpse had been enclosed in a leaden coffin.

The church clock required maintenance from time to time. In December 1795 Jas. Arnold was paid ten shillings for repairing and cleaning it and the following April a further 2s-7d had to be spent *"for repairs to the clock and chimes"*. More recently in 2001 the clock face was renovated.

In 1805 John Dee was paid £4 a year for keeping the churchyard tidy. In July 1806 the following details are shown for the repair of the churchyard wall :-

Jennings	-	for hauling lime and brick	13s-0d
Pople	-	cart load of lime	9s-0d
		bag of lime from Longhope	1s-6d
Havard	-	3 bushels of hair	3s-6d
Tranter	-	500 bricks	15s-6d
Dayer	-	Cart load of stone and hauling	7s-0d
Thos Stone	-	repairing Churchyard wall and other work	£1-15s-0d

The churchyard was surveyed and the tombstone inscriptions recorded in the 1980s. The early parish register (1672-1766) and the Bishops transcripts (1597-1670) have been transcribed and indexed (6)(7). It is not unusual to find mistakes and omissions in the register. For example the wedding of John Baily and Mary Malvern in 1757. In the register his name is stated as Thomas Baylis but on the marriage licence he has signed as John Bayly and even then the spelling is different from the head of the form (16). A nightmare for family historians.

The Communion Plate dates back to 1680, the oldest piece being a plain paten given by William Rogers. A second paten is from 1760, and a chalice from 1762. Two flagons and an alms-dish were given by Robert Foley in 1770, and in 1961 a silver wafer box was given by Mrs Moore in memory of her husband.

There are eight bells, the six oldest of which are inscribed as follows:-

3rd   John Hill John Matthews Churchwardens Thos Mears Fecit 1843
4th   Samuel:Hillman:Artter:Pitt Churchwardens:September:19:1674
5th   Stefanus:Skinner:et:Richardus:Hill:Gardiani Ivly:13:1638
6th   Thomas:Masters:John:Clarke:Church:wardens:Anno:Domini:1649
      Recast AD 1909 W.H.Connor Rector E.Conder
      junr.L.J.Smith Church Wardens
7th   Aylward Parsons & Arthur Hope Chwardens 1724 Recast 1899
      Barwell founder Birmingham W.Martin - vicar
      T.Day:F.Powell:Church Wardens
8th   Lavdate xdeum in cymbalis bene sonantibus Iohn Hill Iohn
      Matthews
      eccleslae custodes C & G Mears founders 1850 dia 45 Eb

All the bells were re-hung in 1909 when the sixth bell was re-cast.

On 7th January 1861 a peal of 5040 changes was rung in a time of 2 hours 57 mins. This has been repeated a dozen times up to 1982 when the two smaller bells were added.

The War Memorial in the Churchyard was formally dedicated on November 3rd 1920.

In June 1970 St Mary's Church and the Methodist Church made an Act of Union, and the congregations now share services and pastoral work.

With the growth in population in the 19th century outlying parts of the Parish needed their own church. In 1892 the foundation stone of Christ Church, Gorsley was laid and the building dedicated by the Bishop of Gloucester in July 1893. The building work was carried out by John Bidmead at a cost of £1030. Gorsley became a separate ecclesiastical district in 1872 although the original chapel, built in 1863, was in Clifford's Mesne (14). The new St Peters was built in 1882.   In 1985 they became a United Benefice with St Mary's, Newent.

In 1712 Sir Robert Atkyns stated that a chapel dedicated to St Hillary and St Helias had previously existed at Kilcot but *"is now wholy demolished"* (15). A field called "Chapel Meadow" is the probable site, although Rudder calls it St

Tilley's Nap. This may well be the Chapel referred to in the Bull of Pope Alexander III in 1242. William Green calls it St Syblys and St Ekas in 1707.

There is another field called "Chappells", north east of Ford House, where it is said a chapel once stood, although the only reference to it now is the name on the 1840 Tithe Map.

The Newent Congregational Church in the High Street dates from 1846. The site was purchased the previous year from Mr William Young for £200 and had been the site of a Public House called the Swan, formerly the Lower Horseshoe (8).

Previously there was no non-conformist place of worship in the town. In 1843 George Hayes, a carpenter, and Mr Sutherland, an Excise Officer approached Congregational ministers in Gloucester and Cheltenham and hired a room in the High Street. The first recorded preacher was Rev. Dr. Brown from Cheltenham. This caused quite a stir in the town, the opposition being led by the local aristocracy. Windows were broken and constables had to be hired to control the crowd.

The school room was completed and opened in 1845 as a day school, under the superintendent Mr Joseph Stratford, and a Sunday school run by Jonathan Williams until his death in 1885. The new chapel was completed and officially opened on May 6th 1846. The Church was built to seat 300 people and the first service was taken by Rev. S. Martin of London. The list of ministers is as follows:-

1846-1847	John G Guennett
1847-1850	John Burrell
1851-1854	Josephus Chapman
1854-1860	Thomas Roberts
1861-1863	Thomas Gough
1864-1874	John Henry Hughes
1875-1888	William Harris
1888-1902	W. H. Dash
1902-1904	John Riordan
1905-1916	Kenfig Morgan
1917-1921	William Bailey
1922-1926	Arthur Shand
1927-1933	Robert Coveney
1933-1937	Wilfred G Walton
1938-1957	Ben Davies
1957-1960	Bert Deary
1960-1996	Pulpit supplied

Fig.65 United Reformed Church 1846

At the instigation of Mrs Luke a Manse was built in Culver Street in 1869 on land bought from Mr Hartland, a grocer, for £80. There had been some local opposition to several other sites before the one in Culver Street was finally acquired. The total cost of the building was £537-2s-11.5d

In 1870 Mr John Beach of Redmarley died and left the Chapel £500. This was invested and the income is still being received. The Chapel was repaired and redecorated in 1883. The high pulpit was removed and the pews lowered. The stonework at the front of the church was removed and replaced after it was struck by lightning.

The number of people attending was never very high and by the end of 1891 the membership of the church stood at 43. This declined in the early years

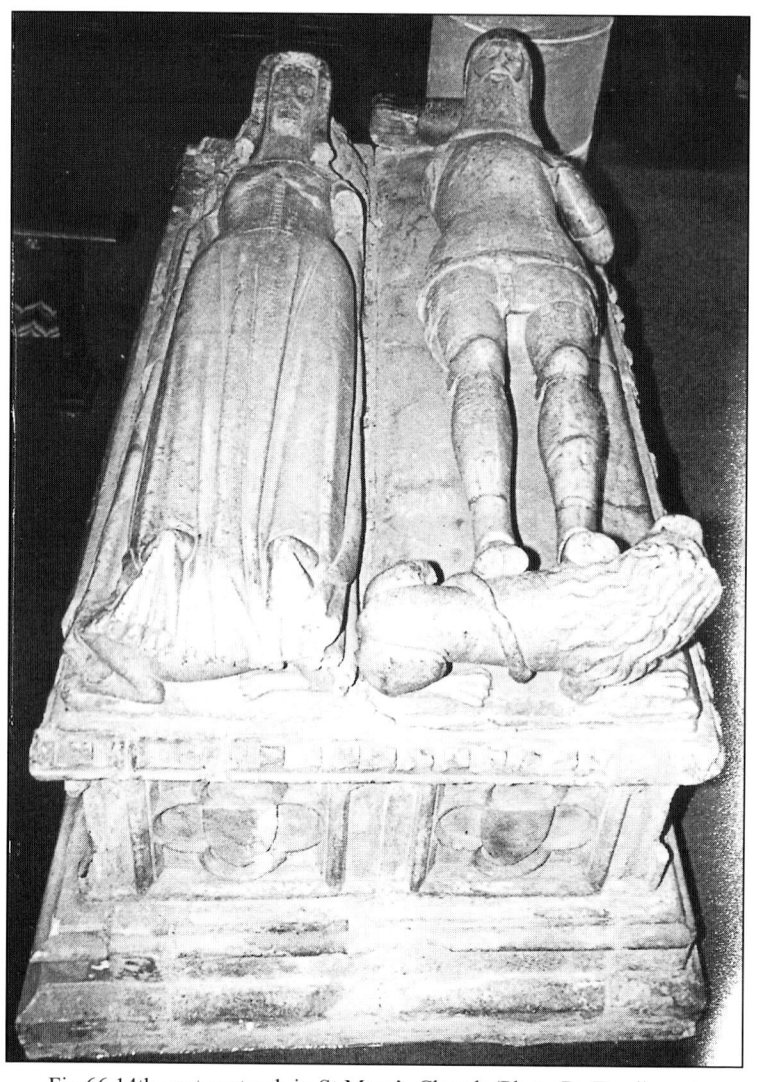

Fig.66 14th century tomb in St Mary's Church (Photo Dr Tomlinson)

of the 20th century and at a special meeting called to pass the accounts on 10th January 1904 only six people attended. The Rev. Kenfig Morgan became Pastor in 1905 and the congregation increased considerably.

In 1911 Mr John Bidmead senr. died. He had been a member of the church for nearly 60 years and had done all of the brickwork, painting and papering of the Manse when it was built. He had been a Sunday School Teacher for 52 years of which 27 were as Superintendent. He had been a Deacon for 35 years. A tablet in his memory was erected towards the back of the church.

It was practice for some members to pay a rental on their chosen pew but in 1919 this was discontinued *"members to retain their usual seats, but without any priority of use"*. For insurance purposes the church was valued at £2,400 at this time, for which they paid a premium of £1-16s-0d. For a time in 1920 the Women's Institute used the school room for their meetings.

In 1925 the vestry, originally built as a Ladies Room, a wash house and lavatory were added at the rear of the church.

The Church was always in financial difficulties, especially between the two World Wars, and to help out in 1930 Rev. Coveney agreed to take a cut in his stipend, which at that time was £190 per annum.

Central heating was installed in 1929 and electricity in 1931. When Rev. Coveney left in 1933 the old Manse, which was in a poor state of repair, was sold and the proceeds invested. The building of a new Manse was not started until 1937 in Bradfords Lane, on land purchased from Mr Ackerman for £56.

In 1938 the Rev Benjamin Davies became pastor. He was not in good health and one Sunday morning he collapsed in the pulpit still reciting the Lord's Prayer. He regained his health and continued as Pastor until 1957.

The centenary of the church was celebrated in June 1946 and a souvenir booklet about its history was produced at the 150th anniversary in 1996. The small graveyard at the rear of the church has been surveyed and the inscriptions recorded in 1999.

In 1960 the Rev. B. Deary resigned and from then on no permanent Pastor has been appointed, and the Manse is rented out.

In 1969 the spire of the parish church, St Mary's, was declared unsafe and the church was closed for a time. As a result morning services were transferred to the Congregational Church. On 12th July 1969 a unique ceremony took place when the Rev. C.W. Earle was instituted as Rector of St Mary's in the Congregational Church. A symbolic induction then followed at St Mary's Church gates while the congregation watched from the street.

In 1972 the Congregational Churches and the Presbyterian Churches in England and Wales combined to form the United Reformed Church and in consequence the Church in Newent changed its name to The Newent United Reformed Church. Since then there has been no permanent Pastor.

In 1687 a small number of Newent Residents emigrated to America, probably as a result of religious persecution. They founded a colony near Norwich, in Connecticut which was originally called Newent, but changed its name to Lisbon in 1786. Some of the emigrants were Josiah Read, Hezekial and Jabez Perkins, and the Bishop family. The church they built is still called Newent Congregational Church and their pewter communion set was given to them in 1723 by their friends in England.

Fig.67 The Catholic Church in Ross Road, built 1959

Until 1939 the Catholic Church had not been represented in Newent since the reformation.

In 1935 the Salesian Fathers came to Blaisdon Hall and four years later they opened a Mass Centre in the house of Mr and Mrs Clifford Deacon at the Scarr. Mr and Mrs Deacon moved in 1943 and services were transferred to Newent Market House (9). The congregation was swollen at times by Italian and German prisoners of war.

In 1952 Father W. Boyd was appointed and, with the help of Richard and Greta Ovington, and Mrs Chris Robinson, set about raising money to build a church. He persuaded Mr Andrew Ford to sell a plot of land on Ross Road, from where he had previously run his cider business, for £475. The site contained two old sheds, one of which was made of doors and beams from the old workhouse. The doors had metal peepholes. Much of the brickwork was done by a former pupil of Blaisdon, Billy Udell, helped in the later stages by the more experienced Norman Marcovecchio. Much of the work was carried out by volunteers giving them great satisfaction, although some mistakes were made. The two side doors in the porch were initially made too narrow to allow a coffin through and had to be widened (23).

Building work commenced in August 1957 and took three years to complete, the first Mass being celebrated in the unfinished interior. The official opening took place in December 1959 by the Rev. Father Hall, Provincial of the Salesians in England. The church is 70 ft long and 26 ft wide and is built in an attractive golden brick made by the National Coal Board. It has a wooden shingle roof. The oak doors were made by the staff of the Salesian School. The cost of building the church was £2,848 but this took no account of the enormous amount of voluntary work put in by the congregation. (fig.67)

The church is dedicated to Our Lady of Lourdes and the ministers have been as follows:-

1939-1945	Father Payne (Rector of Blaisdon)
1945-1952	Father Coppo
1952-1970	Father William Boyd
1970-1972	Father Chadwick
1972- 1995	Father James McGuire
1995-	Father Aidan Murray

A Wesleyan Centenary meeting was held in Newent on 15th January 1839 but it was not until 1855 that a Wesleyan Chapel was built in Culver Street (fig.68) which became part of the Ledbury Circuit. The land was given by William Green, gent, and gratefully received by the Superintendent Preacher on

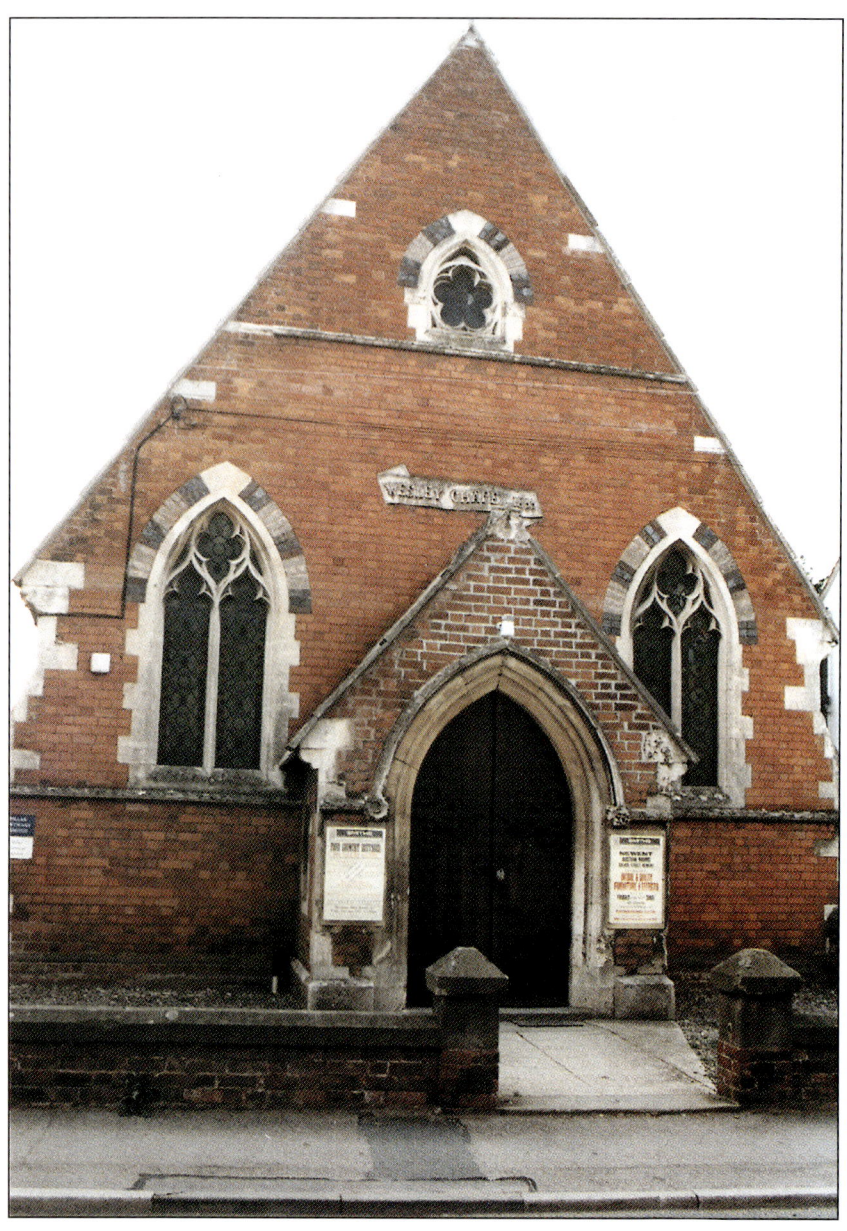

Fig.68 Former Wesleyan Chapel in Culver St., built in 1855

the Methodist Circuit, Rev. Thomas Sheers of Ledbury (20). The following is a list of ministers between 1898-1969 (10):-

1898	H Gorton Edge	1936-38	Norman B Cooper
1902	W G Davies	1939	J Eric Thorp
1911	A S Higson	1940-42	M H Jelbert
1913	G Dyer	1943-45	M O Darwin
1918	Frederick W Smith	1946	F W Gear
1919	C Wesley Garratt	1947	Derek Burton
1920	W D L MacKenzie	1950-51	John J Vincent
1921	B R K Paintin	1952	J Neil Graham
1922-4	A Simmons	1953-54	E Kenneth Coles
1925	N A Priestly	1955-58	Edmund B Potts
1926	W H Bridge	1961-63	W Edmund Thomas
1927	T C Brown	1964	John W Williams
1929-30	W Gollins		W Edmund Thomas*
1931-33	W J Hill	1967-69	J S Pyke
1934	J H Denis Jones		W Edmund Thomas*
			(*supernumerary)

One of the ministers Rev John J Vincent (1950-51) reached the highest Methodist Office in the country by becoming President of the Conference in 1989. He came back to preach at St Mary's during his presidential year.

In the early 1950s the Ledbury Circuit consisted of 15 places split into two sections with two ministers. The Newent section consisted of Newent, Upleadon, Kents Green, Redmarley d'Abitot, Pendock, Staunton, May Hill, and Pool Hill.

Typically the minister would conduct two or three services each Sunday. He would sometimes cycle from Newent to preach at Ledbury at 11-00 am, have lunch with some church officers, then cycle to Upton Bishop for 2-30 pm and back to Newent for tea and evening service at 6-30 pm, followed by a youth fellowship run by Gorsley Baptist Church at the Griffith's family home.

There was a good Sunday School at Newent, as well as a Guild, a Ladies meeting, a Junior Club, and a Youth Club. The original church has now been turned into an auction room.

Other religious sects have been represented in Newent from time to time. The Plymouth Brethren used to meet in the building next to the Tan House in Culver Street. Later they built a small chapel at the rear of No 8 Church Street, which has now been moved to the Shambles Museum. They then built a new church in Glebe Close but this was closed in 1999 and converted into a nursery school.

The Newent Christian Fellowship (Assemblies of God) began meeting in the Community Centre in 1981. The present Pastor is Mark Preston.

The non-conformist churches in Great Britain are split into several sects and it is not the intention to provide a history of how they developed, only to give a brief account of how they affected Newent.

In 1577 a list of recusants in Newent comprised seven names with an annual value of their property (21) :-

James Collwell	worth £28
William Dobbins	worth £20
William Wall	worth £43
Roger Huntley	worth 5 shillings
Philip Ebbes' wife	-
Elizabeth Fawkener	worth nothing
Clement Cooke	worth nothing

This could mean that they were either Catholic or "Puritans".

In 1779 a list of dissenters included, William Beale, John Prosser, William Morgan, Samuel Washburton, John Malvern, and Thomas Wood, when they petitioned the Bishop of Gloucester to hold meetings of worship in the house of Mary Ballinger. In 1792 a house in Culver Street was registered for worship (24).

An early reference to the "Dissenters" occurred in 1805 when the local meetings were disrupted and a number of people were arrested (13).

It began on Sunday March 3rd *"while Mr Macklow, one of our local Preachers was conducting the worship of God in Newent, two young men disfigured and disguised came into the place of worship, interrupted the service and put the congregation into disorder"*

On Good Friday April 12th when they went to open the new licensed Meeting House they were *"interrupted and prevented by a crowd of men gathered around a table, drinking, singing, shouting and swearing"*. The same problems occurred again on May 26th and June 9th, when *"Some hundreds gathered and held a mock service"*.

On June 21st the preachers were followed out of town and pelted with stones and dirt, and on July 5th it was decided that the problems made the meeting untenable and the chapel was shut. On October 25th they were again set upon by the crowd and the following month the chapel door was *"thrown down"* during the service.

The interference was not tolerated for long and thirteen rioters were arrested. Richard Jones and William Buddens, both of Newent were brought to trial at the next Spring Assizes at Gloucester but both were treated leniently after they promised to behave.

In 1816 a licence was granted for the dissenters to use the house of William Nelmes, and two years later Richard Allan, a Methodist minister from Gloucester, was allowed to use the house of Daniel Robins, a cordwainer, for religious purposes. There are several references over the next 25 years of private houses being used for worship (24).

The Baptist movement started in Newent in 1831 when John Hall, from Minsterly in Shropshire, took over the Gorsley Baptist Chapel ministry, although the foundation stone for the present building was not laid until 7th May 1851. In these early days baptisms were performed in Gorsley Pool. In the autumn of 1831 he started a small chapel in Gloucester Street, Newent but it only lasted a few months as it was difficult for Mr Hall to get there (11).

Mr Hall did most of the collecting of the money to build Gorsley Chapel. One day he called on an aged respectable attorney in Newent to solicit a subscription. The attorney replied *"You ought not to come to me for assistance, seeing you have been mainly instrumental in taking away our prosecution fees, for before you came to Gorsley we mostly had half a dozen cases a year, but now we do not get one in that number of years"* Mr Hall had the reputation of turning people away from crime and into more Christian pursuits. The attorney, despite his remarks, still made a donation. John Hall died in 1885 aged 79.

A temporary Sunday School building was erected south of Kilcot Cross and in June 1934 a new Baptist Chapel was opened alongside it. This was closed in the 1990s and converted into a private house.

Another non-conformist group, usually known as Christian Brethren, appeared in the Newent area in the summer of 1930 when some Christians from Cinderford began open air gospel meetings at Clifford's Mesne (11). The following summer an itinerant evangelist, Luther Rees, returned and erected a tent in the orchard of Mr Caleb Warren. The tent was moved to Aston Ingham for the month of July, and evening meetings were held at Mr Warren's house.

In the autumn of 1931 Mr Arthur Notley came to live at Ravenshill Farm in Clifford's Mesne and meetings were held at his farm house on Sunday mornings. In December it was agreed to build a mission hall in the village, in the orchard where the tent had been erected the previous summer. This was achieved in just six weeks at a cost of only £59. The humble construction was built by W G Hall of Aston Crews and was mainly timber and corrugated iron sheets. The opening service was held on Friday 5th February 1932.

In 1934 a Bible study group was started in Oxenhall by George Harpur which continued until 1945, but there was a growing wish to bring the movement into Newent. In October 1944 a series of evangelistic meetings were held in the former "Nags Head" on the corner of Culver Street, the home of the Women's Institute at the time. These continued for two years. In July 1946 a tent was erected in a field adjoining the Holts (now Johnstone Road) for a children's mission.

It became clear that a more permanent place of worship should be found, and this came about when Mr R H Goulding offered a room in his business premises in Ledbury Road. It was named the Gospel Hall and the first service was held there on 13th June 1948. It continued in use for 14 years.

The site in Ledbury Road was not ideal and many inquiries were made over the next few years to obtain some land for a purpose built chapel. A building fund was started in 1952 but it was not until November 1960 that a quarter of an acre of land was purchased in Glebe Close for £450.

In 1951 Mr Alfred Cracknell, a retired builder, moved into the area and together with Mr Arthur Goulding they provided the main spiritual leadership in the church for many years. Mr Cracknell was able to provide experienced advice and supervision as the new Glebe Chapel was constructed. It cost £5,400 and was opened with two special services on Sunday 4th March and Monday 5th March 1962. The architect was Mr Charles Booth of Hereford, who gave his services freely.

The new congregation expanded rapidly and in 1966 it was necessary to build a new hall extension at the rear of the chapel. The Sunday School reached its peak in 1967 when 149 children attended one Sunday afternoon meeting.

A Baptistry was built into the new Chapel and the first baptism by immersion took place in November 1962. The first wedding in the Chapel, between Alan Waters and Evelyn Goulding, was performed on 15th November 1963.

In the 1960s a small bookstall was started in the Chapel. This gradually grew and before Christmas in 1974 and 1975 this was moved to the front room of a house overlooking a main street in the town. Then for six months in 1976 it moved to an empty shop. Sales escalated and a Charitable Company was formed to buy the Old Parish Rooms in the High Street, opposite Watery Lane for £10,000. It was purchased in 1978 and opened as the "Good News Centre" in March 1980.

Since then over £100,000 has been spent refurbishing the property and it is now a well known Christian bookshop and Coffeehouse.

In the early 1990s the Elders of the Chapel were Dr Eric Church, Douglas Bell, and Theo Cracknell. Dr Church moved to Devon in 1997 and the Elders in 2002 are; Theo Cracknell, David Dexter, John Cox, Tim Dean, and Ian Cracknell. The deacons are; Alan Waters, Andrew Cox, Arthur Lowe, Steve Smeaton, Tim Cracknell and Mark Goulding. In order to cater for the mothers of young children two mid-week morning meetings are now held on Tuesday, called "Stepping Stones", and on Friday, called "Koffee and Kids".

Another group of non-conformists, The Quakers, used to meet in the Community Centre in Ross Road.

Fig. 69 The former tannery building used by the Plymouth Brethren
Originally built in 1695

References

1.	G Zarnecki	1953	Trans Bristol & Glos Arch Soc
2.	R M Bradfield	1999	Newent Carved Stones Unravelled
3.	Church Guide	2000	
4.	Nourse Manuscript	c1725	GRO
5.	S Rudder	1779	History of Gloucestershire
6.	Parish Register	1672-1766	GRO P225
7.	Bishops Transcripts	1597-1671	GRO GDR/VI/164
8.	United Reformed Church Booklet	1996	
9.	Catholic Church Silver Jubilee Pamphlet	1985	
10.	Rev J J Vincent		Private correspondence
11.	Theo Cracknell	1992	From Tent Campaign to Town Chapel
12.	J C Shambrook	1886	Life and Labours of John Hall
13.	Thoughts on the Evil of Persecution	A Pamphlet	
14.	L Hines	2001	Millennium Memories, The History of Gorsley and Kilcot
15.	Sir Robert Atkyns	1712	Ancient and Present State of Gloucestershire
16.	R E Bailey	2002	History of the Bailey Family
17.	F Penney	1965	Parish Magazine Article (churchwarden's accounts)
18.	Vestry Minutes	1768-1820	GRO
19.	Beale Correspondence	1752-1805	NRA
20.	Gift of Land	1853	GRO EL523
21.	Bristol & Glos Arch Soc		Vol 5 p.222-237
22.	J Douglas	1912	Historical Notes on Newent GRO PA225/2
23.	Rev W Boyd	2001	Private correspondence
24.	Hockaday Abstracts		GRO Vol 292/3

16. From the Church Records
Frances Penney

In addition to recording baptisms, marriages and burials the Parish Register (1) also gives details of unusual deaths, scandals and praise. The Reverend Thomas Jackman who died in 1690 was said to have been the *"learned, pious, and charitable late vicar here to the great good of all his parishioners"*.

In the case of baptisms the name of the father is given, often with his occupation, but the name of the mother is not recorded until 1684. Illegitimate children are recorded under the name of their mother but the name of the reputed father is also given. The strangest entry is that of the daughter of Alice Barnwood in 1710. She had given birth to a son, John, in March 1707 when she was recorded as the wife of John Barnwood *"as they say"*. But she and John were not married until April 1708. In August 1710 the entry reads *"Mary the daughter of John Barnwood, by Alice his wife, was baptized (as in wedlock but by affidavit made by the said Alice one John Hawkins is the father)"*. John Hawkins later fathered sons by Mary Taylor (1711) and Margaret Jones (1714), married Elizabeth Freame in 1720 and had two daughters by her.

The ages of those buried are not usually given unless they had lived to a great age, such as Ann Hopkins who died aged 100, in 1760. Ann Knowles, who died in 1726 aged 79 was worthy of note as she had *"taught school in this town 46 years"*.

Burials during the period of the first parish register (1672-1766) averaged 32 but in some years there must have been severe epidemics (1682 = 94, 1683=72, 1727=84, 1728=95, 1729=70, 1741=94, 1765=67). Smallpox was noted in Newent in 1755 (burials = 55) and again in 1756.

Many people were buried under the floor of the church. These memorial stones are now hidden under the carpet but they were recorded in 1988 (2), as were the memorials on the walls, and reveal details of several families. Four generations of the Nourse family are recorded in the Lady Chapel. The first Walter Nourse was married to Mary Engham from Gunstone in Kent. She died in childbirth in 1636, leaving a daughter, Mary, and a son Walter, born in 1631. The widower remarried and is commemorated in a memorial on the wall of the chapel together with his second wife. Their son was Timothy who lived at Southerns. He married Lucy Harwood, daughter of a prebendary of Gloucester Cathedral, in 1691, and in his will of 1699, left money to pay for apprenticeships for poor children. Lucy, after his death, married Thomas Stokes and left money for her own charity to provide clothes for poor widows.

The wife of the second Walter (1631-1663) was also named Mary. She died in 1695, aged 76, and their children were Walter and Mary. The third Walter (1655-1743) wrote (c1725) "The Reminiscences of Life in Newent" in the late 17th century, giving details of the rebuilding of the church in 1675-9 and the building of the Market House in 1668. His wife was Dorothy Bourne, daughter of John Bourne, Lord of the Manor of Kilcot. This Lordship passed to Walter Nourse on his marriage to Dorothy in 1686. Walter and Dorothy had three sons Walter, John and Timothy, and two daughters, Mary and Elizabeth.

The Nourse family were also Lords of the Manor of Boulsdon, the first Walter having purchased it from Thomas Estcourt in 1630. It passed from father to son until 1758 when John, the only son to survive Walter, died. The Lordship then passed to William Nourse of Weston-under-Penyard, there being no member of the family left in Newent.

John Bourne (1620-1708), originally from Sutton Bourne in Somerset, is buried in the south isle of the church. In his will he said that he had already disposed of his lands to his daughters, Nourse and Clarke, and to his grandson John Smith. It appears that he was living part of each year with his daughters because he left each of them *"the furniture that I have in my chamber at her house"* together with various books. His granddaughter Elizabeth (sister of John) received *"a great brass kettle, pewter and brass in a hogshead, an iron-banded trunk and all the linen in it, and all the bedding and household stuff that my daughter Clarke knows to be mine in the house"*. All this was valued at £50 in his probate inventory. Walter Nourse was his executor and residuary legatee.

Also in the Lady Chapel are several memorials to the Woodward family who lived at the Moat. Christopher (1629-1699) was the man who took the plans prepared by Edward Taylor to London for the installation of the roof, in the restoration of the church (1675-79). Three pillars had been erected to support the roof in the middle of the isle, but several objections to these were raised as they *"take up too much room"*. Taylor, a carpenter, told them that when he worked *"in London after the fire he saw at St Brides and some other places such blades as would soon run up this building"*. Although his draft, for a roof without pillars, was liked it was considered advisable to show it to somebody that understood it and Taylor suggested his *"old master in London who was accounted the best carpenter there"*. The plan met with his approval with the comment *"they need not fear the building"*.

Christopher's son, also Christopher (1660-1710), lived for part of his life in Oxenhall where three of his six children were baptized, including his posthumous son, Christopher, who died in 1731 aged 21.

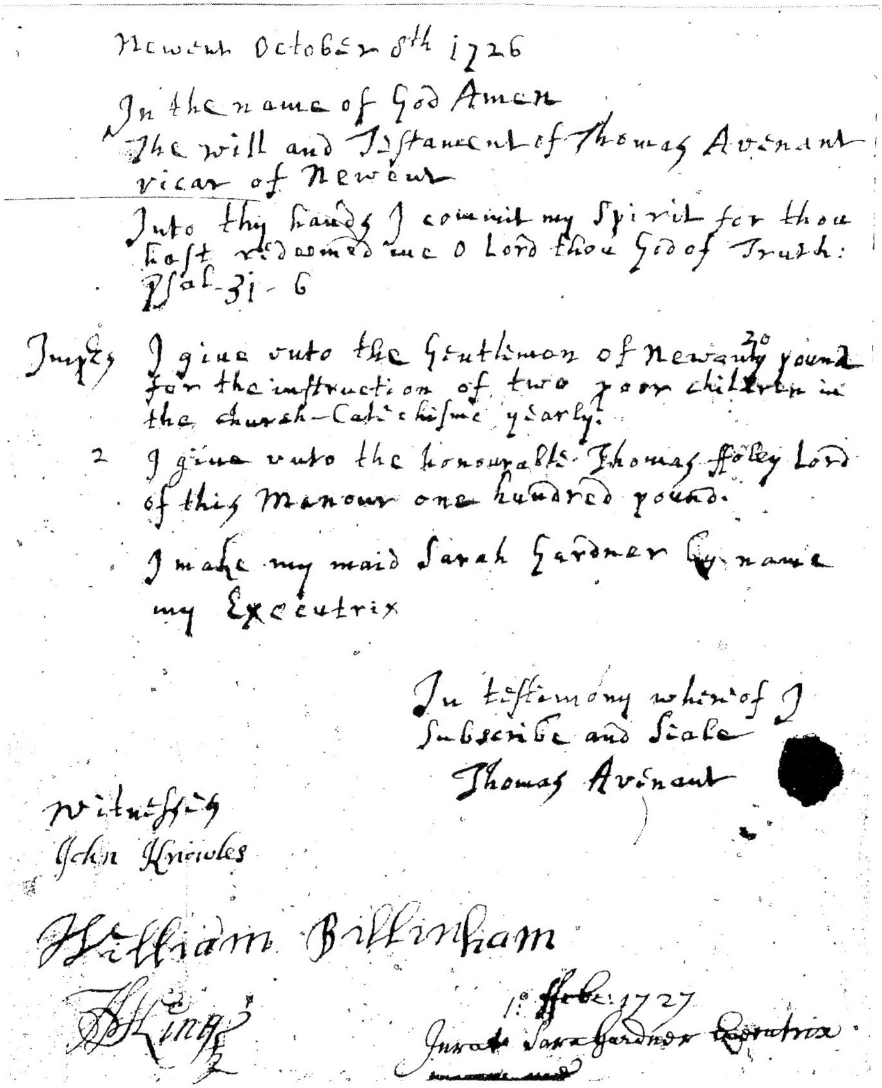

Newent October 8th 1726

In the name of God Amen

The will and Testament of Thomas Avenant vicar of Newent

Into thy hands I commit my Spirit for thou hast redeemed me O Lord thou God of Truth: Psal. 31 - 6

Imp^s. I give unto the Gentlemen of Newent 30 pound for the instruction of two poor children in the church-Catechisme yearly.

2 I give unto the honourable Thomas Foley Lord of this Manour one hundred pound.

I make my maid Sarah Gardner by name my Executrix

In testimony whereof I subscribe and Seale

Thomas Avenant

Witnesses
John Knowles
William Billingham
[illegible]

1° Feb: 1727 Jurat Sara Gardner Executrix

Fig.70 The Will of Thomas Avenant, vicar of Newent, 1726
(courtesy of Glos Record Office)

Transcription of Thomas Avenant's will (fig.70) :-

Newent October 8th 1726

In the name of God amen. The will and testament of Thomas Avenant Vicar of Newent. Into thy hands I commit my spirit for thou hast redeemed me O Lord thou God of truth.   Psal 31-6

1. I give unto the Gentlemen of Newent 20 pounds for the instruction of two poor children in the church Catachisme yearly
2. I give unto the Honourable Thomas Foley Lord of this Manour one hundred pound

I Make my Maid Sarah Gardner by name my Executrix

Witnesses : John Knowles, William Billinham, H Kinge

In Testimony where of I subscribe and seale
Thos Avenant

Transcription of Symon Parsons Probate Inventory (fig.71) :-

A true & pfect inventory of all & singular ye goods chattles cattles rites & creadites of Symon Parsons of Hayes in ye pish of Newent in ye County of Gloucester yoman deceased, taken vallued & aprized ye 25th day of February Ano 1709 by wee whose names are here unto subscribed

	£ s d
The deceased wearing apparell & money in purse	25 -16 - 9.5
One bill of eighteene pounds due from Zach Shrapnell	18 - 0 - 0
One bill due from Mr Wm Attwood of three & twentie pounds ye first of May next	23 - 0 - 0
One bill of five pounds from James Holeday where of part haud beene reced in the deceds life time but w remains now due cannot yet know & when reced shall be charged	
Owing from Tho Haynes of Dymocke for two years rent for land at Crowfield at 3 £ p ann where of one pound & five shilings was reced in the deceds life time soe there remains due	4 - 15 - 0

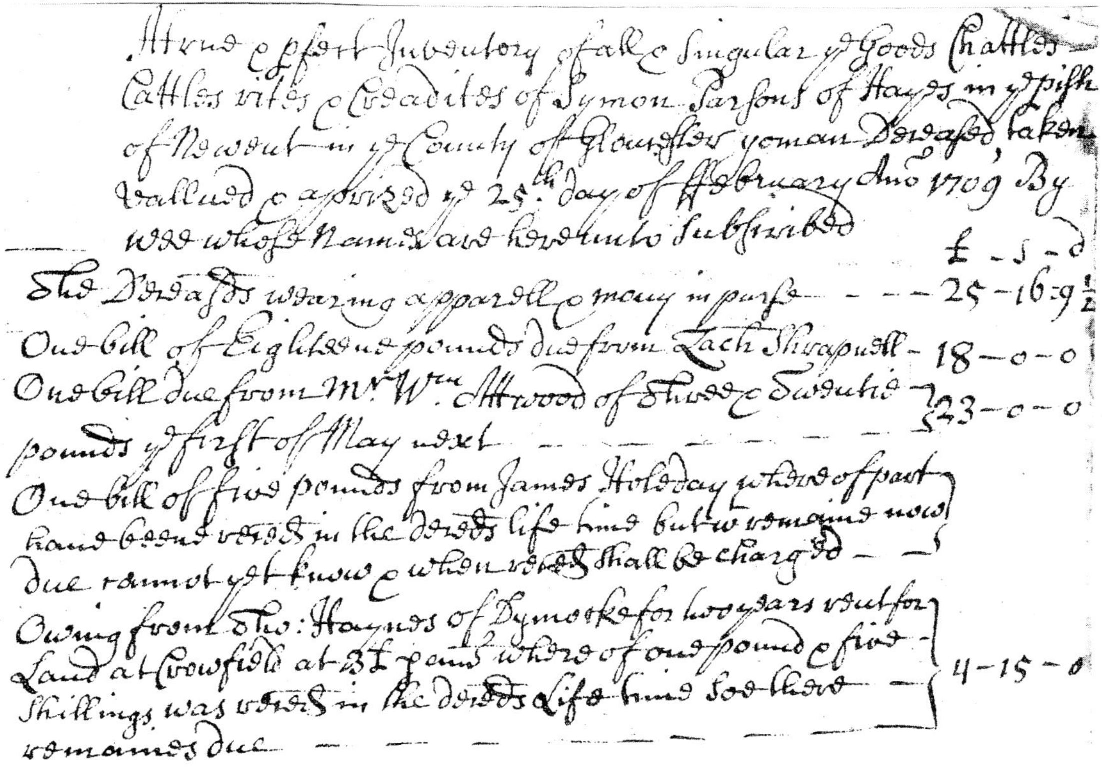

A true & perfect Inventory of all the singular the goods Chattles & Credits of Symon Parsons of Hayes of Moutiuton in the County of Hereford taken & valued exhibited the 28th day of February Anno 1709 By vs whose Names are hereunto subscribed

	£	s	d
His Wearing apparell & money in purse	25	16	9½
One Bill of Eighteen pounds due from Zach Shropnall	18	0	0
One Bill due from Mr Wm Attwood of Sussex Susqhia	23	0	0
pounds ye first of May next			
One bill of £105 pounds from James Hileday at Interest past			
from August 1698 in the Hands of ... life but ...			
Due them of ... upon Bond shall be charged			
Owing from Tho: Haynes of Bymocks for 10 years ... for			
Land at Crowfield at £1 p ann ... of one pound fire	11	15	0
Shillings was owing in the days of his time ...			
... moneys due			

Fig.71 Part of the Probate Inventory of Symon Parsons of Hayes, 1709 (courtesy of Glos Record Office)

In the chancel, between the organ and the Lady Chapel, are stones recording several clergymen of Newent. Francis Singleton, vicar from 1627-1642, a native of Gloucester, was educated at Queen's College, Oxford, and was awarded a masters degree by Jesus College in 1626. He was also appointed Rector of Somerfield, Herefordshire in 1631.

Thomas Avenant, vicar from 1691 to 1727, came from King's Norton, in Worcestershire, was educated at New Inn Hall, Oxford, and held livings at Avon Dassett (Warwickshire) and Dormington (Herefordshire) before coming to Newent in 1691. He was probably the brother of Richard Avenant who, from 1669 to 1713, was in partnership with the Foley family in the ironworks at Oxenhall. Thomas, in his will, left £20 for the instruction each year of two poor children in the catechism, and £100 to *"the honourable Thomas Foley, Lord of this Manor"*. His estate was valued at £704. (fig.70)

Dr John Craister, vicar 1728-1737, was a fellow of Trinity College, Cambridge, becoming a B.A. in 1701, M.A. in 1705 and a Doctor of Divinity in 1723.

A Curate, Nathaniel King, who came from Woodchester, was educated at Magdalen College, Oxford. In 1711 he applied for a schoolmaster's licence but several people in Newent protested saying *"it was contrary to the will and mind of many substantial inhabitants of our parish"*, but on the stone recording his death in 1724 he was said to be learned and eloquent, preached strong sermons and defended the sacred principles of England's church.

Above the south door of the church are two marble memorials. The top one, decorated by the sculptor John Flaxman, is to Barbara Bouchier (1751-1784) who died at sea on a journey home from India, where her husband Charles had been a member of the council at Bombay. Charles had the memorial erected *"in testimony of his affectionate regard for one of the most blameless and deserving of her sex"*.

Barbara was the daughter of James Richardson (1703-1776) surgeon and apothecary. He was born in Knockshinnock, near Dumfries, in Scotland, and his memorial said he was skilled in his profession while *"his superior understanding and pleasant conversation greatly enhanced his society and friendship, whilst his humane and liberal heart gained him universal esteem"*. He established in Newent one of the first medical spas in England.

In 1734 James married Anne Nest (born 1712) daughter of Thomas Nest, a glazier from Gloucester, and Elizabeth Morse (1675-1756) daughter of Abraham Morse, Clerk. James and Anne had eight children, of whom two died in childhood. Their youngest daughter, Sarah Morley (1756-1784) is commemorated by another Flaxman tablet in the nave of Gloucester Cathedral.

Their son Samuel (1738-1824) married in 1786 Harriet Davey, the widow of Major William Davey who had served as Chief Persian Secretary to Warren Hastings, Governor of Bengal. They had two children, Samuel and Harriet. In 1769 Samuel brought his African servant, Thomas Bloomsbury to Newent (see later).

James' eldest daughter Anne (1734-1772) married Christopher Sundius, a Swedish naval officer serving with the British Navy. She had ten children of whom five died in infancy.

Thomas (1743-1823) James' third son, is commemorated in a memorial on the wall of the church (the pillar to the left of the Lady Chapel) . It was erected *"in grateful affection"* by his nephew, Henry Richardson. Thomas was a J.P. with *"an integrity of principle which prompted him to spurn any action that was sordid or dishonourable"*. He also had *"a kindness of disposition, a warmth and serenity of heart, and a cheerfulness of temper. By the inhabitants of Newent he was more especially beloved as a father and benefactor whose purse was always open to encourage improvements or relieve distress"*.

On the north wall of the church is a memorial to Elizabeth Draper, wife of Samuel. He was the third son and middle child of the family of nine of Edward Draper, shoemaker and cordwainer. The Draper family, through marriage, were connected with many families in the 18th century (4).

Samuel was the most successful of this family financially, owning property in Newent and London. Born in 1705 he went to London in 1719 as an apprentice to a cheesemonger, started his own business in Shoe Lane in the City of London and became a Freeman of a City Guild. He and his wife returned to Newent where he was a member of the Vestry and a Churchwarden. He had no children but was very generous in his will to all his nephews and nieces and their children, many of whom were named Samuel.

The earliest member of the Draper family of whom we can be certain is Richard, a shoemaker, who died in 1682 and whose inscription on a headstone is still legible. He married in 1664 Bridget, daughter of Edward Wall, a yeoman, from whom she later inherited a malt house in Culver Street. Her brother John, a blacksmith, was responsible for the ironwork in the rebuilding of the church.

Richard's eldest son Edward (1665-1723) married, in 1698, Elizabeth daughter of Giles Lingen, a butcher. They were the parents of five sons and four daughters. Their eldest son Edward (1699-1776) was a student at Merton College, Oxford, and was ordained in 1722. His tutors said he had *"conducted his life and morals devoutly, soberly and honourably"*. After a period as a curate at Huntley he became Rector of Horton in 1730 and vicar of Minsterworth. In 1733 he married Dorothy Beale who was born in London, daughter of John Beale, *"a citizen and cheesemonger of London"* and cousin of Miles Beale, clothier of Newent. Their son, Edward, followed his father to Merton and into the church. After serving as curate to his father he became rector of Leckhampton from 1767 until his death in 1825 at the age of 92. He never married and in his will he left money to his sister-in-law (widow of his brother Samuel) and her children. One of these, Thomas, lived at that time in Quebec but he returned to England and, with his wife and children, lived in Cheltenham. His son Thomas, listed as a shoemaker in the 1851 census, emigrated to Australia.

Edward and Elizabeth's second son Richard (1704-1762) was at one time an innholder *"at the sign of the George"*. His son, Richard, was executor of Samuel's will in 1780. The fourth son, Cornelius (1707-1757), was another successful man who lived at Southerns where he farmed. His probate inventory showed the extent of his farm stock, crops and animals, and the possessions in his house; his total estate being worth just under £1,000. Cornelius married Margaret Taylor, the granddaughter of Edward Taylor (see later). In his will he makes provision for her, his son Samuel and his five daughters.

Samuel married in 1769 Elizabeth, daughter of John Astman, member of another large Newent family. John Astman's sister, Sarah, married Thomas Hartland and their son was the Lieutenant in the Royal Company of Invalids (see later). Samuel's marriage was short lived as Elizabeth died in 1772. He never remarried and in his will of 1813 he left generous legacies to his sisters and their children. Cornelius' daughter Mary (1733-1789) married Peter Parkington from Westbury-on-Severn in 1756 and, after six daughters, had a son, Samuel, born in 1769, and another, Cornelius, in 1770.

Elizabeth (1753-1816) married John Ellis, a widower from Bristol, in 1774. She had two sons, John and William and, after the death of her husband, returned to Newent and married Thomas Griffiths, a widower, in 1792. After his death she kept house for her brother Samuel who, in his will, left all his household furniture and goods to his nephew, John Ellis of the George Inn, the goods to be sold and the interest from the sum raised to be paid to Elizabeth. The names of two of John's daughters, Sarah and Urania, are inscribed on the top of the chest tomb of Cornelius their great grandfather.

Margaret (1739-1801) married John Cadle from Westbury-on-Severn in 1758. They had two daughters and five sons, two of whom, Thomas and Cornelius, emigrated to America, and their great grandson, Joseph, went to Australia in 1852.

Hannah (1745-1780), Cornelius' fourth daughter, married John Green, a plumber and glazier. This family stayed in Newent and their grandson, Joseph, was listed as a plumber in the census of 1851.

William (1709-1741) the fifth son of Edward and Elizabeth, was apprenticed at the age of 14 to Anthony Edmonds, a glover. In 1733 he married Anthony's daughter Elizabeth, by whom he had four children. He died in 1741, a year in which there must have been an epidemic, for there were 94 burials instead of the average 32. Soon after Elizabeth's death in 1746 their son William was sent to London to be apprenticed to a cheesemonger and made contact with his uncle Samuel who was later godfather to some of his children. He also became a liveryman of the Clothworkers Company and, in 1768 at the election of Lord Mayor, was listed as a cheesemonger of Bishopgate Street.

As far as we can tell the Draper name died out in Newent, though the Cadle connection is still here. William's line continued in London, and later in Ireland, for six more generations.

The earliest gravestone in the Churchyard is that of Samuel Clark, who died in 1681, and the latest that of Susannah Sophia West in 1948. But her name was recorded on an existing family stone for no new graves were dug after 1865 when the cemetery was opened in Watery Lane.

32 of the gravestones are listed monuments of historical interest; 17 are of the 17th century; and 8 are double-sided with inscriptions about 100 years apart and not, as far as is known, of connected families.

The inscriptions on the 535 tombstones were recorded between 1982 and 1986 (3). Many prompted further research to find the stories behind the names.

Edward Taylor, who died in 1721, aged 87, is shown as the, *"head workman contriving and rebuilding the roof of the Church in 1679".* His son William was a butcher and died in 1762, aged 89.

Thomas Warn (died 1777, aged 82) built the Church organ in 1737. According to a report in the Gloucester Journal (7th June 1737) it was the first organ he had built *"all of his own composing and tuning."*

Another Church musician was Richard Warjohn (died 1834, aged 85) who had been a member of the Parish Church Choir for 77 years. At the top of his headstone is inscribed an open music book giving the words and musical notation of the first line of Psalm 40.

The chest tomb of the Reverend Thomas Jackman (died 1690, aged 75) has an inscription in Latin showing that he was a popular preacher, a theologian noted for his piety and a driving force behind the restoration of the Church.

John Hartland (died 1803, aged 80) had *"The honour of holding His Majesty's Commission of Lieutenant in the Royal Invalids and that of Town Adjutant of Berwick-upon-Tweed".* Information from the library at the Ministry of Defence showed that Companies of Invalids consisted of pensioners fit for garrison duty and were deployed from 1703 to 1803. Two Army lists show that

It: Twenty four Planes, fourteen Augers, four hand
Sawes, four Axes, two Hatchets, four Adzes,
thirty Chissels and Gouges, three Drawing knives
two Iron Squares, one Gimblet and Bitts three
Hamers, one Iron Barr, four Iron Pins, two Pulleys,
two Rules, two pair of Compasses, two Screw Bitts
one hold fast and other working tooles 3:0:0

It: Timber for two Tableframes, one Ever for an Oval
Table, one lath Bench, one Poole Box, Some Boards 0:18:6
Timber, wood and Lumber

It: Moneys due to the deceased 10:0:0
It: In ye Stye one Stone Pigg valued at 0:6:8

Apprized by us
Thomas Rudge
John S Jentson

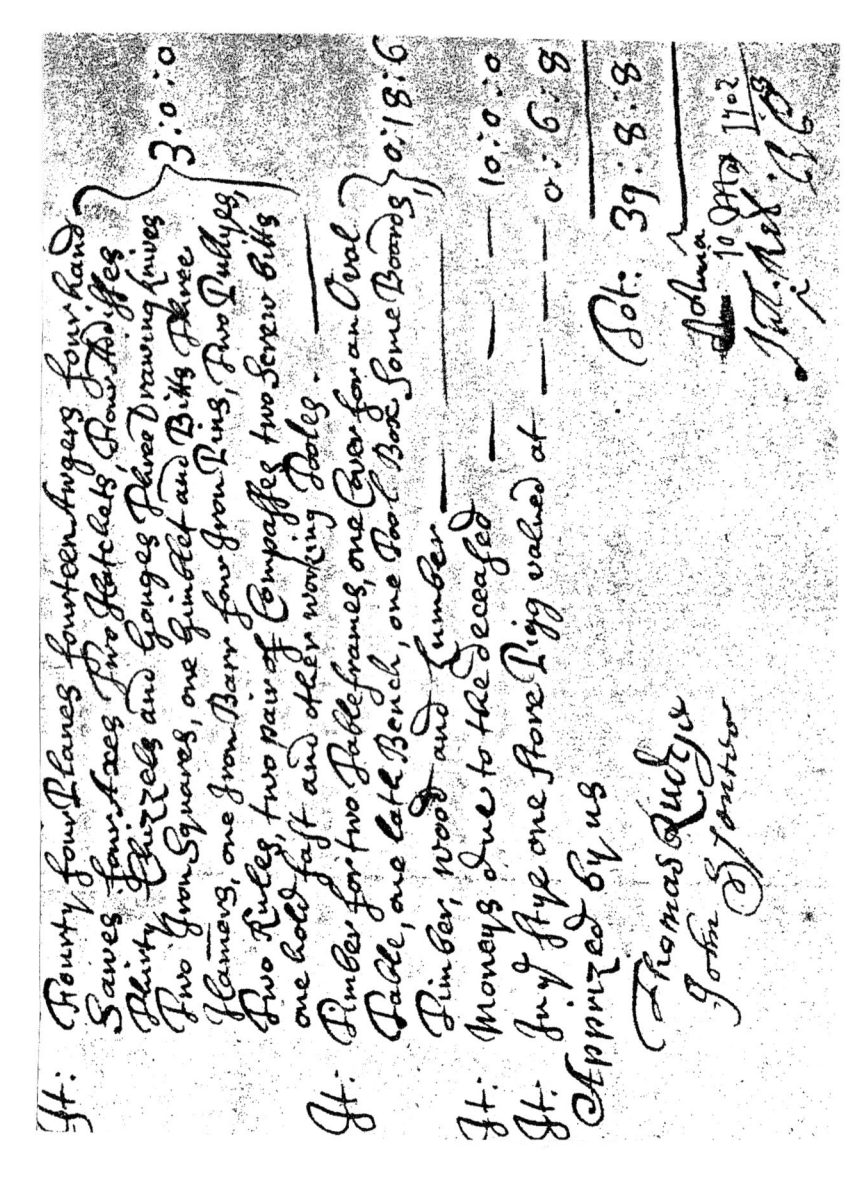

Tot: 39:8:8

Johua
10 May 1702
Inl. Reb. 3 6

Fig.72 Part of the Probate Inventory of Edward Taylor, 1702 (courtesy of Glos Record Office)

Transcription of part of the Probate Inventory of Edward Taylor (fig.72) who was a carpenter and son of the Edward Taylor who rebuilt the church roof, showing some of his tools :-

It	Fourty four planes fourteen awgers, four hand sawes, four axes two hatchets, four addisses thirty chizzels and gouges three drawing knives two iron squares, one gimblet and bitts three hamers, one iron barr four iron pins, two pullyes two rules, two pair of compasses, two screw bitts one hold fast and other working tooles	3 - 0 - 0
It	Timber for two tableframes, one cover for an oval table, one lath bench, one tool box some boards timber, wood and lumber	0 - 18 - 0
It	Moneys due to the deceased	10 - 0 - 0
It	In ye stye one store pigg valued at	0 - 6 - 8
	Tot	39 - 8 - 8

Apprized by us   10th May 1702
       Thomas Rudge
       John Spencer

John joined such a Company in 1775, was at Berwick-upon-Tweed in 1780 and still receiving full pension in 1803.

    Another military man was William Underwood (died 1830, aged 67) who had been a Yeoman Warder of the Tower of London for 43 years.

    Perhaps the most unusual memorial is that on a large flat stone in a section of the churchyard holding several stones of the Richardson family including Thomas, a J.P., and James, a surgeon. This records Thomas Bloomsbury, a native of Africa, who died in 1829, aged 75. He had been a faithful servant of Samuel Richardson for 55 years, having come to Newent at the age of 15 in 1769. His master Samuel, had died in 1824 but his family looked after Thomas *"who had borne repeated attacks of illness with Christian patience"* and had shown *"honesty, integrity, strong affection and attention to his master's interest"*.

References
1. Newent Parish Register 1672-1766   GRO P225 IN1/2
2. Frances Penney   1988   St Mary's Church Survey
3. F Penney/D A Pearce   1987   St Mary's Churchyard Survey
4. G C Draper   1990   The Drapers of Newent

17. Transport
David Bick

Roads

Most of the narrow lanes that criss-cross the district were probably there before the Roman occupation, for their often deeply sunken character testifies to very remote beginnings (1).

Newent's location in low ground between the Forest of Dean and the Malvern Hills made it a natural route into Wales and the Marches, and at the town the two ways diverged. You could go westwards via Kilcot and Ross, or more towards the north via Dymock. The Ross route through Oxenhall, Gorsley and Linton is very ancient. Much survives as country lanes, but between Fidler's Cross and Bollitree Castle it is no more than a deeply sunken hollow-way.

The Romans used the Dymock route, and its course beyond the village seems pretty well established. However, between Gloucester and there, old trackways were probably improved and pressed into service, and thus the road never existed in classic form. Of several likely routes the one via Pauntley is intriguing. West of Ketford was a very fine but narrow road obliquely climbing a cliff-face, and cut out of the solid rock for the purpose, much as was Roman practice on the Continent. It is now a public footpath (map reference 725308).

Another route, from Gloucester to Dymock via Newent ran along the Oxenhall parish boundary, and a grid-like street pattern in crop markings behind Lyne House Farm lies on it. Other ancient ways, perhaps salt-ways from Droitwich, run south-westerly via Redmarley, Three Ashes and Gorsley, and via Welsh House Lane and Shaw Common.

There were once two high roads from Gloucester to Newent, the present one, and another through Tibberton, entering Newent via Kent's Green down Bury Bar. The final mile or two was abandoned in the 18th century, but can still be traced as footpaths and a sunken lane (724256).

The roads round Newent were almost useless for vehicles and even horses until the Turnpike Acts improved them, but the once familiar pike-houses with a gate or chain across the road where tolls were collected have nearly all gone. There is one near the garage in Huntley, and another near Lea Line. A few of the old milestones can still be found at the roadside, and how keenly the weary traveller must have sought them.

The present B4221 from Kilcot through Gorsley to the M50 and beyond was opened in 1810 as a new road to Hereford. The advertisement made much of the wonderful scenery, and with all the hills to climb at a snail's pace there was time enough to enjoy it.

During the 19th century, many minor roads were closed to save the cost of maintenance (2), and some examples, from north to south are given below. Those marked with an asterisk are still open as public paths, and well repay exploring (3).

* Ryton to Redmarley (Poet's Path)	1.5 miles
* Ketford towards Dymock (Poet's Path)	1
Kempley Green to Old Rock	1.25
* Botloes Green to Paunt House and Ketford	1.25
Near Peter's Farm to Shaw Common	1
Furnace Lane, Newent, to Winters' Farm	0.5
* Bury Bar, Newent, to Caerwents	1.5
* Southend to Caerwents	1
* Woodgate, south through Newent Woods	0.5
New House Farm to May Hill Common	0.75

Fig. 73 An old milestone, now removed

The Botloes Green route is of particular interest; thirty years ago an old man told me that pack-mules went that way, carrying stone from the Forest of Dean for the building of Eastnor Castle, begun in 1812.

Fig.74 Bob Beachus in his 1910 Belsize Taxi, c1920

Canals

The only canal in our district ran from the River Severn at Gloucester via Newent and Ledbury. 34 miles long, it was launched during the years of a "Canal Mania" at the end of the 18th century, mainly on the promise of coal deposits just west of Newent. In fact, the coalfield with its serious limitations in quality and potential had long been known, but served its purpose very well in the glowing promotional literature. In order to bring the new canal closer to the mines, the original plan for a route up the Leadon Valley was changed for a much more difficult course involving a tunnel well over a mile long at Oxenhall. Combined with the failure of the collieries, this proved a fatal blunder, and by

1798 all the authorized capital had been spent in barely reaching Ledbury, only half way to Hereford.

The only source of traffic was thus reduced to that of two small market towns and their environs, but somehow the canal contrived to stay in business but with no hope of a dividend, until in 1827 a new manager, a young man of 23 named Stephen Ballard, was appointed manager. Full of enthusiasm, he soon increased trade to the point where the old dream of reaching Hereford, seemed not only possible but even a sound commercial option. Capital was raised under a further Act of Parliament, and after many difficulties the goal was at last attained in 1845. But already, railways were threatening much of the traffic, and trade never developed to any great degree.

Fig.75 The partly restored canal showing the entrance to Oxenhall tunnel

Fig.76 Lock Cottage, Oxenhall, showing the lock chamber in course of reconstruction
(photo Derek Lemarchand)

Eventually the canal came under the control of the Great Western Railway, who between 1882 and 1885 converted the Gloucester-Newent-Ledbury section into the new mode of transport. However, a length of two or three miles including the notorious tunnel was bypassed, enabling it to survive, providing an historic amenity of great interest in the area.

The publication, in 1979, of my book, The Hereford & Gloucester Canal (4), brought sufficient attention to this long abandoned waterway to encourage formation a few years later of a Trust with the avowed intention, not only to preserve certain features, but actually to re-open the whole 34 miles and 21 locks from beginning to end even though much of the route has gone without trace and long since sold off to different owners. However, men have flown to the moon, so nothing is impossible.

Aided mainly by grants and volunteer labour, the Trust has certainly got off to a good start, and close to Newent alone a mile has been largely restored, including the derelict Lock Cottage at Oxenhall, now refurbished and inhabited, and the adjoining lock. Once quite overgrown and impassable, the towpath from here now makes a picturesque walk as far as the tunnel just beyond Cold Harbour Lane, and opposite the cottage a part of the branch canal to the forgotten coalfield again holds water. These sections have at least been saved from oblivion. They will be a constant reminder of a brave old enterprise financed mainly by local capital which for generations served the community well, but for its investors never stood much chance from the beginning.

Railways

As early as 1836 the ambitious England and Ireland Union Railway was projected to run via Gloucester, Newent, Ross and Abergavenny to the west coast, but it came to nothing. Thereafter, many other proposals arose for routes via Newent, including the Worcester, Dean Forest and Monmouth Railway, upon which work actually commenced in 1862. An isolated stretch of embankment in a field south-east of Pauntley church and a deep cutting in Collinpark wood (746280) for a proposed tunnel under the ridge bear testimony to this forgotten venture. The new form of transport finally arrived as the Gloucester-Newent-Ledbury Railway, built by the Great Western and opened on 27th July 1885, largely on the route of the old canal. It was a typical rural line, never of much benefit to the shareholders but of great service to the locality.

The section from Ledbury to Dymock was laid as double track and the remainder to Newent and Gloucester was single track, although it all became single track during the first World War when the second track was lifted for use overseas. It was constructed by Appleby and Lawton from Manchester.

In 1928 the third class return fair from Gloucester to Ledbury, via Newent was 2/5d, and in 1939 it was possible to buy a cheap evening return from Ledbury to Gloucester for 1/1d. The line closed to passenger traffic on 11th July 1959, the last train being hauled by locomotive No 3203, driven by Jack Folley and Jim Kavanagh (fireman). Many local people travelled on this final journey and a carnival atmosphere prevailed with the Leadon Valley Skiffle Group providing music on the platforms. One of the passengers on this last train, Mr Smith from the Scarr, had also travelled on the first train in 1885. The line continued to be used for freight but was finally closed on 20th May 1964 (5). Ten days later locomotive 78001 travelled the line for the last time collecting empty trucks. But such is the power of nostalgia that some years ago a resurrection was proposed with Emmett-style tramcars rocking through the daffodil fields from one end to the other. A delightful dream!

References

1.	David Bick	1985	The enigma of Holloways, Local History Bulletin
2.	David Bick	1999	Lost roads & Houses in Oxenhall, Oxenhall Anthology
3.	David Bick	1992	Old Newent and District
4.	David Bick	1994	The Hereford and Gloucester Canal
5.	D Postle	1985	From Ledbury to Gloucester by rail

18. 20th Century Wars
Eric Warde

First World War

"No one can guarantee success in war but only deserve it"

Winston Churchill

One keystone of Britain's foreign policy was based on the The Royal Navy retaining control of the seas. Support was provided by a small force of rigorously trained, highly motivated regular soldiers, regrettably thinly spread across the Empire. From 1914 until 1916 Britain survived the First World War with a completely volunteer Army, uniquely by comparison with friend and foe alike.

When the First World War commenced men from all over the country received the King's shilling on signing their Territorial Army papers. They subsequently served with great gallantry on the many fronts on which British Forces campaigned. It was only after the passing of the Conscription Act in January 1916, an attempt to restore British military power subsequent to the fiascos of Loos and Gallipoli, that manpower was directed into military service. Loos goes down in history as a situation in which the British Army *"in a single day were to lose more men than any other army in the history of the world"* (1).

During the First World War as many as 40,000 men served with the Gloucestershire Regiment so that it expanded to 16 Battalions. At the outbreak of war the regiment comprised four Regular Battalions together with a Territorial Battalion that had been raised for Home Service. Some of the "Terriers" were Regulars, who had served in South Africa's Boer war and since retired, but enjoyed soldiering. Over 8,000 men from the "Glosters" were killed or wounded.

The War Memorial in St Mary's churchyard lists the names of 55 men from Newent who served but did not survive the First World War. Additionally there are numerous other men who did not return to surrounding villages, hamlets and parishes where they had lived prior to their military service. These include L/Corp. George Burlow, 2nd Battalion, died of wounds, May 1915; Pte Albert Bowkett, 5th Battalion Glosters, killed in action, November 1916 and Corp. Frank Philpotts, Royal Engineers, killed in action, November 1918. All lived at Pool Hill, one of the smaller hamlets surrounding Newent whose population was some 70 people.

The first Newent man to die was A/S J Hodgetts. He was killed in an engagement between HMS "Pegasus" and the German Cruiser "Konigsberg" off the coast of Zanzibar in September 1914. The last to be killed included Pte C H Beard of the Labour Corps, Driver W Cox, and Major T Merrick, DSO, both of whom were serving with the Royal Field Artillery. All died in November 1918. Major Merrick is the only one listed as being married.

Two soldiers named Beard died but it is not possible to say if they were brothers. Similar remarks apply to two men named Dallimore. Twin brothers, Pte James Faulks and Pte John Faulks, were killed at Basra (7th Btn Glosters) and in France (2nd Btn Grenadier Guards) respectively. It is likely that two members of the Jacques family, Ass. Steward A. Jacques and W H Jacques (who cannot be traced), also come into this category. It is also possible that three members of the Rickards family, Pte E Rickards (1st Btn Glosters), Sgt. H Rickards (Royal Field Artillery), and Pte P Rickards (7th Btn Glosters), all gave their lives for their Country. The first two are brothers as they are listed with the same parents, but information about P Rickards is limited.

A number of those listed on the Memorial cannot be adequately traced. Included in this category are :- J Archer, R L Bidmead, W H Jacques (already mentioned), C Newman, J Racker, W H Smith, W F Webley, G C Williams, and H M Winfield. Others, about whom doubt exists, include H W Hall, A N Marshall, A A Williams, and J Woodward. None of these men are listed on the Commonwealth War Graves Commission web site.

Of the 55 names recorded on the St Mary's First World War Memorial no fewer than twenty served with one of the 16 Battalions of the Glosters while a further three saw service with Worcestershire Regiments. Curiously a man from South Africa and a man from New Zealand are also named on St Mary's Memorial.

The saddest entry must be that of 15 year old Apprentice R Trubshaw, who was lost on the SS Sandhurst, out of London, in May 1918. His parents, Howard and Bertha Trubshaw, resided in Newent's Ross Road.

Newent men killed in the First World War

Name	age	Unit	died	Commemoration
P O Allsopp, stoker	27	H M S "Defence"	May 1916	Plymouth
J Archer		(unable to trace details)		
Pte W A Apperley	18	13th Bn Ox & Bucks	June 1918	Boulogne
Pte W A Baldwin	29	13th Bn Glosters	Sep 1917	Heuvell
Pte C H Beard	?	328th Work Co	Nov 1918	St Albans
Pte T C S Beard	?	2/4th Bn Glosters	Aug 1917	Teper
Pte A Berkley	27	4th Bn Worcesters	Apr 1918	Ploegstreert
R L Bidmead		(unable to trace details)		
Pte J Bodenham	28	47th Gen Hospital	Feb 1919	Mont Huon

Name	Age	Unit	Date	Place
Pte W Brace	25	14th Bn Glosters	Oct 1917	Medingham
Pte C Cale	?	12th Bn Glosters	Oct 1917	Tyne Cot
Sapper R Colwell	?	173rd Tunnelling Co RE	Jan 1918	Canada Farm
Driver W Cox	27	B Bty, 306 Bde Royal Field Artillery	Nov 1918	Delsaux farm
L/Cpl J Dallimore	25	12th Bn Rifle Brigade	Mar 1918	Pozieres
L/Cpl M Dallimore	?	1/6 Bn Glosters	Oct 1916	Tyne Cot
Pte J Dee	37	2nd Bn Glosters	May 1915	Menin Gate
Pte W Elliott	25	9th Bn Glosters	Oct 1916	Karasouli
Pte James Faulks	21	7th Bn Glosters	Feb 1917	Basra
Pte John Faulks	22	2nd Bn Grenadiers	Oct 1918	Tourgeville
L/Cpl G Griffiths	?	10th Bn Glosters	Apr 1918	Pozieres
H W Wall	?	Worcs Yeomanry	Aug 1915	Mudros
2nd Mate A Hankins	25	HMS "Falaba"	Mar 1915	Tower Hill
A/S J Hodgetts	?	HMS "Pegasus"	Sep 1914	Zanzibar
L/Cpl C Hope	42	B Co, 1st Reg S. A. Inf	Sep 1917	Wimbereux
Pte W Hopkins	28	18th Bn Machine Corps	Mar 1918	Busingy
Sgt B Humpherson	22	Canterbury Reg, NZEF	Aug 1915	Chunuk Blair
A/Steward A Jacques	35	HMS "Vicknor"	Jan 1915	Plymouth
W H Jacques	(unable to trace details)			
Pte F Jones	?	RAMC	Oct 1918	Blakeney
L C Jones	(unable to trace details)			
Pte N Jenner	20	Royal Glos Hussars	Aug 1915	Green Hill
Corp. H Lane	?	1st Bn Glosters	Sep 1916	Flatiron
Pte J Lewis	19	Glosters	Sep 1917	Kamasouli
A N Marshall	?	1st Bn Bedfords	Jul 1916	Thiepval
Bomb. A Meek	23	A Bn, 110 Bde	Sep 1917	Lijssenthoek
C Newman	(unable to trace details)			
Maj. T Merrick DSO	?	Royal Field Artillery	Nov 1918	Mont Huon
Pte J Moore	31	2/5th Bn Glosters	Jun 1918	?
L/Cpl L Parry	?	8th Bn Glosters	Mar 1918	Arras
Pte A Phillips	26	10th Bn Glosters	Mar 1918	Loos
L/Cpl H Phelps	23	8th Bn Glosters	Aug 1917	Somer Farm
L/Cpl W Price	?	2nd Bn Glosters	May 1915	Menin Gate
J Racker	(unable to trace details)			
Pte E Rickards	31	1st Bn Glosters	Nov 1914	Menin Gate
Sgt H Rickards	22	A Bn, 178 Bde RFA	Sep 1918	Queant Road
Pte P Rickards	?	7th Bn Glosters	Apr 1916	Basra
Pte G Simmonds	?	14th Bn Glosters	Jul 1916	Thiepval
N S Smith	(unable to trace details)			
Pte W Sysum	?	59th Bn Machine Gun Co	Mar 1918	Arras
Sgt O Thomas	?	12th Bn Glosters	Aug 1917	St Severs
App R Trubshaw	15	SS "Sandhurst"	May 1918	Tower Hill
Pte W Wadley	27	1st Bn Worcs	Sep 1916	Vermelles
W F Webley	(unable to trace details)			
G C Williams	(unable to trace details)			
A A Williams	?	2nd Bn Royal Irish Rifles	Nov 1918	South Cerney
H M Winfield	(unable to trace details)			
J Woodward	?	4th Bn Glosters	Oct 1916	Thiepval

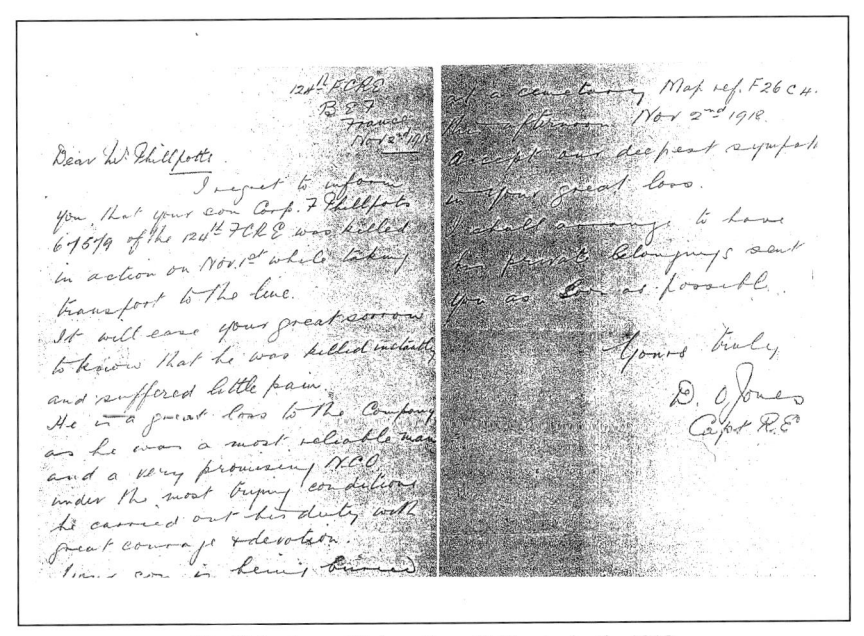

Fig.77 Letter notifying Corp Phillpots death, 1918
(courtesy Mr Hickman, Hardwick)

Transcription

Dear Mr Phillpotts,

I regret to inform you that your son Corp F Phillpotts 67579 of the 124th FCRE was killed in action on Nov 1st while taking transport to the line. It will ease your great sorrow to know that he was killed instantly and suffered little pain. He is a great loss to the Company as he was a most reliable man and a very promising NCO. Under the most trying conditions he carried out his duty with great courage and devotion. Your son is being buried at a cemetery Map Ref F26C4.0 this afternoon Nov 2nd 1918. Accept our deepest sympathy in your great loss. I shall arrange to have his private belongings sent you as soon as possible.

Yours Truly
D O Jones Capt R.E.

World War II

"We are such stuff as dreams are made on, and our little life is rounded with sleep" William Shakespeare, The Tempest

The declaration of war with Germany, broadcast by Premier Neville Chamberlain at 11-15 a.m. on Sunday, 3rd September 1939, was received by a nation that had expected the event to occur for the previous twelve months or so. It did not come with any surprise nor was the emotion that was evident on Monday, 3rd August 1914, to the fore. Living as I did on the South Coast Chamberlain's announcement was immediately followed by the screech of an Air Raid Warning Siren and the appearance of the local Air Raid Warden, fully equipped, to make the never forgotten statement "I interpret that as the All Clear". He then shut the front door of his home only to return subsequent to the siren stopping and restarting, with a completely different note, to announce that the new note was a warning. This was my introduction to the Second World War.

Conscription was already in place so that the mad rush of August 1914 did not exist, except for those who wished to serve in elite units such as The Royal Air Force as Air Crew, or at a later stage in the war, not serve as conscript Coal Miners, the so-called "Bevin Boys". The British Expeditionary Force duly arrived in France and the killing started, albeit on a small scale.

Commonwealth troops also disembarked in the UK. All that stood between England and the German Army in 1941 were two Divisions of the newly arrived Canadian Army, mostly volunteers. Hitler's Intelligence Services were miles adrift, and if only he had known England might have had a totally different structure to that existing today.

St Mary's Church holds a Roll of Honour for Newent and district that lists, albeit incompletely, the names of the 120 local men and women who comprised the various branches of the Nation's military forces in the Second World War. Some of those listed arrived in Newent and district subsequent to the end of the War, others have, for whatever reason, been omitted, but are added to this list (shown *).

The Roll of Honour for Newent and District, Second World War

F Armitage	T H Gibson	E S Pitman
A Awford	J R Gladwin	C Powell
O Bagnall	J Graham	E W Powell-Chandler
F C Baker	E H Groves	D A Pritchard
F Ballinger*	P R Harris	D Prout
C Barber	G Hartland	W J Ralph

F J Beachus
F Blewitt
P J Bisco
R J Bisco
P W Bodenham
B J Brawn
J Buckland
R B Burroughs
M A Carter
V D Chamkin
A V Chandler
S K Clayton
B Clifford
H Clifford
R J Clifford
L C Clifford
D R G Clissold
F C Clissold
R G Cole
J W Cooper
T J R Coleman
T J Coleman
G A Crowther
D Davis
L G Davis
O J Day
T F Day
W F Day
G Draper
D Driscoll
M Duffield
B C Elgood
E W Eversham
P J Flaron
G T Fenech
B Freeman
R Gardner

E Hayward
R J Hayden
D L Hudson
J F L Johnstone
J P Johnson
B F Jones
C E Jones
D O Jones
E L Jones
M J Jones
R V Jones
J Lane
C C Large
E Leiper
F W Locke
C J Lodge
L S Loveridge
S Loveridge
H T Manns
H Matthews*
S D Matthews
D V Meek
H I Markey
J Mitchel
L D Millar
J Mills
P P Monaghan
H W Morgan
R Morris
H S Napier
P E Neal
G L Necker
M Newcombe
R T Nunley
F Parry
D G Phillips
W Phillips

L H M Reece
A K N Rickards
E Roberts
P J N Russell
F C Sargent
D Saunders
P Shaw
A Simpson
C Simpson
L Simpson
L M Smith
A T Steele
M W Stephens
R Stranger
R C Taylor
J G Thurston
A R Tilling
T A Timney
K M Tomlinson
R H Wadley
T D Weaver
E A Williams
D A Williams
L S Williams
H J Wirdman
D A Wood
J W Yeoman

    Among the saddest is the demise of Cadet D Hudson, the sixteen year old son of William and Jessica Hudson and former pupil of Newent Grammar

229

School. He died aboard the SS "Harpagon", out of London, in April 1942. The earliest recorded deaths are those of Corp R Burroughs (4th Royal Tank Reg, RAC) at Pont-Remy in June 1940; Sgt O Day (2nd Glosters) at Dunkirk in May 1940; Pte T Gibson (2nd Glosters) at Calais in May 1940; Gdsm J Graham (2nd Grenadiers) at Esquelmes in May 1940 and Pte L Williams (Glosters) at Cassel in May 1940. All must have been killed in the battle for France that resulted in the evacuation from Dunkirk in May 1940 of the residue of the BEF and other Allied troops and their return to the UK.

Newent's Second World War dead number 25 on the Church Memorial, less than half the number listed for the First World War. Only four members of the Glosters are included but six Newent men served with the RAF. Pte F Ballinger of the 5th Dorsets; LAC H Matthews, RAFVR and Pte P Russell of the Ox and Bucks Airborne Light Infantry were killed in the early stages of the liberation of Europe in the summer of 1944.

Gunner J Buckland, a 19 year old in an Airlanding Anti-Tank Battery of the Royal Artillery was killed in March 1945 during Montgomery's advance into Germany, the last Newent demise on record.

Deceased past pupils of the former Newent Grammar School are commemorated in the present school hall. No less than thirteen names are listed of whom eight are neither included on the town war memorial nor listed on the War Graves Commission web site. Robert Houldey, Ralph Jennings, Colin Morley, Frank Mustoe, Alec Park, Frank Robinson and John Smith (all serving with the RAF), and Edwin Butler (RASC), are the war memorial/web site omissions.

Former Pupils of Newent Grammar School killed in World War II

Robert Burroughs	Royal Tank Corps
Edwin Butler	Royal Army Service Corps
Robert Houlday	Royal Air Force
Derek Hudson	Merchant Navy
Ralph Jennings	Royal Air Force
Cyril Lodge	Hong Kong Volunteer Defence Force
Colin Morley	Royal Air Force
Royden Morris	Royal Army Service Corps
Frank Mustoe	Royal Air Force
Laurence Reece	Royal Air Force
Alec Park	Royal Air Force
Frank Robinson	Royal Air Force
John Smith	Royal Air Force

Once again Newent men gave their lives in most theatres of war, from Hong Kong to the D-Day landings and on the advance into Germany. They served on land, in the air and at sea. Three of them were buried in Newent Cemetery; AC Frederick James Beachus, RAFVR, Pte William Phillips, Pioneer Corps and Flight Sergeant Leonard Mervyn Smith, WOP/Air Gunner, RAF.

Newent men killed in World War II

Name	age	Unit	died	Commemoration
Chief Eng Room Art G Baker	31	HM Sub Regulus	Dec 1940	Chatham
Pte F Ballinger	30	5th Bn Dorsets	Jul 1944	Banneville
Chief Off. C Barber	46	MV Swedru	Apr 1941	Tower Hill
A/C2 F Beachus	34	RAFVR	Nov 1941	Newent
Gunner J Buckland	19	3rd Airlanding Anti-Tank Bty, RA	Mar 1945	Reichswald
Corp R Burroughs	21	4th Royal Tank Reg	Jun 1940	Pont-Remy
Sgt O Day	28	2nd Bn Glosters	May 1940	Dunkirk
Sgt T Day	37	1st Bn Glosters	Aug 1942	Rangoon
LAC W F Day	22	RAFVR	Nov 1944	Glos Old Cemetery
Pte T Gibson	19	2nd Bn Glosters	May 1940	Calais
Gdsman J Graham	22	2nd Bn Grenadier Gds	May 1940	Esquelmes
Sgt G Hartland	23	115 Sqdn RAF	Dec 1940	Runnymede
Cadet D Hudson	16	SS Harpagon	Apr 1942	Tower Hill
Staff Sgt D Jones	32	18th Div. Trans. Co. RASC	Nov 1943	Thanbyuzayat
Gdsman J Lane	22	2nd Bn Coldstream Guards	Dec 1942	Medjez-el-Bab
F W Locke		(unable to trace details)		
Pte C Lodge	25	Hong Kong Volunteer Defence Corps	Dec 1941	Sai Wan
LAC H Matthews	31	2788 Sqdn RAFVR	Aug 1944	Mazargues
R Morris		(unable to trace details)		
Pte W Phillips	28	Pioneer Corps	Nov 1942	Newent
Sgt L Reece	?	235 Sqdn RAFVR	Jul 1940	Runnymede
Pte P Russell	30	2nd (Airborne) Bn Ox & Bucks Lt Inf	Jul 1944	Ranville
Ft Sgt L Smith	30	207 Sqdn RAF	May 1942	Newent
D A Williams		(unable to trace details)		
Pte L Williams	22	Glosters	May 1940	Cassel

Korea

The invasion of South Korea by the Communist North became the cause of the next involvement of the Glosters in fighting. As part of the United Nations' Force the 1st Btn., The Gloucestershire Regiment played a major part in the subsequent fighting. In particular the Battalion was almost annihilated as a result of its stand on the Imjin River in April 1951. Out of some 650 members of all ranks, 622 were either killed or captured. Among those captured was Lt. Col. J P Carne DSO, who was later awarded the Victoria Cross. Quartermaster Sergeant Major Phillips, the father-in-law of the Rev. Patricia Phillips, formerly of St Mary' Church and currently rector of Redmarley D'Abitot, was among the members of the Glosters who served in Korea. In 1970 Major Phillips MBE, MSM finally retired from military service having risen from Drummer Boy to Major and served in two world wars.

Personal memories of World War II

Newent itself saw little of the fighting during the Second World War with only a few bombs falling in the area. However many residents took part in the conflict and survived. The Town also became the site of a prisoner of war camp. The following stories are from some of the Newent people who took part in the hostilities, some who were very young but remember what life was like, and also the experiences of both sides POW camps. Some sections have been written by the people themselves and others as a result of interviews.

<u>Harold (Pym) Markey</u> 17118, Young Soldiers Btn., Glosters and later The 3rd Parachute Btn.

"One of the lasting things about being a soldier is that friendships with comrades in arms are the deepest and most enduring"
General Frederick Franks Jnr

Harold Markey volunteered to join the Army at the age of 17 but was rejected as being under age. A quick walk around the block aged him by a year and he was accepted into the Young Soldiers Battalion (70th Btn) of the Glosters.

Later he volunteered to join the Paras, the incentive being the extra two shillings a day pay. He was sent for training at Hardwick Hall, Chesterfield and Manchester's Ringway Airport and on passing was posted to the 3rd Parachute Battalion in Tunisia, North Africa in 1943. He was then part of the airborne landing into Sicily and on returning to North Africa the Paras formed part of the seaborne troops landing in Italy at Taranto. The Battalion moved forward to Bari at which point the 8th Army took over and the Paras returned to Algiers where later they embarked for England arriving in time for Christmas 1943 and subsequent training for the invasion of Europe.

After fourteen aborted missions the Paras took off from Folkingham, Lincolnshire for Arnhem on 17th September 1944. Eventually out of ammunition and related resources surrender was inevitable and he spent the next six months or so in a German prisoner of war camp.

During an allied night air raid on the town adjacent to the camp he escaped with a fellow prisoner of war from the Airborne Recce Corps. They "hot wired" a stationary Opel and drove it until they ran out of fuel. Walking at night and hiding by day they approached the Allied lines. One day they hid in a barn but had to stay overnight because of the increased German activity in the area. They were noticed in the barn by a Polish slave labour girl who gave them bread and her scarf knitted from string (which he still has to-day). Eventually they met a US Jeep Patrol and were taken to their Unit for their identification to be verified. They were given a shower, clean clothing and their first good meal in some six months. From here they were flown to Brussels, the British Army's Headquarters, and later to the UK.

Harold was finally demobbed in 1946.

Over the years Harold and his wife have regularly attended Arnhem reunions and, in particular, at Oosterbrook, where his group made their last stand prior to capture.

Andy Russo (2) One of Mussolini's infantrymen.

Andrea Russo, one of five sons of smallholders Domenic and Foresta Russo, was born in April 1920 at Maddoloni, some 10 miles south west of Caserta in Southern Italy. His mother had inherited wealth that was lost as a consequence of the Second World War. All five sons served in the Italian Forces, one being lost on the Russian Front.

Andy served in Albania and North Africa and was captured by "men in skirts" in 1942. He was shipped to Liverpool where he was badly received by the Liverpudlians, due to recent bombing raids on the City. He was transferred to Gloucestershire to work on the land in Coleford, Taynton, and Boulsdon. While working at Boulsdon he met his future wife, Helena Ruby Mary Ballinger of Clifford's Mesne.

When he was repatriated to Maddaloni in 1947 he was issued with an Italian passport, obtained a visa to travel through France and a permit to enter England until 12th January 1948. The UK entry permit cost him 19s-3d .

Fig.78 Andy Russo, Italian Infantryman
(courtesy of Mrs Helena Russo, Newent)

On arrival at Dover on 6th January 1948 he managed to obtain a 12 month work permit, conditional on his registration with the Police on his arrival at his destination. He registered with PC R F Webb (No 116) who endorsed his passport at Newent Police Station on 7th January 1948. In March 1949 he was granted an indefinite extension to continue to work and stay in the UK. In the meantime he had married Helena at Gloucester's St Peter's Church. In due course two daughters arrived, Yolanda and Marilyn.

He worked at Boulsdon until the farm was sold when he joined the Wildsmith organization. Winston Wildsmith graciously provided accommodation for the Russo family in the, now demolished, gatehouse to Newent Court. Andy later purchased land from the Freeman family, which evolved into America Gardens. The family took up occupation in 1963 and he later purchased his widow's current home in Brookside . Helena moved from America Gardens after his demise in 1994.

Andy was granted British Citizenship in 1958. He continued working for Wildsmith until he became involved in the restoration of the Newent Community Centre, work he continued until his retirement in April 1984. Paul Marland, the West Gloucestershire M.P. wrote him a most gracious letter of thanks for his work both in the Town and at the Centre.

Along with fellow former POWs, Guiseppi Perillo (see later) and Antonio Marcoveccio, Andy was one of the team that built Newent's Roman Catholic Church, Our Lady of Lourdes, in the late 1950s (See chapter 15).

Anne Solesbury (nee Hinds) (3)

Having been born and bred on a farm I was, to a great extent, cushioned from the realities of war. I was aware of strange new words coming into daily use; shrapnel, anti-aircraft batteries, doodlebugs, Lord Haw-Haw, coupons and dockets. I knew about search lights because I had watched them at night, the soldiers manning them were camped in a field at Hayes Farm. There were conversations that I did not understand about dogfights at night (how could this be when the dogs were fast asleep on the hay in the barn?) and where was the Siegfried Line and why were the soldiers going to hang their washing on it?

World War II was well into its second year when I started at Pauntley C of E School, Pool Hill. I had seen from the outside that the windows were criss-crossed with tape, in case of bomb blast. When war was declared on 3rd September 1939 there were 52 children on the roll. Numbers increased with the coming of the Land Settlement Association in 1938 and gradually evacuees moved into the area.

The Head Mistress was Mrs Edith Somerville: Infants' Teacher was Miss Emily Freeman, later replaced by Miss Kate Rogers who became Mrs Kate Taylor. Being a Church School the Vicar, the Revd. W S Irving, visited once a week, cycling from the vicarage at Oxenhall on his tricycle.

Entrance to the School was through the Boys' Porch (just a few coat hooks here) into the Big Room with its huge tortoise stove. An oilcloth map of the world (lots of pink!) hung on the wall, a great globe stood on a cupboard, there was a piano and, of course, desks. In a corner was a shelf with an enamel bucket and a mug: my father brought a churn of drinking water to the School every day. When you needed a drink, the mug was dipped into the bucket of water. In the winter hands were washed here too, a chipped enamel bowl, carbolic soap and rainwater from the butt outside, the roller towel hung on the door going into the Girls' Porch. A great glass and wooden sliding screen divided the Big Room from the Little Room and this had an open fireplace with a basket grate, small tables and chairs and the usual cupboards. The Girls' Porch ran along the back of this room.

"The Offices" (as they were called in the School Log Book) were about 15-20 yards away. It was a brick shed, divided into three; The Teachers, The Big Ones and The Little Ones, the only difference being the height of the wooden seat, the size of the bucket and the size of the hole! The boys used a brick trough which ran along the side of the shed, open to the elements. I have described this setting to help the reader imagine what it was like in 1941 when there were 70 children! 23 evacuees from Birmingham had been billeted in the area and an Assistant Teacher, Mr Grunnill, had come with them to help with teaching duties.

When I began school in 1941 the war effort was well organized. All paper and cardboard was saved for salvage in the School salvage shed and organized by the newly formed Youth Squad. All sorts of metals were collected for scrap. National Savings Stamps were an important part of the war effort. A National Savings Committee had been formed and these people organized concerts, whist and beetle drives, fetes, anything to raise funds. The School was the venue, as we had no village hall then and the Post Office and Shop was just across the road. In June 1941, £260 was raised during War Weapons Week, a lot of money in those days. The School entered a tableau in Newent Carnival that summer.

The children were expected to raise money by various means. They picked rose hips, 28 lbs were sent to Gloucester and raised four shillings. Over 1 cwt of chestnuts were sent away to raise 9s-8d. Most weeks we sent £1 to the Soldiers' Cigarettes Fund. Dig for Victory was supported from the school garden, the boys worked this and sold produce. In the Big Room both boys and girls knitted for servicemen: boys did scarves but the older girls managed socks, balaclavas and mittens.

The ARP Warden, Mr J Millard, came regularly to check gas masks, the little children had "Mickey Mouse" ones.

August 1944 was a memorable month. Queen Mary visited the Land Settlement Association at The Scarr and took tea with the Howard family at No 17. She also visited Pauntley Church, the children lined the way and waved flags.

Slowly, some of the refugees and evacuees were returning home. Back on the farm, prisoners of war (German and Italian) were working in gangs on the land. The Italians made baskets for us in exchange for cigarettes or bay rum (for their hair). If you could save cellophane, they would make a pretty belt, using cigarette packets, beautifully woven, it just needed a buckle. The Germans would make rings, if you gave them coins or old metal to melt down, a bit of coloured glass made a pretty stone.

My brothers were still busy with blanco, brasso and the pull-throughs, the Home Guard did a grand job, amongst other things guarding Brand Green Reservoir.

When VE-Day came on May 8th 1945 the Government announced a two day holiday. The vicar held a Service of Thanksgiving and the School Bell could be rung again, and the Church Bell too. On August 15th it was VJ-Day, another two day holiday. These followed "Thanksgiving Week" when £176 was raised and collected and invested in National Savings.

How very fortunate I am to have experienced a country childhood in a village school during World War II and how proud I am of our War Effort, however small it may seem, by today's standard.

Edmund Potts (4) Worcestershire Regiment

"No man, however he may talk, has the remotest idea of what an ordinary infantry soldier endures"   Sergeant H Green

After Oxford and Sandhurst I was commissioned into the Worcestershire Regiment in 1941 and was sent to the 8th Battalion in Northern Ireland. From there I went to the 8th Battalion in Madras, where we joined the newly formed 19th Indian Division. After lengthy training in India, we took over from the British 2nd Division at Imphal on the northern Burma border.

We were very lightly equipped. Each man had a Lee-Enfield rifle or a Bren Gun, a knapsack and a blanket. The blankets were carried in bundles of ten on mules. Each company of about 100 men had a jeep to carry cooking equipment. This was the only mechanized transport. Food and necessary equipment (including petrol) was dropped to us from the air. We advanced on foot for some 450 miles in jungle country, across the River Chindwin as far as Irrawaddy, where the Japanese had planned to make a stand. In the process, we encountered delaying parties of Japanese and suffered casualties, from both rifle and artillery fire and scrub typhus. Casualties were rescued by flying Jeeps and Dakotas and flown back to India.

The Japanese put up very determined resistance along the Irrawaddy and we had quite heavy casualties, especially among the junior officers and mules. I was shot in the stomach and my batman was hit in the throat. We were both taken to a temporary casualty clearing station in a tank and then flown back in a Dakota to hospital in India. My batman was invalided back to England, but I returned to the Battalion which was then advancing up the Chin Hills towards Thailand. We managed to capture the Jap Headquarters at the hill station of Kalan in August 1945, just before the Japanese capitulated.

After my Army experiences, I decided to make a career in teaching which took me to Strathallan, Perth, in Scotland and then to Wrekin College in Shropshire, where my two daughters were born. I finally retired to Springfield Grange, Cliffords Mesne, in 1982, to the house where my mother was born.

Dennis Little BEM (5) Corps of Royal Engineers.
   Prior to the start of the Second World War Dennis Little worked on a farm, for very poor wages, outside Bristol. He signed up with a Bristol based Territorial unit of the Corps of Royal Engineers, by which means he obtained a "paid" holiday each year. On the outbreak of war his unit was posted to Lechlade, thence to France and the French-Belgian border. Consequent upon the May Blitzkrieg, along with most of the UK Forces, his unit was forced back to the Dunkirk beaches where chaos reigned supreme. The exception was the personnel associated with a ranking naval officer who made significant attempts to control the troops entering the beaches prior to embarkation on the "little ships" returning the remains of the retreating British Army to England.

Included in the Royal Engineers' kit were a number of flat bottomed rowing boats, each capable of holding eight passengers. These were used on no fewer than four occasions to ferry men from the beach to a paddle steamer located some distance offshore before the rowers themselves finally climbed aboard.

After arrival at Harwich they remustered at Hereford and set up a canvas camp at Monmouth. A spare rifle was sold to the local Home Guard for £12, doubtless beer money, and the squad kept fit by walking the local hills and mountains. Then commenced the long drag working up to D-Day. Much time was spent wiring and mining Cornish beaches, and this was followed by a period at Bridgwater destroying unsafe explosives. This activity continued elsewhere in the UK and their skills became honed.

When D-Day arrived the unit drove off their landing craft and over the beaches towards the "action" line to serve as a mine clearing/disposal squad. At the "fag" end of the war they took part in the crossing of the Rhine as back-up to the Paras and Glider-borne troops that made the initial assault. Because of his time on a farm Corporal Little enjoyed an ability to perceive mined areas by observation of soil surface differences. The end of the fighting saw the unit stationed at the German Naval base at Kiel, the home of the German Pocket Battleship fleet. One had capsized as a result of RAF bombing while the other was still moored to the quayside. Much time was spent demolishing bunkers and pill boxes, and destroying explosives that were surplus to demolition needs.

Prior to de-mob Dennis Little was awarded the British Empire Medal for his work with explosives in France, Belgium and Germany. He resumed his pre-war activity on a Land Settlement Association holding on Redmarley Road, and has now retired to Ross Willis Court in Gloucester Road, Newent.

Harold Wirdnam (6) Wiltshire Regt and Corps of Military Police.

In late 1934 Harold Wirdnam was employed by a Swindon horticulturist and approaching his 17th birthday. He was unfortunate enough to have failed to close a greenhouse door so his employer, as was the wont at that time, threw a potted plant at him. Harold proceeded to enlist in the Wiltshire Regiment at Le Marchant Barracks, Devizes on 12th December 1934, only to be granted immediate Christmas leave. A six month basic training course was followed by advanced training at Aldershot's Talavera Barracks, having been assigned to the Wilts 2nd Battalion.

After two weeks embarkation leave the battalion sailed from Southampton on HMT Nevasa for India in December 1935 and three weeks later they were based at Bangalore, Mysore. The outbreak of World War II resulted in a posting to Madras where most of the time was spent boarding and searching shipping that entered the harbour. Subsequent to the Japanese invasion of Burma they moved, first to Bangalore and later to Lucknow, to undergo rigorous training for jungle warfare.

The Wilts were moved to Dinapore, Bengal, to assist in coping with an outbreak of famine and it was here that Harold applied for a posting to the Corps of Military Police (India). He successfully passed out from the Military Police Training Establishment, Faizabad, and was posted to the 73rd Line of

Communication Provost Unit, at Chittagong, a town now included in Bangladesh, adjacent to the Burmese border. The unit was responsible for local security and military traffic control.

In late 1944 some "squaddies", because of their length of overseas' service, were eligible for repatriation to the UK under the so-called "Python" scheme. Lance Corporal Wirdnam was posted back to his parent unit, the Wiltshires, and began a lengthy journey back to the UK. En route he was informed of the death of his brother, Geoffrey, who had been killed in action with 42nd Royal Marine Commando. Eventually he arrived at Swindon, via Bristol, after an absence of nearly eleven years.

On expiry of his leave he reported to 3rd Combined Infantry Depot, Colchester and requested a transfer to the "Red Caps", which was eventually granted. Re-training at the CMP School, Mitchet, was followed by a transfer to the CMP, Portsmouth Division. The balance of his time with the Military was spent with the Red Caps in London, based at Chelsea Barracks and Great Scotland Yard. It was while on street patrol in London that he met his future wife Maud (see later).

Maud Wirdnam (7)

Observing Maud Wirdnam today who could guess that, some 60 years ago, she was a corporal in charge of barrage balloon sites at Sheffield, Birmingham, Dagenham and London's Dock Land. She, together with 16 young women and a mass of heavy equipment, helped to defend Britain's cities from Luftwaffe attack. Many of the sites were both isolated and devoid of even menial comforts.

She was born Maud Dennis, the daughter of a sergeant in the 5th Dragoon Guards, who died when she was 11 years old, and lived in Clerkenwell, EC1. In the summer of 1941 she volunteered for service as a WAAF, hopefully as an instrument fitter. On arrival at RAF Innsworth she was told that all vacancies had been filled and she was advised to apply for a posting to Balloon Operations.

Initial training took place at Newcastle upon Tyne and this was followed by further training at Cardington. Then came her first operational posting, to Sheffield with a crew of 16, who worked two hours on, four hours off. She was responsible for the flying and maintenance of a barrage balloon and its associated equipment, located in a field in the middle of no-where. One of life's luxuries was to be invited into a "civvie" home to indulge in a hot bath in domestic surroundings.

A compassionate posting was granted to Dagenham; her mother needed some degree of comfort due to the continuing Luftwaffe raids on London. For a while she was engaged in the defence of the Ford Plant. While at Dagenham her balloon was hit by an ack-ack shell splinter and burst into flames. She was later posted to London's Albert Docks to provide protection for Allied troops embarking for the Normandy campaign.

Because of the progress of the war in Europe she was posted to RAF Stanmore, Fighter Command HQ, and promoted to Sergeant. She was responsible for a group of wireless and phone operators who were located in the underground tunnel. After the Stanmore posting she and a fellow Sergeant were enjoying a day out in London and approached two Military Policemen for advice regarding local pubs. The Red Caps subsequently joined them and Sergeant Maud Dennis became Mrs Harold Wirdnam on 3rd November 1945. She was demobbed a month later.

Joe Perillo (8) An Italian infantryman

Fig.79 Joe Perillo, Italian Dispatch Rider
(courtesy of Joe Perillo, Newent)

The only son of Vincento and Annuziata Perillo, Giuseppi (today Joe) was born in August 1915 in Somma Vesuviana, adjacent to Napoli (Naples). The family also had four girls. Joe's father's first wife had died in childbirth and Vincento remarried, at the ripe old age of 50, to a widow some twenty years his junior. Joe left school at the age of eleven to help on the family smallholding that grew grapes, lemons, peaches, apricots etc.

At the age of 18 he sat, and failed, the exam for the Italian Customs and Excise Authority. When he was just 20 he was conscripted into the Italian Infantry, seeing service on the country's northern borders. After about five months service his father managed to obtain his release to work the family smallholding. By this time his father was in his early seventies.

In May 1940, after Italy's entry into the Second World War, he was recalled to the colours and posted to Tripoli. The war in North Africa waxed and waned and November 1941 saw him stationed near the Egyptian border as Infantry protection for a German 88mm anti-tank battery. Conditions were primitive, food was in short supply and the troops were both starving and lousy.

On 22nd May 1942 another British attack outflanked the strong point and Joe found a new role as POW of the British Army. After some months in an Egyptian cage he was shipped to Glasgow, via Durban, on the "Viceroy of India", and thence to Sheffield. In the autumn of 1942 he was camped in Ledbury and encouraged to work on the land. A posting to Madresfield Court, Lord Beauchamp's estate and living on the farm, was followed by work at Burley Gate and Newent. Prior to repatriation to Napoli in April 1946 he worked for a horticulturist in Ashby-de-la-Zouche.

He returned to England and worked in a local hospital until 1947 when he married a Newent girl, with whose family he had been billeted during his POW days. After his Neapolitan marriage he returned to Newent to take up a successful career running a shop in Culver Street, a task he relinquished only recently. Joe has no regrets about his change of lifestyle and was naturalized some thirty years ago. He is exceptionally proud of a letter he received in 1966 when his old friend, Angelo Rafaele Servolino, became Minister of Transport in the Italian Government. Servolino's daughter is currently Mayor of Naples.

Phyllis Shaw (née Jones) (9)

I was born in Broad Street, Newent in March 1917 and educated at Picklenash and Newent Grammar Schools. On leaving school I trained as a children's nurse in Bristol and then the Children's Hospital in Gloucester, now demolished. Following that I went on to train as a State Registered Nurse at the Royal Berkshire Hospital in Reading and in 1943 volunteered to join the Queen Alexandra Army Imperial Nursing Service.

After mobilization at Hatfield House, the 150th General Hospital embarked at Liverpool to join a convoy, not knowing where we were being sent except we were equipped with tropical uniform! We were five weeks at sea down the west coast of Africa, eventually reaching Cape Town and Durban. After a few weeks there we joined another convoy up the east coast of Africa to Mombassa. I was then attached to No 1 General Hospital and proceeded to Nairobi (Kenya) by rail. The 150th Hospital was destined for Burma to be with the East African Division and the 14th Army. Tragically the ship was torpedoed by a German destroyer near Ceylon (Sri Lanka) with 44 nursing sisters on board who were all lost along with 1,300 other troops and all the Hospital equipment.

I was very fortunate to have been nursing in Moshi (Tanzania) in the shadow of Mount Kilimanjaro and was not sent on that convoy to Burma. However I was soon at sea with other nursing sisters crossing to Colombo and Chittagong, forming small units to proceed from Imphal to Rangoon. The Japanese were just in retreat and many battles were being fought. It was difficult nursing under canvas during the monsoons with only hurricane lamps.

There were all races to be cared for including many Burmese civilians but my unit mainly nursed East African troops. I had learned a reasonable amount of Swahili by then. The African dressers were excellent. I was able to see General William Slim knighted on the Imphal plain by Lord Louis Mountbatten. Our Hospital section moved to Palel, Meiktila and Pagan and eventually reached Rangoon just as the last Japanese had fled.

We joined the Hospital there, which had been the University, and after a terrific cleaning campaign we were ready to receive the prisoners of war who had been held by the Japanese in Burma. It was very sad to see them but they were so happy to be with us. Many were very, very ill and did not live to reach home.

I was given a short leave to go to Darjeeling in the Himalayas. It was a wonderful and memorable short leave before I was to return to East Africa where I was demobilized in June 1946. Although my nursing career had ended then, I married and spent many happy years in Kenya before returning to England in 1963.

Sidney Beddis (10)

It was July 1942: the Germans seemed to be making progress everywhere and on the Eastern Front the hard pressed Russians were in urgent need of war supplies. To provide this sorely needed aid, a large convoy, to be known as P.Q.17, was assembled at Loch Eyre and for the perilous trip to Murmansk was given a strong, close escort of destroyers, frigates and cruisers. This escort was intended to protect the convoy against U-boats and aircraft based in Northern Norway. Another threat existed from the "Tirpitz" which was based in a Norwegian fjord and ideally placed to raid the convoy. As protection against such an eventuality a long range escort, consisting of battleships, heavy cruisers and the aircraft carrier HMS "Victorious", shadowed the convoy.

At this time I was a Paymaster Sub-Lt with only four months service as an officer. I was ordered to join the staff of VA2HF, Vice-Admiral Sir Bruce Frazer, who was flying his flag on the Aircraft Carrier. Prior to becoming an officer I had served as a coder on a minelayer and to say that I felt lost on joining a large front line unit of the Navy would be a gross understatement. However they soon made me feel more at ease.

We sailed from Scapa Flow that night and I soon learned the nature of our mission. For a couple of days nothing untoward happened, then came the first alarm signals. I was a cipher officer whose job it was to decode signals from the Admiralty and take them to Admiral Frazer. Bad weather had prevented continuous surveillance of the "Tirpitz" and after a couple more days the Admiralty reported that the berth previously occupied by the "Tirpitz" was empty. She could not be located and it was assumed that she had put to sea with the object of attacking the convoy which had already been spotted by German aircraft.

Spotter aircraft were sent off but nothing was seen. This state of affairs continued until we were near Spitzbergen when the convoy was ordered to scatter and for each ship to make her own way to Murmansk. This proved to be an utter disaster. Stripped of their protection the merchant ships merely provided target practice for U-boats and aircraft. Only a handful managed to reach port.

For the long range escort, there was nothing to be done once the convoy had scattered and we returned to Scapa Flow.

History has shown that the "Tirpitz" was never a threat to the PQ17 as she had not been fully operational and had only been moved to another fjord.

Apart from the drama of the events connected with this great disaster my other memory is of the surprise I had when I first went from below decks to take a message to Admiral Frazer and found that at midnight in these northern waters it was as light as at mid-day.

Anthony Montague (11)

Anthony Montague was educated at Newent Community School until the summer of 1976 when he enlisted in the Royal Navy. After various postings and training in Stores Accountancy he was posted to HMS "Amazon" in late 1981. The outbreak of the Falklands War saw "Amazon" based on Mombassa from where she was recalled to Devonport and re-equipped for the Falklands in nineteen days.

Because of the damage to HMS "Antelope" and HMS "Sheffield", "Amazon" was dispatched to participate in a fire fighting course at Portland and thence to Ascension Island. Argentina had capitulated by this time so "Amazon" waited at Ascension Island until Antelope arrived. They then sailed to Port Stanley to begin coastal patrols.

A second three month tour of duty in the Falklands was completed two years later. At the age of 26 the decision was made to leave the service in 1986 and not run on until reaching his 40th birthday. Today he works for the Xerox organization, not surprisingly in a stores capacity.

General Sir Peter de la Billiere, KCB, KBE, DSO, MC and bar

Although not a native of Newent Sir Peter de la Billiere now lives close to the town and his contribution to the defence of the Nation should not be omitted.

Sir Peter enjoyed a most distinguished military career. The former 17 year old squaddie in the King's Own Shropshire Light Infantry rose to be appointed Commander of British Forces in the Middle East during the Gulf War and, subsequently, Special Advisor on Middle East matters to the Minister of Defence. Not only did he receive awards for gallantry in the field but his services to the Nation resulted in the award of a KCB and a KBE. President Bush confirmed American appreciation of his contribution to the successful conclusion of the Gulf War by presenting him with the Legion of Merit, Degree of Chief Commander. The full story of his life can be read in his Autobiography "Looking for Trouble".

Eric Jones DFC (12)

I suspect it was the spartan three seat biplane which occasionally visited a field near the Traveller's Rest Public House which first aroused my interest in flying, an interest which intensified after an outing to Alan Cobham's Flying Circus at Ross-on-Wye. Many years later, having passed my School Certificate examination at Newent Grammar School, I became eligible for a school prize. I chose a book about the Royal Air Force with the School crest prominently displayed on the front cover. I still have it. So, as the war loomed ever closer it was to be the Royal Air Force for me, if possible in aircrew, if not in some other capacity.

But I am jumping ahead, lets go back to the beginning. My father was crippled by polio at the age of nine but this didn't prevent him from successfully

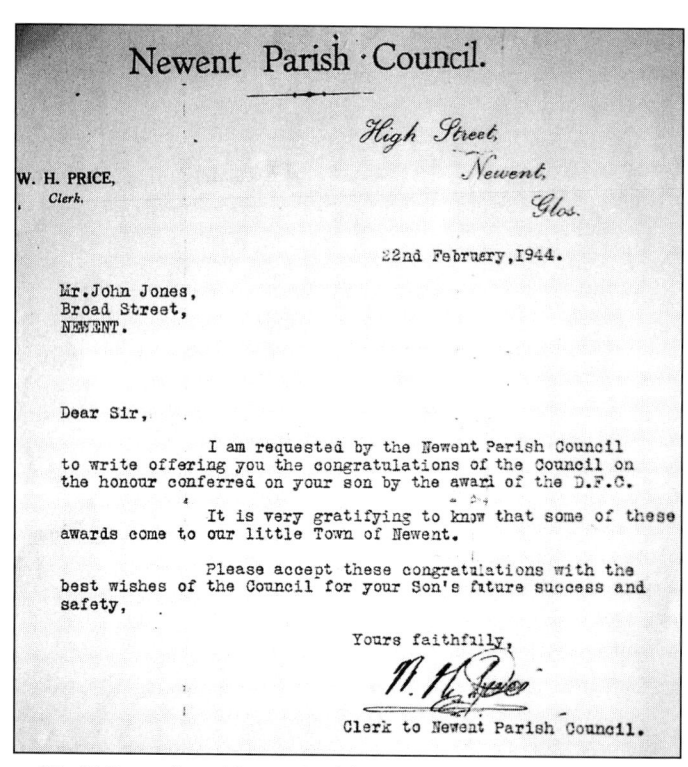

```
                    Newent   Parish · Council.

                                      High Street,
W. H. PRICE,                              Newent,
   Clerk.
                                             Glos.

                              22nd February, 1944.

     Mr. John Jones,
     Broad Street,
     NEWENT.


     Dear Sir,
                I am requested by the Newent Parish Council
     to write offering you the congratulations of the Council on
     the honour conferred on your son by the award of the D.F.C.
                It is very gratifying to know that some of these
     awards come to our little Town of Newent.
                Please accept these congratulations with the
     best wishes of the Council for your Son's future success and
     safety,

                              Yours faithfully,

                                  [signature]

                              Clerk to Newent Parish Council.
```

Fig.80 Letter from Newent Parish Council concerning the award of a DFC to F/Lt Eric Jones. (courtesy Eric Jones, Poole)

---

running a shoe retail and repair shop in Broad Street, Newent. I was born in a room over his workshop in 1922 with sisters already three and six years old. My mother, in addition to having three children, also, when the war came, looked after a continuous stream of evacuees. Some of my earliest recollections involved sitting on a box on the work-bench watching my father at work and listening to all the local gossip.

The Junior School at Picklenash was housed in the old stone buildings in Bradfords Lane. I remember little of those days before leaving for the more modern building which housed the "Senior" School. Success in the School Certificate exam saw me leaving school. I was just 16 years old when I attended Gloucester Technical College for a year's course to learn book-keeping and typewriting. War with Germany had broken out during this period and as I was slowly approaching that magic age of 18 it was difficult to settle to any form of learning.

Two short clerical jobs followed and during this period my part in the war effort was limited to volunteer service in the St John Ambulance Brigade whose headquarters were in the Oxenhall Road. We were never involved in enemy action.

So I reached the volunteering age of 18 and I was over the moon when, after two medicals I was accepted for training as a pilot in the Royal Air Force. The only thing I could drive was a bicycle. However, I had to wait until April 1941 before I was called up and ordered to report to the Air Crew Receiving Centre in London.

After training in Devon and Booker Elementary Flying Training School I was sent to Canada. This flying school was in Southern Saskatchewan and the new plane to master was the American T-16, we called it the Harvard. All went well here, flying in clear summer skies until one dark night I managed to turn my aircraft over on its back and they needed a crane to lift the wreckage off me. I thought this is it, I'm finished, but I wasn't and once again someone, somewhere was on my side.

All trainee pilots wanted to be fighter pilots and it wasn't until I returned to England and was introduced to the twin engined Oxford that I realized that bombers were to be my destiny. It was my next unit where I took a big step forward. To me, at this stage in my training, the Wellington was a huge aircraft and so presented a huge challenge. It was here that I collected most of my crew. The method of selection, equal numbers of pilots, navigators, wireless operators, bomb aimers and gunners were directed into a hanger, the door was shut and we were told to come out as complete crews.

With the Wellington mastered it was my good fortune to be posted to a Lancaster conversion school. Everyone knows what a Lancaster looks like and if they think it is superb, well, that's the way it handled, super. I arrived at 49 Squadron, Fiskerton in Lincolnshire two years and four months after my initial call-up and during my short training period on the squadron twelve aircraft were sent to raid the flying-bomb site at Peenemunde. Four aircraft failed to return, one third of the force. I then realized that I was at the cutting edge of the war and flying would no longer be quite the same again.

Every "sprog" pilot was expected to fly one operation with an experienced pilot. Mine was to Berlin, the "Big City", on 23rd August 1943. Over Berlin there wasn't a cloud in the sky. It was a clear night and the scene was a frightening example of what lay ahead of us.

Fig. 81 F/Lt E J Jones DFC (left) with his crew and ground crew in front of their Lancaster during World War II (courtesy Eric Jones, Poole)

So our tour of operations, twenty-nine in number (I never understood why we were not asked to do the full thirty) all of them against major German cities, got under way. Our very first trip as a full crew saw us twisting, diving and turning to get out of the clutches of a searchlight cone over Nuremburg. Our thoughts were, how can we survive thirty operations like this.

Losses on the squadron mounted, both Hodgkinson and Brunt, pilots I had trained with, went missing. Richardson, returning from his first operation, crashed on his approach to landing with only the rear gunner surviving. At this period of the air war only one out of every two aircrew would survive. Walls of flak (anti-aircraft fire), searchlight cones and fighter attacks all had to be survived if crews were to return safely. Through all of this morale was high and our chief "Bomber" Harris (known affectionately to all aircrew as "Butch") was held in great esteem.

Two of my crew, the rear gunner and wireless operator, both missed some of our operations and had to complete them with another crew. They were both shot down. Just a common cold had cost them their lives. After five of my twelve raids on Berlin I was awarded the Distinguished Flying Cross which I wear with pride on behalf of all the members of my crew whose ability and loyalty was unsurpassed. Miraculously I completed my tour of operations with four members of my crew. Madam Luck was, indeed, riding with us over the skies of Germany all those years ago.

Valerie Diana Hooke (nee Oerton) (13)

I joined the Wrens in Spring 1942 at the age of 17, having just left boarding school. My initial training was at New College in London which had been taken over as a WRNS training "ship". There we had to learn the ways and jargon of the Navy, cabins, bunks, and galleys etc. and were instructed by Officers and a very frightening Chief Petty Officer from the 1914-18 war! None of us knew where we would be sent and at the end of three weeks I, and some 40 other raw recruits, were told that we were to be posted to Felixstowe on the East Coast to take over a hazardous job from the Royal Marines.

"Operation Outwards" purpose was to harass the enemy with balloons filled with hydrogen gas. Attached to them were either incendiary devices to cause fires or trailing wire to short-circuit electrical power cables. The results were impressive, causing damage over the whole of Germany. The handling and launching of these balloons was very dangerous and quite a few of my friends were seriously burned when the hydrogen exploded. I still jump out of my skin if a balloon bursts!

I was promoted to Leading Wren and then Petty Officer during this time and the order came through that we had to form a band to release bandsmen for active service. So this became my responsibility. We were taught to play and march by the bandsmen of the Liverpool Irish and very good we were.

When D-Day came our job was over, so we were returned to New College to re-categorize, and, being a Petty Officer, I was quartered with all the old ones who had frightened us so much in 1942! I had a confrontation with a rather jumped-up Officer, who was badly treating my girls, which resulted in being stripped of my rank and transferred to a driving course in Leeds.

After several postings I arrived in Newcastle and was interviewed by the Admiral. This Transport Depot was like no other. The Admiral's Wren drivers were his pride and joy; we were to wear white lanyards at all times. His girls were literally hand-picked and many of them were daughters of his personal friends. It was a very happy "ship" in every way. In those days the Tyne was full of shipyards, with every sort of craft being either built or repaired, a busy place, and driving was a difficult task as we had no signposts or proper lights.

When the war in Europe ended I was driving the Admiral Engineer and was with him when he took the surrender of a very large oil tanker called the "Nordwark", which, on closer inspection was a ship bristling with guns. I drove my Admiral and the German Captain back to Newcastle and was so proud of the Admiral who treated the German with great courtesy and good manners.

Before I got my discharge I had a spell of duty in Hull, and finally at the First Air Arm Base at St Mirren in Cornwall. I have to say that it was a great privilege to work with so many marvellous girls. We were all proud to be Wrens and proud to be English.

Royston Edward Cadle (14)

Royston Cadle presently lives in Brookside, Newent with his second wife Olga (Micklethwaite). His first wife Doris (nee Preece) whom he married in 1940, died in 1991. He is the eldest child of Joseph and May (nee Fisher) Cadle and spent most of his early life in Huntley. His father was in business as a Building and Decorating Contractor trading as J Cadle and Son.

In 1899 the US branch of the family established a direct lineage to Richard Cadle of Boswell, who was born c1619. It is probable but not proven that the family originated from William Cadle who was one of the grantees of Forest of Dean rights in 1220. Royston is also related to Thomas Cadle, the Newent Solicitor, who had Edmund Edmonds as a pupil in his Newent practice as long ago as 1840. Edmonds is well known for his acquittal for his wife's murder. (see chapter 5).

On leaving school at the age of 14 he was apprenticed to his father and spent most days on the job site, cycling home for a meal and then riding to Brunswick Road Technical College to continue his education. On the outbreak of the Second World War his wife, Doris, worked in the Eastgate Street Accounts Dept. of the Gas Company. He was called-up in the following year and joined the Royal Engineers at Aldershot. He became a driver and much of his time was spent tented in Scotland.

Fig.82 Royston Cadle, 1945 (courtesy Royston Cadle, Newent)

On D-Day he landed on Arromanche Beach at 16.00 hrs through a sea covered in dead bodies. His squad's task was setting up camps for the subsequent waves of "squaddies", and unloading ammunition, tanks and other supplies. They slept in ditches soaked in sea water. He clearly recalls the battle for Caen, in particular the bombing and shelling. He remembers one returning bomber falling into the sea after being hit by German flak. He cannot recall firing a shot in anger.

As the Allies advanced into Europe his squad went to Brussels and finally to Lubeck from where he was demobbed in 1946. To get back to the UK he spent two days on a train with wooden seats, no food and no water. On arrival in London he spent the night in a Church Army Hostel, then home to Huntley and back to work.

Women at War, by Kath Rees (15)

During World War II there was a hidden workforce in this country - Women. The reaction of many women, while coping with their changed circumstances, is summed-up by the words "we just got on with it". This was the title of a book by Bette Anderson, about the role of women in World War II and the following are some of the experiences of women from around Newent.

Mrs Alma Bagnall (16)

In 1939, when war broke out I had just left school and was working in an office. As it was a transport office I could have continued to work there but my older sister, Barbara, had to join up. We wanted to stay together and I suggested the Land Army but as Barbara was afraid of cows we opted for the NAAFI. We were sent to Longmore, in Hampshire. Barbara had been away from home before but I hadn't and I felt very homesick at first.

We started work at 7-30 am by cleaning the floor and the tables and getting out all the cakes, sweets, and cigarettes ready to sell to the servicemen. I was not used to cleaning but we all mucked in together. We worked all morning and then from 6 pm to 9 pm in the evening. Once we were open we worked non-stop. I didn't mind the hard work because as we lived in married quarters we had our meals cooked for us. We had to wear a uniform at work but we could please ourselves when we were going out. I remember once when we went on leave we reached St Pancras and the train was just pulling out. The Guard stopped the train because we had our uniform on, so I thought I would not go out without it again !

I certainly gained confidence from what I did in the War, it helped me no end. I was a different person completely. I was able to stand up for myself, which I had to do when I returned home and went to register for employment. The young girl in the office told me that cleaning the hospital was the only job available for women. I was very annoyed and said "Look here, you go and do the cleaning, I've been away from home and done my bit. Don't you dare offer me jobs like that !" After that they gave me a job in an office, typing and doing the invoices as I did before the war.

When my husband-to-be returned from the war we got married and we resumed the management of his grocery business. My experience in the NAAFI helped because ration coupons made it all very complicated.

Mrs Geraldine Beaman (17)

Mrs Beaman spent the war years in the Women's Land Army and now lives at Lyne House Farm. Her memories of that time are as follows.

I left boarding school in July 1939 and spent the summer holiday enjoying myself before I embarked on a career. Many members of my family, including my brother, were lawyers and I had thoughts about a similar career. However when war broke out, in September 1939, my sister and I joined the Women's Land Army as we lived on a country estate in Warwickshire. We had 16 weeks training at Moulton before we were sent to the farms. We earned 14 shillings for a 52 hour week, in winter, and a 72 hour week in summer. Of course as we lived on the farms we received free board and lodging. I worked on both large and small farms.

We were expected to do everything from milking the cows, harnessing the horses to driving tractors. The only thing physically impossible was cutting the required amount of hay and silage.

When the war ended I could have remained at work on my last farm but I must admit I was extremely tired and had had enough, anyway most of the farming jobs were given to men from war service. Mike, who had seen active service in Africa, and I got married. We moved to Cambridge where Mike studied Agriculture and I got a job looking after a lecturer's children. I hated it as, being the youngest child in my family, I knew nothing about children. There was no chance of studying law at this time and eventually we bought Lyne House and I helped out on the farm whilst bringing up my five children. I knew more about farming than Mike after my experience in the Women's Land Army.

Mrs Diana Bendle (18)

During the war Mrs Bendle ran a Newsagents' business in Newent. Mrs Bendle says; Before the war I worked in a shop in London but had moved to Oxenhall with my parents. My fiance and I were going to run a Newsagents' business in Newent and I thought "Oh well it's a quiet little place I shall be able to sit behind the counter and knit !" Instead of that it was harder work than London was because my husband was called-up and I had to run the business alone.

At 6-00 am each morning I collected the papers from the station on my trade bicycle with the carrier at the front. Often I had to deliver the papers too as we were not allowed to employ young girls and boys in those days and obviously most of the young men had either been called up or were working. I did receive help from a nice old man who lived at Kilcot. He was a cobbler who was too old to go to war and combined the delivery of my papers with delivery of his shoes. In addition to selling newspapers and magazines I also ran the library which was set up by my in-laws in 1920. If I hadn't run the shop it would probably have closed just like some of the other shops in Newent.

After a long day at the shop I helped my mother cope with the evacuees that lived in our house. I don't think I did a lot. In those days there was no counselling, we just got on with it. I was quite a shy person but running the business and travelling around the country, visiting my husband, gave me confidence. I believe I was often the only woman on the trains as I frequently travelled through the night, arriving in Newent with the papers ! I felt quite safe. After the war I helped my husband run the business as much as I could but I had two children to bring up.

Mrs Frances Penney (19)

In 1943, after leaving Reading University, I registered for war work and was drafted to Bletchley Park, the code-breaking centre. The first thing I had to do was sign the Official Secrets Act and then I was taken to Hut 6, which was the centre of the code-breaking section dealing with Enigma. In the Registration Room of Hut 6 the coded messages, intercepted at various stations in England, were identified and marked with a coloured cross (e.g. red being the main Luftwaffe code) or by a name given by the code-breakers. My job was to register, or list, the details at the start of the message. These showed the operator how to set up his machine to decode the information. If the code had been broken the message was passed through a hatch to the decode room where operators, at electrically operated replicas of "Enigma" machines, typed in the 5-letter groups and the German message appeared

I had been warned at my interview that the work was repetitive but there were slight variations in the intensity and the amount, depending on whether one was listing a busy code such as Red or a little used one.

My grade was Temporary Assistant (Foreign Office) and my salary £4-1s-8d a week, exclusive of war bonus whatever that was! Quite literally I was part of the "hidden workforce" of women who helped the war effort. We never knew what the messages said or what happened to them after they left our hands. This fact, together with the idea that there were parts of Bletchley Park that I had never seen, surprised people with whom I toured Station X in September 2000.

Mrs May Goulding (20)

Mrs Goulding, who is in her 90s, and still lives at Holder's tells us; When war broke out I was a newly married farmer's wife in Oxenhall. Three of my four children were born during the war but as well as being a busy wife and mother I had to share my home with evacuees. At one time we had children from Birmingham and their parents visited them on a Sunday. They were not naughty children. Farmers were asked to take on prisoners of war and as a farmers wife I had to cook them a meal at lunchtimes. For dinner I gave the Italians some cooked vegetables and things. I gave them a dish of carrots but they didn't touch those. They didn't know what carrots were.

Before the war I was one of the few women in the area to drive a car. It was very useful because my parents, who lived at Gorsley, were often ill and needed my help. Petrol was rationed and so I had to walk there and back, pushing my babies in the pram. Country people were probably better off for food in wartime because we had our own vegetables, eggs and milk. I know sausages were rationed but we managed to get some once. I was pleased about that as I kept fancying them when I was pregnant !

We still managed to go out to chapel, often on foot. Once when we used the car, at night, the police stopped us. They asked us where we were going and what we were carrying. They were surprised when they saw the children sitting on the back seat with all my parent's washing ! After the war I had another child and continued to help on the farm when I could. We were expected to grow more crops but it was nice to have my home back for just the family, although we made many friends with the evacuees.

Mrs Doris Ralph (21)

Mrs Doris Ralph was 15 when war broke out.

At that time I was working as a domestic servant for a doctor in Spa Road, Gloucester. I worked at Clifford Manor and then got a job at Staverton looking after the children of an RAF Officer. He was moved to Norwich and as I was not allowed to go with them I got a job at Hawksley's the aircraft factory in Brockworth when I was 17.

I lived at Malswick and caught the bus each day to go to Brockworth. We worked from 7-00 am to 6-00 pm every weekday but it was good fun. My job was to count out nuts, screws etc for the aircraft fitters. I have very vivid memories of the day the Gloucester Aircraft Company factory next door was bombed. Luckily it was bombed before we got there but I spoke to the man on the gate when we arrived. He was so upset because it was his job to identify the victims. Men were in charge of us and I remember I took a rabbit into the factory for one particular person, as meat was hard to get. Living in the country we were able to catch rabbits to help with the meat rationing.

After the war we had to leave the factory as the priority was given to men returning from action. I managed to get a job in a sack factory in the Docks doing women's work, cleaning the sacks, there were rats and mice running all over the place. I enjoyed the factory work and it was something I would not have experienced if it had not been for the war and I would not have met my husband either. I would probably have continued to do domestic work locally.

I got married while I was at the factory and after the war I brought up my family and worked part-time.

Fig.83   The Hooke Family of Crookes, Newent

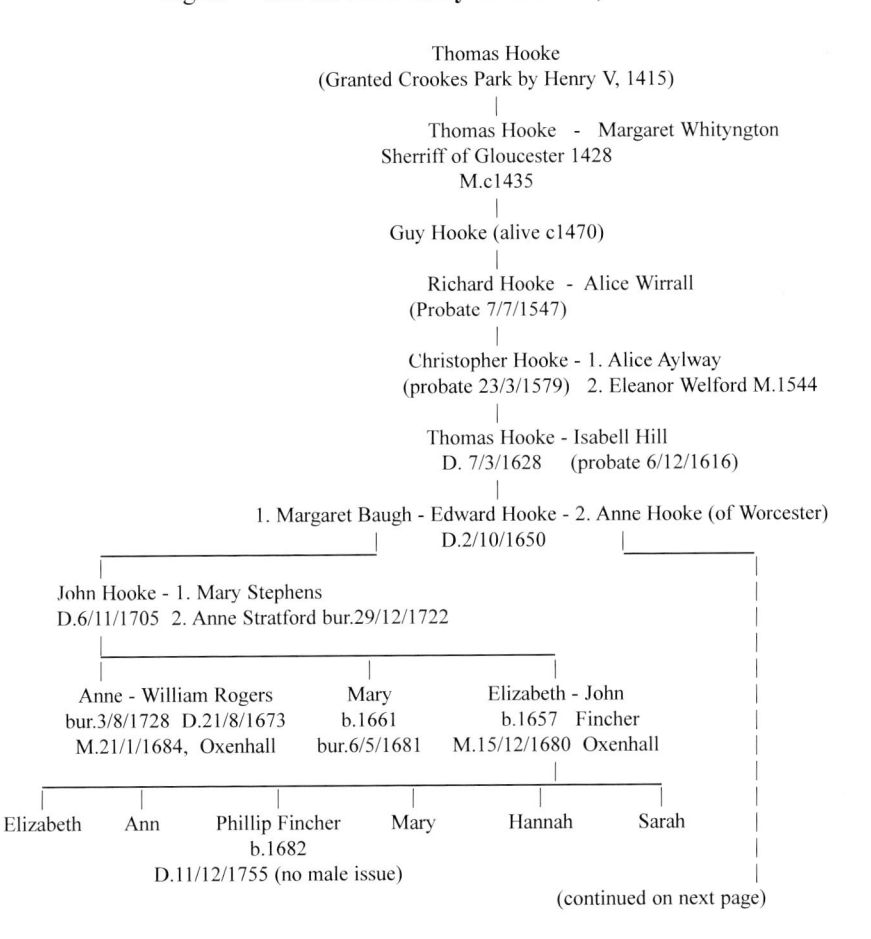

Thomas Hooke
(Granted Crookes Park by Henry V, 1415)
|
Thomas Hooke - Margaret Whityngton
Sherriff of Gloucester 1428
M.c1435
|
Guy Hooke (alive c1470)
|
Richard Hooke - Alice Wirrall
(Probate 7/7/1547)
|
Christopher Hooke - 1. Alice Aylway
(probate 23/3/1579)   2. Eleanor Welford M.1544
|
Thomas Hooke - Isabell Hill
D. 7/3/1628   (probate 6/12/1616)
|
1. Margaret Baugh - Edward Hooke - 2. Anne Hooke (of Worcester)
D.2/10/1650

John Hooke - 1. Mary Stephens
D.6/11/1705 2. Anne Stratford bur.29/12/1722

Anne - William Rogers	Mary	Elizabeth - John
bur.3/8/1728 D.21/8/1673	b.1661	b.1657 Fincher
M.21/1/1684, Oxenhall	bur.6/5/1681	M.15/12/1680 Oxenhall

Elizabeth   Ann   Phillip Fincher   Mary   Hannah   Sarah
b.1682
D.11/12/1755 (no male issue)

(continued on next page)

(from previous page)

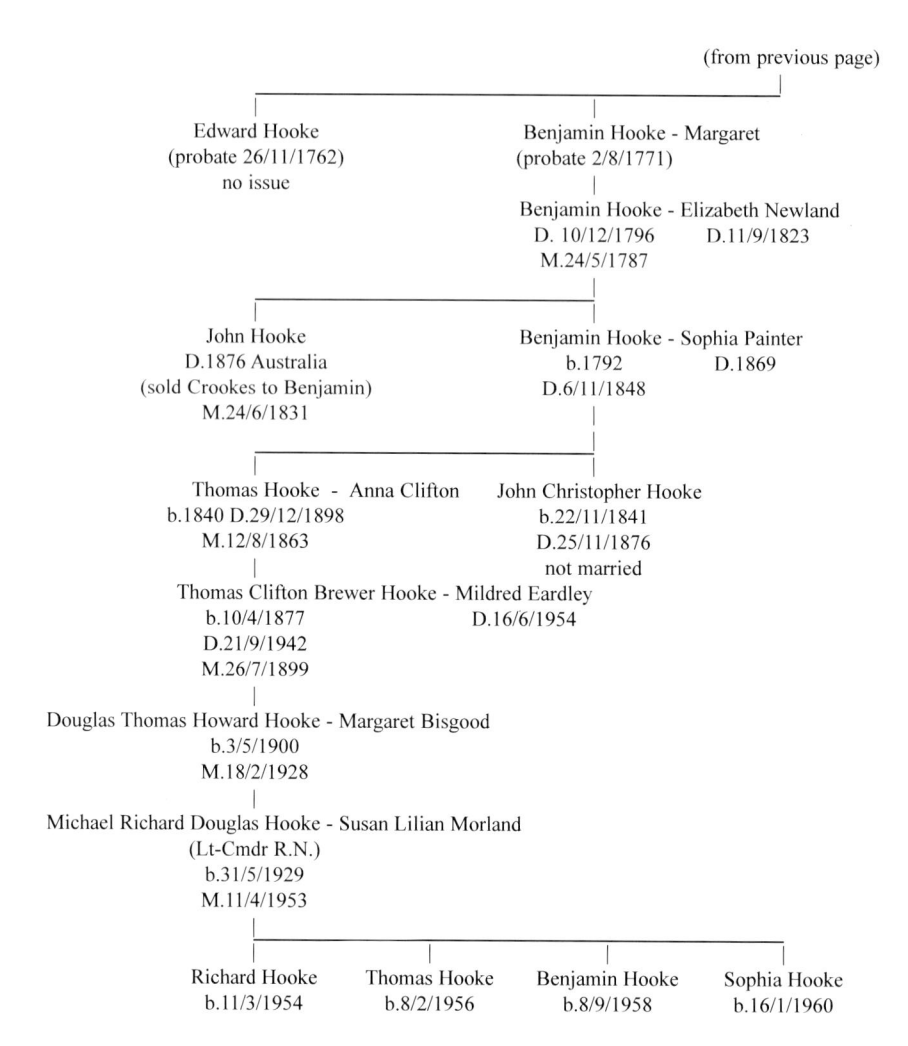

```
        Edward Hooke                    Benjamin Hooke - Margaret
     (probate 26/11/1762)                  (probate 2/8/1771)
          no issue
                                       Benjamin Hooke - Elizabeth Newland
                                         D. 10/12/1796    D.11/9/1823
                                               M.24/5/1787

         John Hooke                    Benjamin Hooke - Sophia Painter
       D.1876 Australia                    b.1792           D.1869
    (sold Crookes to Benjamin)             D.6/11/1848
         M.24/6/1831

              Thomas Hooke - Anna Clifton     John Christopher Hooke
              b.1840 D.29/12/1898                 b.22/11/1841
                   M.12/8/1863                    D.25/11/1876
                                                  not married
            Thomas Clifton Brewer Hooke - Mildred Eardley
                      b.10/4/1877         D.16/6/1954
                      D.21/9/1942
                      M.26/7/1899

    Douglas Thomas Howard Hooke - Margaret Bisgood
                    b.3/5/1900
                    M.18/2/1928

    Michael Richard Douglas Hooke - Susan Lilian Morland
                  (Lt-Cmdr R.N.)
                    b.31/5/1929
                    M.11/4/1953

          Richard Hooke    Thomas Hooke    Benjamin Hooke    Sophia Hooke
           b.11/3/1954      b.8/2/1956       b.8/9/1958       b.16/1/1960
```

Henry Cadle (of Bosley) - Margery
  bur c1541   bur. Jun 1557
         |
  John Cadle - Elizabeth Kilford
         |
   Henry Cadle   -   Joan Brooke
b.c1542 bur Feb1594 bur. Apr 1597
         M.Jan 1577
         |
   John Cadle   -   Margaret Martin
b.Sep. 1585 D Feb 1638   D. Sep 1666
    D. Feb 1638
         |
   Richard Cadle - Ann
   b. 1619 (Bosley)
         |
   Joseph Cadle - Elizabeth
      D. 1652
         |
   John Cadle - 1. Isobel   2. Sarah Seer
   (Mariner)   D. aged 46   (8 children)
   1678-1745   (2 children)
         |
   John Cadle - Hannah Vaughan
   (Mariner)
   1723-1766   M.1748
         |
   John Cadle - Sarah Green
   (Carpenter)
     b.1749   M.1779
         |
   Joseph Cadle - Ann Halls
   (Carpenter)
     b.1787   M.1813
         |
   Joseph Cadle - 1.Alice Haines   2. Esther Toomey
     b.1813   M.1841 D.1863   M.1863 (2 children)
         | (5 children)
   Joseph Cadle - H Toomey
     b.1843   M.1868
         |
   Joseph Cadle - Mary Fisher
     b.1885
         |
   Royston Cadle - 1. Doris Preece   2. Olga Micklethwaite
     b.1911   M.1940 D.1991
         |
   Richard Cadle
     b.1950

Fig.84 The Cadle Family Tree
(only the direct descent is shown)

References
1. Alan Clark — 1991 — The Donkeys
2. Mrs Helena Russo — September 2001 — Private interview
3. Mrs Anne Solesbury — January 2002 — Private communication
4. Edmund Potts — November 2001 — Private communication
5. Dennis A Little BEM — April 2002 — Private interview
6. Harold Wirdnam — July 2001 — Private communication
7. Mrs Maud Wirdnam — July 2001 — Private communication
8. Joe Pirello — July 2001 — Private interview
9. Mrs Phyllis Shaw — August 2001 — Private communication
10. Sidney Beddis — May 2002 — Private communication
11. Anthony Montague — June 2001 — Private interview
12. Eric Jones DFC — August 2001 — Private communication
13. Mrs Hooke — November 2001 — Private communication
14. Royston Cadle — Private interview
15. Kath Rees — Open University degree module
16. Mrs Alma Bagnall — Interview with Kath Rees
17. Mrs Geraldine Beaman — Interview with Kath Rees
18. Mrs Bendle — Interview with Kath Rees
19. Mrs Penney — Interview with Kath Rees
20. Mrs Goulding — Interview with Kath Rees
21. Mrs Ralph — Interview with Kath Rees

19. Memories of the 20th Century

The memories and stories of residents of a town are always interesting and although some of the things may have been everyday happenings, they do give an insight on a previous generation. Perhaps it could be said that things which occurred within living memory are not history, but unless they are recorded they may be lost forever. This section is devoted to such memories and has been contributed by many past and present residents of the town.

During World War II, in the winter of 1942, Newent Court had a disastrous fire. It was a bitterly cold night and the water from the hoses froze as it ran on the ground. Some of the west wing was saved including the kitchen and servants quarters, together with a drawing room to the left of the main entrance. It was used by Ribston Hall High School in Spa Road, Gloucester as a project centre. The Head teacher, Miss Lucy Whittacker, lived there for a time.

The idea was for each form, together with their teacher, to spend two separate weeks a year at Newent learning to tend animals, manage the estate and the house and hopefully gain from the free and easy communal life. Pupils were charged £1 per week and had to take their ration books. In the grounds was the lake with a wishing bridge, tennis courts, lawns, countless trees, rhododendrons, a conservatory, and a flourishing kitchen garden with greenhouses.

The dormitories, with 6 or 8 bunk beds, were all named after the trees that could be seen from the windows; Larch, Pine, Sycamore, Mulberry, and Cedar. Sycamore and Cedar were the most popular rooms because they looked out over the front of the house, although Cedar was the smallest.

The girls all had duties to perform, helping in the kitchen garden and greenhouses, sawing logs, looking after the animals, "Jonathan" the horse, "Mully" the donkey, and the goats, kids, hens, and pigs. Cleaning out the pig sty was the least popular occupation. (fig.87) Every evening supper consisted of cheese and some very strong cocoa made with water. Mid-night feasts and raids on the other dormitories were a regular feature of school life at the Court.

The girls travelled from Gloucester to Newent by train and parents came to visit on Thursday afternoons for tea. On V.E. Day in 1945 the girls celebrated with a huge bonfire and baked potatoes in the ashes.

In May and June the girls were allowed to pick the rhododendrons which lined the long driveway, to take home, but they were charged two shillings for the privilege. Despite the close proximity to the town the girls were not there long enough to mix with the permanent residents. They were split into Houses called Romans, Danes, and Saxons with each House wearing a different coloured cloak.

Fig. 85 Newent Court before the disastrous fire of 1942

Fig. 86 Newent Court Quoits Team c1900. Front row extreme right=Charlie Jenkins, 5th from right back row=Francis Chamberlain (Photo Mrs Clifford)

Fig.87 Pupils of Ribston Hall School at Newent Court in 1950
L to R:- Jane Jackson, Valerie Turk, Hilda ? , Margaret Blewitt, Rita Bunn,
? ,Pat Challice, Valerie Crowther, Margaret Selway, Christie Pascoe.

(photo Margaret Phillips)

Another Gloucester school to have associations with Newent after the Second World War was Denmark Road High School for Girls. Casual labour was scarce and the girls were transported to Newent by lorry to help harvest potatoes grown on local farms.

After World War II the increasing amount of road traffic through Newent was causing congestion. The railway was closed in 1964 and a scheme proposed to build a by-pass on the line of the railway. The new road was opened in 1968 with due ceremony but when the cavalcade set off to drive along the new road one of the owners of the cars parked in the centre of the road could not be found.

This caused more than a little confusion. The by-pass has certainly relieved the town of through traffic but has been the scene of several serious and fatal accidents. It now has a 50 mph speed limit.

The Market House is one of the main focus points in the centre of the town and was used to shelter the town fire engine underneath, for which they were charged £2 a year, before the present fire station was built on the Dymock Road. The last time this fire engine was used was for a fire at the Lancaster Saw Mill in the 1930s (now Ladder and Fencing Industries) There was a weighbridge at the south corner of the Market House, and some stocks and a whipping post were situated near by.

The gallows was sited in "Pinchin Field" at Squirrel Corner on the Ross Road, and it is said that one of the gallows beams was used in Squirrel Cottage. In the 1950's Clifford Manor, near Glasshouse, was the home of a nudist colony.

Burials ceased in Newent Churchyard around 1865 and the last person buried there before the new graveyard was opened in Watery Lane, was the widow of a local vet, Mr George West.

At the beginning of the 20th century the winters were colder than today. The primary school at Picklenash was heated by an old coke boiler which the children were allowed to sit around and warm up. There were two classrooms divided by a large curtain. One day Clarice Huggins, one of the pupils, suffered an epileptic fit and when the doctor was called he was angry with the teacher for allowing her to remain on the wooden floor. He immediately pulled the curtain down and laid the child on it to make her more comfortable. The doctors at the time were Dr Johnstone and Dr Smelt, the latter causing much sniggering among the children of the town. Dr Frank Hayes Smelt practised in Newent for 52 years.

Two of the teachers at Picklenash School at the beginning of the 20th century were "Betsy" Harris, who was quite handy with the cane, and Miss Millard. Before the Grammar School was opened in 1925 children needing secondary education had to travel to Gloucester, usually by train. They would catch the 8-30 a.m. train in the morning, returning on the 4-00 p.m. leaving their bicycles either at the station or Mr Palmer's cycle shop. Unfortunately the train times meant they usually had to miss the first and last lessons of the day.

Sidney Huggins lived next door to the Wesleyan Chapel in Culver Street and was one of the workmen at Lancaster Sawmills, now Newent Ladder and Fencing in Horsefair Lane. He worked there through both World Wars until he retired, looking after the large horses used for hauling timber. It was customary for him and his sons to have their hair cut by one of the other men at the sawmills, which cost 6d on a Sunday because there was no spare time in the week. Sometimes his children would meet him from work and they would go looking for stray hens' eggs in the hedgerows to take home for tea.

Sidney Huggins' uncle, Harry Huggins farmed at Clifford's Mesne.

Many of the workers at the sawmills had small hand trucks which they were allowed to fill with off-cuts of timber to be used as fuel. It was a common sight to see them being wheeled up the High Street empty in the morning and back full in the evening. Newent Ladder and Fencing Ltd took over the sawmills in 1971.

Places to visit in Newent were the Cinema in Culver Street, now Perpetua Press, and the Devonia Tea Rooms in the High Street. The Devonia was quite smart and mainly frequented by the better off.

Daffodils grow wild in the Newent area in profusion and in the first half of the 20th century the children used to pick them. They were put into baskets and taken to the British Legion Club to be transported by train to London Hospitals. Daffodil Teas are still held in the spring at Oxenhall Church Hall.

Fig.88 A decorated float at the Holts garden party c1924. Holding the horse is Ted Chamberlain with Charlie Jenkins at the back

(photo Mrs Clifford)

Fig.89 Francis Chamberlain, head gardener at Newent Court, and his dog "Tiger" (photo c1900, courtesy of Mrs Clifford)

Before the first World war Andrew Knowles owned Newent Court. Two of his staff were Mr and Mrs Francis Chamberlain who lived in the Lodge. Mr Chamberlain (fig.89) was the head gardener and Mrs Chamberlain was the housekeeper. He started a flower business in Bradfords Lane and built the house called "West View" in 1911. For years the business provided the holly wreaths at Christmas and many of the bouquets for local brides. Mr Chamberlain died as a result of falling from a cart taking produce to Gloucester market in 1916. His son Edward (Ted) (Fig.88) and his wife worked at Stardens for a time. Later he helped with the flower business and also ran a bicycle shop at the northern end of the High Street until 1953.

Ted was very friendly with the musician Joe Meek, and when Joe's father, George, died in the early 1950s he had to make over 100 wreaths. George Meek was a property developer, buying and renovating houses.

During the Second World War Ted Chamberlain rented several fields off Bradfords Lane from Lady Raikes. In 1945 the son of Lady Raikes' housekeeper accidentally set fire to the hayricks which were completely burnt out because of the distance to the nearest fire hydrant. The housekeeper left shortly afterwards and then tragically the young lad was drowned in the sea.

Royal Celebrations

Newent has always marked Royal occasions with some form of celebration, for example the proclamation of King George IV in 1820 (see chapter 2). In the 20th century the Coronation of Queen Elizabeth II created the most interest. A seventeen strong committee was set up to coordinate the festivities under the chairmanship of Mr Haswell Dawkins. The Committee members were:-

Chairman	E H Dawkins	Mrs M Field
Vice-Chairman	E N Thurston	Miss M Clapham
Secretary	R Bisco	A Langley
	P F Winfield	A J Williams
	F G Knight	H J Dalby
	R P Ovington	Dr K M Tomlinson
	Mrs E M Jones	J M Smith
	Mrs J Gore	H Davis
	Mrs W Haig	

The celebrations lasted over a week with events taking place in various locations. A marquee was erected on the recreation ground and proceeds were to be used to purchase at least one public seat *"to be placed in a useful position in the Town, as a permanent memorial of this great occasion"* (1). A souvenir programme was published and sponsored by the Newent Private Traders' Association.

The first event was the Carnival Queen dance on Whit Monday 25th May, when the Carnival Queen was chosen. This was held at the George Hotel, tickets 5/-. The music was provided by the Melody Makers, and Marlene Williams was voted in as queen (fig.90).

The following Sunday a special Coronation service was held at St Mary's Church, conducted by the Rev W C Hodgins.

Fig.90 The Carnival Queen and attendants 1953. L to R :- Betty Blewitt Emily Jones, Marlene Williams, Shirley Jackson, Mary White
(photo Elsa Dawkins)

Fig.91 The Coronation Carnival beer tent 1953
L to R :- Mr Watson, Mr Langley, & Dr Tomlinson

Fig.92 Conservative Fete fancy dress competition, Mantley House 1953
(photo Elsa Dawkins)

The celebrations on Coronation day itself, which was a Tuesday, did not start until 4-30 p.m. to allow those with access to a television to watch the London ceremony live. The children were given a free show called "Trixapoppin" put on by the Newent Ladies Toc H, featuring a well known magician, Eric Williams, which also included free ice-creams. In the evening a Coronation Ball was held in the marquee with music again by the Melody Makers. Tickets were 3/6 for adults and included refreshments.

The following day the Newent Amateur Dramatic Society put on a Mock Trial called "Bloomer v Clott" *"an action for damages for breach of promise of marriage which will be tried before Mr Justice Stargreaves"*. It had a cast of over 30 people and admission was free. The judge's name may have been influenced by the trial a few months earlier of a local businessman Eustace Hargreaves (see chapter 5).

On 5th June the Newent and District Music Club and the Newent Orchestral Society put on a joint "Music for All" concert. The programme included the Pomp and Circumstance March by Elgar and a selection from Gilbert and Sullivan Operas. The Conductors were Mr H Davis and Miss C Crampton.

The main festivities took place on Saturday June 6th, after the Coronation, and began with sports on the recreation ground. Seventeen different races were held ranging from a toddlers race for the under six year olds, to a slow bicycle race. There was a ladies egg and spoon race, and even a pram race for married men.

The Carnival Procession commenced at 7-00 p.m. from the Lodge House in Gloucester Street and proceeded along Church street, Broad Street, High Street, Station Road, and then returned to the Recreation Ground via Watery Lane, where the judging took place. (fig.91). Music was provided by the Town band. At 8-15 p.m. the Newent Football Club staged an event called "Football Fanatics".

Besides all the attractions the Carnival Committee gave a £2 prize for the best decorated shop window and also for the best decorated private house. All the children in the parish were given a Coronation souvenir mug. A Conservative fete was held at Mantley House, the home of Admiral Raikes, where a fancy dress competition was held (fig.92).

The list of advertisers/sponsors in the souvenir programme provides an interesting list of the traders in the town at this time :-

| Deane | Broad St | Fruiterer, Florist, Seedsman |
| W Wildsmith & Son Ltd | Culvert St | Building contractor |

C Blunden	Broad St	Grocer
J A Smith	Broad St	Radio, T V, & Cycles
George Hotel	Church St	Proprietor Percy Lodge
John Yeates	Kilcot	Dairyman
E A Donnelly	High St	Hairdresser
Joseph Hill	Lewall St	Funeral Director, Building Contractor
Daffodil Cafe	Broad St	Proprietors C & E Galpin
G & F Thurston	Church St	Grocers
Arthur Barlow	Broad St	Fish Merchant
R M Bidmead & Sons	Culvert St	Builder
Arthur Clark & Son	The Corner	Hardware
International Stores	Broad St	Grocers
Oliver Lewis	Broad St	Tobacconist & Stationer
W W Watson	Church St	Seed Merchant
W & W Akerman	Broad St	Butcher
Gloucestershire Sand & Gravel Co Ltd	Cheltenham	Builders Merchants
W R Field & Co Ltd	Yew House	Coal & Coke Merchants
S & T Harris	Broad St	Green Grocers
Crown Guest House	High St	Guest House
H Bray & Co	Waterloo House	Tailors
P Bendle	The Library	Newsagents
Jeanne Bennion	Church St	Ladies Hairdresser
W E Bennion & Son Ltd	Broad St	Garage
The Toy Shop	Broad St	Proprietress I M Pocock
O A Eves & Son	High St	Garage
W K Evans	Church St	Electrical Shop
I G Jennings	Broad St	Confectioner & Tobacconist
Arthur Langley	Culvert St	Gents Hairdresser
Elizabeth Langley	Culvert St	Ladies Hairdresser
H Lancaster & Co Ltd	Horsefair Lane	Timber Merchants
J Gore	Broad St	-
Osborne & Voigt	Lewall St	Electrical Contractors
Philip J Bisco	Culvert St	Plumber
M E Field & Son	-	Haulage Contractor
J & G Perillo	Culvert St	Grocer
E M Meek & Sons	High St	Dairyman

Later in the year, on August Bank Holiday Monday, The Newent Food Production Club held a Coronation flower show which was advertised as *"the largest show ever held in the district"*. This also included sports, side shows, Punch and Judy, music, and a Floral Dance in the evening.

A mention should be made about the Land Settlement Association (L.S.A) north east of the town as it became a major employer in the 1950s. It was set up in 1934 to provide smallholdings for the unemployed. This national organization initially bought 20 farms all over the country and split them into holdings of about 5 acres. The Newent estate was made up of the Scarr and Ford House Farms which were divided into 51 holdings, all of which would buy and sell through the L.S.A. These estates had originally been intended to re-house unemployed miners and others, mainly from the north, and provide them with a healthy country life-style while they produced various crops commercially and kept a few pigs.

Fig. 93 Mr Hobart at work at the L.S.A. c1955 (photo Wendy Hobart)

It was slow to get started and after initial training only 8 families remained as tenants by 1938. The holdings were then advertised at the beginning of the Second World War in the national press which brought another 8 tenants. Then a further 10 tenants came from South Wales as evacuees. At the end of the war the remaining 25 holdings were let to ex-servicemen.

Tenants and their wives came from all parts of the country and from a variety of backgrounds. Some were previously employed by large growing concerns while others had their own smallholdings and decided that the L.S.A. co-operative way of growing would suit them better. A few of the wives had experience in the Land Army but for most it was a completely new way of life, smart office clothes being exchanged for old coats and muddy wellies!

After the war the L.S.A. policy was to control tenants so that approximately half were local Gloucestershire people. Initially the L.S.A. was very self contained with its own community centre but under the estate management of Mr Ward tenants were encouraged to create social links with Newent. Many L.S.A. tenants later bought their own small holdings around Newent and became independent.

Workers were employed in the propagating department, in the estate office and packing shed and on individual holdings. Although most of the workers who arrived for work in the mornings were women, the estate provided employment for men as maintenance staff and as lorry and tractor drivers. Occasionally, students training at Pershore College of Horticulture also found valuable work experience.

Only a few tenants had their own transport in those days and would walk or cycle into Newent. Several shops, including the butchers, delivered and there was also a mens outfitters and a Bata shoeshop. There was not the inclination or the time to "pop" into Gloucester as there is now, although one lady in the thirties and forties was known to walk into Gloucester and back with her shopping! Much of the social life at the Scarr revolved around the hall with regular W.I. meetings and other gatherings taking place.

In the 1950s the L.S.A. became the largest single employer in the Newent area with 200 workers, the Ladder and Fencing timber yard being the second largest. In the 1970s casual labour became scarce so they ran free buses from Ross-on-Wye and Cinderford to bring in labour. In 1976 there were 195 employees.

In the early years mobile glass houses on tracks were popular as they could be moved over two or three sites making cultivation easier. As the years went by the need for larger areas of glass resulted in half acre blocks and larger being built, complete with heating, irrigation and automatic ventilation. All the produce was collected from the holdings and taken up to the central packing shed where it was graded and packed into the appropriate container with the L.S.A. logo on it. This was a symbol of quality and deliveries were made on a regular basis to large outlets and supermarkets. (fig.93)

The produce was transported far afield. In 1947 they sold £27,000 worth and by 1976 this had risen to £939,000 (2).

Sadly, for a variety of reasons the Land Settlement Scheme came to an end and in the 1980s the houses were sold to the tenants. Barely a handful of growers continue to produce crops in the area now. Commuter cars now stand in the driveways where once stood battered lettuce crates, and tractors trundling along the narrow lanes are a thing of the past.

Fig. 94 Queen Mary visiting the L.S.A., Newent in 1944 (photo Terry Jackson)

Fig. 95 Richard Phillips of Watery Lane and his wife with his B.E.M. presented in 1969 for 32 years service with the L.S.A.
(photo Terry Jackson)

Fig.96 Laying the foundation stone for the new Church Vestry, 30th May 1912

Some Newent families have been residents in the town for hundreds of years, and have immersed themselves in its activities. Not all have become famous but their lives have helped to shape the town as we know it today. Such a family are the James. William James was born c1828, the son of John James and Elizabeth. In 1853 he married Anna Jones in St Mary's Church and they lived in Upper Church Street. Anna had eleven children and was therefore tied to the family home, but she earned extra money by taking in laundry, as her grandmother had done.

Their eldest son Thomas married Hester Squires in 1872 and became a farm labourer. After a time Hester took over the laundry from her mother-in-law and used to get clients from as far away as London sending their clothes to be laundered. The washing was sent by train with Hester collecting it from Newent Station, then she would busy all the women in the family to help.

Thomas worked at Moat Farm and died in 1893. He had been hay making on a very hot day, and when he came home he was really ill. His wife

Fig. 97 Annie James (nee Hughes) 1873-1930 (photo Vanda Evans)

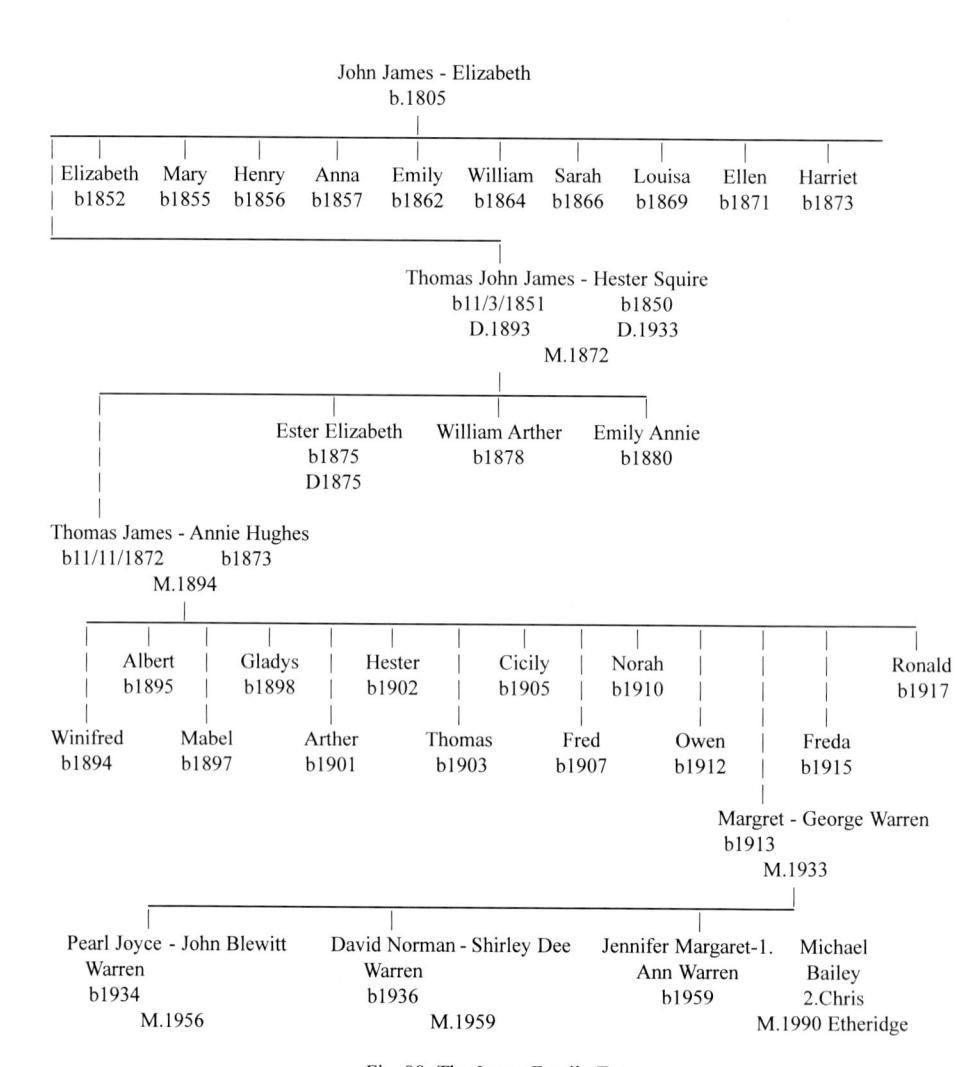

```
                          John James - Elizabeth
                                b.1805
   ┌──────┬──────┬──────┬──────┬──────┬──────┬──────┬──────┬──────┐
Elizabeth Mary   Henry  Anna  Emily William Sarah Louisa Ellen Harriet
 b1852  b1855  b1856  b1857  b1862  b1864  b1866  b1869  b1871  b1873
```

```
                    Thomas John James - Hester Squire
                         b11/3/1851         b1850
                         D.1893             D.1933
                                M.1872
              ┌──────────────────┬────────────────┐
          Ester Elizabeth    William Arther    Emily Annie
              b1875              b1878            b1880
              D1875
```

```
Thomas James - Annie Hughes
 b11/11/1872    b1873
         M.1894
```

```
   ┌──────┬──────┬──────┬──────┬──────┬──────┬──────┬──────┐
       Albert  Gladys  Hester  Cicily  Norah                Ronald
       b1895   b1898   b1902   b1905   b1910                b1917
Winifred  Mabel   Arther  Thomas  Fred   Owen   Freda
b1894    b1897   b1901   b1903   b1907  b1912   b1915
```

```
                                    Margret - George Warren
                                      b1913
                                            M.1933
   ┌──────────────────┬──────────────────┬──────────────┐
Pearl Joyce - John Blewitt  David Norman - Shirley Dee  Jennifer Margaret-1.  Michael
   Warren                     Warren                      Ann Warren           Bailey
   b1934                      b1936                       b1959               2.Chris
      M.1956                       M.1959                                 M.1990 Etheridge
```

Fig. 98 The James Family Tree

called the doctor who threw a bucket of cold water over him to try and cool him down. The shock killed him.

Thomas and Hester's eldest son, also Thomas, worked at the Waterworks in Horsefair Lane. In his spare time he played the trumpet in Newent Town Band, and his brother Bill played the big drum. Thomas, junr., married Annie Hughes (fig.97) from Oxenhall and they had 14 children. Following the family tradition two of the children, Fred and Owen, played in the Town Band, whilst two others, Arthur and Ronnie played football for Newent Town. Two of the daughters, Norah and Margret worked together at Stardens.

The children were very good at getting into mischief such as "cherry knocking". They used to tie cotton on the door knockers across the street from the church and then hide in the churchyard pulling on their cotton. They took great delight in watching people come to answer the door to find no one there. The first time the road surface of Upper Church Street was covered in "tarmac" the workmen left a pile at the top of the town. Nora and Margret had an argument with their sister Freda and covered her hair in it, which resulted in poor Freda having to have all her hair cut off. Their brother, Ronnie, used to go out snaring rabbits and pot roast rabbit became quite the thing for Sunday lunch.

Newent has many local organizations catering for various needs and pastimes of the inhabitants. It is not possible to mention all of them but some will stir the memories of those who became involved.

The Newent tennis club had three grass courts in Watery Lane on the ground now occupied by the Community School. In the 1920s it had been a golf course. There was no car park and access was gained via steps cut out of the roadside bank. A very basic wooden hut served as a pavilion which was shared by the Cricket Club, each organization having its own room with a kitchen in between. The cricket ground was on the brow of the hill away from the road.

Sybil Pratt (nee Freeman) joined the tennis club in 1948 and remembers many matches against other local clubs, as well as the club's own annual tournament. In those days, for those without cars, it was practice to have a clip on your bicycle forks to carry the tennis racket. The club thrived in the 1950s and 60s with many local people being members. Jim Smith (of Conigree Court) was the President, and Frank Chidley often marked out the courts.

Both the tennis club and the cricket club were forced to vacate their facilities in 1968 when the new school was built. The tennis club folded up in the early 1970s but the cricket club moved to a ground at Three Ashes.

The Newent badminton club was founded in 1954 and was the first organization to regularly use the newly built Memorial Hall. Initially it attracted a large membership with many of the tennis club members joining. After a few

Fig.99 Newent Mens Hockey Team 1927/8. L to R rear:- Millard, Jones, Nunn, Smith, Hawkins, Beachus. Front:-Reece, Ling, Cowles, Hawkins (photo Sybil Pratt)

Fig. 100 The Black Dog Darts Team c1950 (photo Terry Jackson, extreme left)

Fig. 101 F. W. Dickinson Headmaster of Newent Grammar School dressed for a part in the Amateur Dramatic Society's show "Ruddigore" in 1928

(photo Sybil Pratt)

years the membership dropped to the keen players who met twice a week and played many matches against other clubs. The floor of the new Memorial Hall was highly polished and was slowed down with a sprinkling of Omo (washing powder). The club prospered for over 20 years and held an annual dinner at various hostelries in the area.

Both tennis and badminton as well as squash, swimming, table tennis, and other sports are now catered for in the form of a leisure centre which is also used by the Community School.

The Newent Amateur Dramatic Society is one of Newent's older organizations and was very active in the 1920s and 30s when they performed at the Plaza Cinema in Culver Street (now Perpetua Press) It was founded in 1927 with J M Scott as President and J L Slade as the Secretary. In 1927 they put on a performance of The Mikado with Claud Cliff playing the Mikado, Derek Jones (Ko-Ko), Muriel Reece (Beep Bo), Aileen Cook (Yum Yum), and Emily Freeman (Pitti Sing).

Emily Freeman (1901-1983) was a keen member who lived at Town House and was the daughter of George and Hannah. She was a teacher at Pool Hill School. Other productions before World War II included Ruddigore (1928), Yeoman of the Guard (1929), Iolanthe, the Pirates of Penzance, The Sport of Kings (1931), Tilly of Bloomsbury, and A Flitch Trial.

After the war the society was very popular and moved their productions to the Memorial Hall when it opened in 1954. Besides those already mentioned many Newent people, from all walks of life, became involved in the society including the following :- Gladys Davis and Eileen Wilton (teachers at Picklenash School), F.W. Dickinson (Headmaster of the Grammar School) (fig.101), Andrew Bidmead (a builder), Richard Ovington (the local vet), Cis Cowles (woolshop owner), Elsie Thurston, Doris Lodge, Philip Cowles (a farmer from Caerwents), Noah Clarke, Jack Price, Eric Lodge, Evelyn Holder, and three teachers from the Grammar School; Alan Mathews, Dorothy Spencer and Raynor Brooks.

At the beginning of the 20th century Newent held an annual music festival and a cricket week.

A number of small businesses in the town were started many years ago. Ivor Markey set up his blacksmith shop in Culver Street in 1927. He had previously worked with his uncle, Frank Jenkins, in premises on Wharf Pitch (fig.102) near the present Fire Station. The main work then was shoeing horses but repair work to farm machinery was undertaken during the Second World War. Ivor's son, Donald, joined him after the war and Ivor continued to work until 1974, by which time his grandson, Keith, had joined the family firm. The

Fig. 102 Frank Jenkin's Blacksmith Shop in Wharf Pitch c1920.
Left is Frank Jenkins, Ivor Markey is shoeing the horse. (photo Ivor Markey)

Fig. 103 John Jones (right) and his son Eric standing in front of his shoe shop in Broad St., Newent c1925 (photo Eric Jones)

fourth generation, Gavin and Duncan, are carrying on the tradition. Now the work is more ornamental, with gates for important buildings, chandeliers for St Mary's Church, a steel structure for Hampton Court Flower Show and many other objects being produced. The tools and materials used remain much the same, and the workshop is a reminder of an earlier age.

One Newent resident who became well known especially with the farming community was Richard Ovington, the Veterinary Surgeon. He qualified as a vet in 1938 and came to Newent at the height of the Second World War in 1941. Being in a reserved occupation he was unable to join the Army. Mr Ovington and his wife first moved into Croft House in Church Street, then to the Verger's Cottage (now the Good News Centre), before finally buying Shirley House in High Street, where they lived for over 50 years.

His memories of those wartime years include milk being delivered in churns on the luggage rack of the farmer's car and ladled into the customer's jug. Alongside the churn was a dustbin in which swill was collected. What would a modern hygiene inspector make of that !

In the early days of his practice most of his work was with cattle and sheep, and with only very primitive local anaesthetics great care had to be taken not to get kicked. Before the war there were a lot of quite small farms of less than 50 acres, with perhaps 20 cows, but as tractors and other mechanization came in the farms got larger and herds increased to 200-300 cows. He recalls a number of outbreaks of foot and mouth disease in 1940, 1947 and 1967 which greatly affected trade in the town because of the restrictions on movement.

Mr Ovington was a member of the Parish Council and the Rural District Council, until its demise in 1974. For a time he was chairman of the Housing Committee and recalls the dispute over the site of the new Secondary School in Watery Lane because it took over the local cricket pitch, golf course and tennis courts.

Newent Community School has helped many pupils achieve success in their chosen careers. One such pupil is Professor Christopher Pearce FReng, Bsc, CEng, FIMechE, FIEE, MRAeS, MAIAA. He was born and brought up in the parishes of Hartpury, Staunton and Corse and came to Newent Community School in 1963. He graduated from Bath University with a 1st Class degree in Mechanical Engineering and started work with the Dowty Group in 1974. He is now the Group Technical and Quality Director of INBIS, a major design engineering consultancy.

In the 1990s he became involved in the attempt on the World Land Speed Record, led by Richard Noble, that led to the construction of Thrust SSC. He was responsible for the technical performance of the team that designed the composite nose and engine nacelles, and validated the structural integrity of the chassis and tail. A new record was set of 1.02 times the speed of sound (over 1,227 Kph).

Chris has received many honours during his career and lectures all over the world. He is married with two daughters and is an active church member. He says "Newent School will always have positive memories for me. I learnt there so many of the basic skills I use every day. From mathematics to public speaking, from team working to acting, my education was rich and varied. I shall always treasure memories of the fine teachers and fellow students I had the privilege to meet".

Fig. 104 The works outing to London of W Wildsmith & Son Ltd, Building Contractors, Newent on 28th November 1953 (Photo Terry Jackson)

Contributors Mary Heggie
Sheila Forrester
Sybil Pratt
Bob Bisco
Maureen Garwood
Evelyn Howland
Mrs Clifford.
Mrs Elsa Dawkins
Vanda Evans
Mrs Wendy Hobart
Margaret Phillips
Keith Markey
Richard Ovington
Chris Pearce

References
1. Coronation Souvenir Programme   1953
2. Peter Leaver   A-Level project on the L.S.A. GRO S154/29 1/24

Index

Abbey of Cormeilles, 57,86,92,184
Agincourt, 86
Almshouses, 145
Amateur Dramatic Society, 32,281,282
Anchor, the, 20
Andrews, Ted, 115
Anthony's Cross, 3
Apprentices, 52
Atherlord's Place, 29,48
Avenant, Thomas, 58,98,99,207,208,210
Awford, Geoffrey, 72
Aylescroft Farm, 163

Badminton Club, 279
Bagnall, Alma, 252
Banker Nash, 78
Barclay's Bank, 19
Barn Survey, 32
Baron, William, 36
Beachus, Bob, 219
Beale, Miles, 212
Beale, William, 40
Beaman, Geraldine, 253
Beauchamp, Lady, 148
Beddis, Sidney, 243,244
Beeby, Miss, 133
Bells, 46,191
Bell, the, 20,70
Bendle, Diana, 253
Bisco family, 81,123,167
Bishops Transcripts, 174,186,190
Black Dog Inn, 19
Blacksmith, 282,283
Bletchley Park, 254
Bloomery slag, 8
Bloomsbury, Thomas, 215

Bodkin, 178
Boer War, 90
Boothall, 49,68
Botany Bay, 107
Boughton, Rutland, 73
Boulsdon, 3,13
Bower, Edward, 24,188
Bower family, 19,24,53,66,67,83
Bower, Hubert, 24,49,66
Bower, John, 53,66,70
Bradfords Lane, 31,36
Brand Green, 3
Brickworks, 162
Bronze Age, 5
Bruton, Henry, 16
Buildings, 17,18,23
Bull Inn, 19,42
Bull ring, 33,37,50
Bury Bar, 12,33
Business Park, 9,10,11,12,13
By-pass, 263

Cadle family, 212,213,259
Cadle, Royston, 250,251
Canal, 45,54,157,162,219,220,222
Carnival Procession, 279
Carnival Queen, 268
Carswells, 48
Cartulary, 185
Castle Tump, 158
Catholic Church, 23,196,197
Cattle Market, 34
Celtic gravestones, 184
Chain, the, 20
Chantry Chapel, 126
Charcoal store, 24,158
Charities, 72
Charity School, 126

Christian Brethren, 201202
Church burials, 190
Church House, 19
Church plate, 191
Church roof collapse, 187
Churchwardens, 45
Church window collapse, 187
Churchyard, 264
Cider, 73,165
Cinema, 20,32,33,72,265
Civil War, 61,90
Cleeve Mill, 3,33,52,62
Cleeve Mill Business Park, 13
Clifford Manor, 32,77,173,177
Clocks, 166,167,190
Coal, 19,153,154,158
Cock fighting, 50
Coins, 179,181
Colliery, 19,159,160,161
Collinpark Wood, 222
Common Fields, 2,47
Community Centre, 24
Community School, 282,284
Comprehensive School, 24
Conder, Edward, 28
Conder, Elizabeth, 21,36
Congregational Church, 192,193,195,196
Conigree, 3,4,5,28
Corn Mills, 163
Coronation, 267,268,269,270
Council housing, 36
Court Rolls, 64,65,66
Court, the, 25,28,261,262,266
Cowdy Glassworks, 179
Cricket Club, 279
Crime Museum, 110
Crockett's Hole, 28,69
Crookes, 61,87
Crop prices, 47

Cross shaft, 20,184
Crown House, 19,66
Crown House Cottages, 5
Cugley, 3,44,47
Culver St, 3,6,20,30
Curriers Lane, 36

Daffodils, 265
Dame School, 126
Dark ages, 13
Darts, 280
De la Billiere, Sir Peter, 245
De Visme, James, 25,82
Dickinson, F W, 281
Dissenters, 200,201
Dissenters Licences, 101,102
District Council, 42
Dobunni, 5
Dobyns, Samuel, 48
Doctors, 103,104,105
Dolocindo, 7
Domesday Book, 57,163
Draper, Cornelius, 29,47,48, 212
Draper, Edward, 50,99
Draper, Samuel, 211
Ducking stool, 36
Dymock, 12

Edmonds, Anna, 28,71
Edmonds, Edmund, 71,105,119
Edred, 184
Education, 126
Electoral roll, 67
Electricity, 118,119
Elmbridge Furnace, 24

Fairs, 51
Farm implements, 47
Farming, 46
Field names, 12,22,154

Firebacks, 154,155,156
Fitz Osbern, William, 57,79,184
Fives court, 50
Flint tools, 1,2,3,4
Floods, 50
Foley, Andrew 28,100
Foley, Elizabeth, 128
Foley family tree, 80
Foley Road, 5
Foley, Thomas, 64,99,154
Ford, Ethel May, 71
Fordhouse, 47
Fordhouse Lane, 3,4
Forty, Walter, 20
Fotheringhaye, 95
Frowde, James Henry, 29,74,75,76
Furnace, 158

Gallows, 69
Gas conversion, 122
Gas supply, 119
Gas Works, 24,121
George Hotel, 19,20,119,145,160
Glasshouse, 2,171
Glass making, 171-176
Glebe Chapel, 202
Good News Centre, 24,202
Gorsley Common, 157
Gorsley stone, 161
Goulding, May, 255
Graces Pitch, 36
Grammar School, 24,135,230,282
Grandison tomb, 20,61,194
Graveyard, 213
Grimke-Drayton, 32,77

Hargreaves, 29,73,74,165
Hayes Farm, 77,96,235
Health Centre Clock, 28
Hengler, 74
Hennezel, 172

High Street, 31
Highways, 42,43,44,45
Hill House, 156
Hill, John, 48,70
Hilly Field, 180,182
Hockaday, 86,92
Hockey, 280
Holders Lane, 154
Hollister, Dr, 105
Holts, the, 28
Hooke family, 61,257,258
Hooke, Thomas, 86,96
Hooke, Valerie, 249
Horne, Edward, 28,69
Horsefair Lane, 165
Horton, Elizabeth, 28,69
Huguenots, 171,172
Huntley Lane, 3

Industry, 153
Inoculation, 137
Inquisition post mortem, 60
Irelands Hill, 4
Iron Age, 5
Iron making, 7,8,153
Iron works, 24,64,154,168,169,210

Jackman, Thomas, 205,213
James, Annie, 277
James family tree, 278
Jones, Eric, 245,246,247,248,283

Kilcot, 5,12,60,92
Kilcot Chapel, 191
King Charles I, 90
King Charles II, 187
King George III, 51
King George IV, 16,267
King Henry II, 184
King Henry V, 61
King Henry VIII, 103,187

Kings Arms, 19
Kings Head, 19
Knowles, Andrew, 25,90,267
Korea, 232

Lancaster, 165
Land Settlement
    Association, 236,272,273,274
Land speed record, 284
Leisure and entertainment, 49
Lewall St, 20,36
Lime kilns, 162
Linton Hall, 157
Lloyds Bank, 78,128
Lock Cottage, 221,222
Lodge House, 27
Loggins, Joseph, 54
Lords of the Manor, 55
Lower Horseshoe, the, 23
Lux Lane, 36
Lyne House Farm, 12

Madams Wood, 111,114
Malswick, 3,12,44
Malt House, 24
Mantley House, 32
Market, 92
Market House, 16,264
Markey, Harold, 232
Markey, Ivor, 282,283
Marriage allegations, 98
Meek, Jo, 73
Mesolithic, 2
Military survey, 87,88,89
Mills, 163,164
Ministers of the Church, 58
Mitre, the, 19
Moat Farm,
    7,29,35,153,162,206,276
Montague, Anthony, 244,245

Morse family, 68
Morse, John Nourse,
    29,41,68,158,165
Mortuary chapel, 23
Moses Meadow, 175-178,180-182
Mote, the, 46
Motor cars, 77
Mynne, Colonel, 19,90

Nags Head, 19
Nanfan and Dobyn, 25,72
Nelfields Farm, 5,6,13
Neolithic, 4
New Inn, 19
Nicholson House, 110
Noel, William, 29
Nourse manuscript, 21,37
Nourse, Timothy, 73,127,188,205
Nourse, Walter,
    32,72,187,188,205,206
Nurthen, John, 40,41

Occupations, 52
Okle Clifford, 32
Olbas oil, 78
Old Court, 20,28,35,69,71
Old Maids Walk, 36
Old Rectory, 26,42
Onslow, Archdeacon, 19
Onslow family tree, 80
Onslow, Richard Foley,
    16,102,114,128
Onslow, Richard Francis,
    100,101,102
Organ, 46
Owner, Joseph, 54
Oxenhall, 3,4,5,61

Palstave axe, 6
Parish registers, 205

Parish room, 24
Parsons, Simon, 48,52,70,208,209
Pauncefoote, Lawrence, 29
Pauntley School, 235
Payne, Gordon, 115
Peacock Brook, 36
Pearce, Christopher, 284
Penney, Frances, 254
Perillo, Joe, 241,242
Perillo, Mrs, 131,133
Perpetua Press, 32
Phillips, Richard, 275
Phillpots, Corp F, 227
Picklenash School,
     30,128-130,132-135,264
Pigeon House, 28
Place names, 63
Ploddy House Farm, 5
Plough, the, 20
Plymouth Brethren, 24,199,203
Police Station, 33
Policing, 109
Poors land, 47
Poor Law Institution, 24
Population, 52,60,151
Porch House, 66,132,133
Porter, Roger, 65
Porters Place, 25,65
Porter, Thomas, 65
Postal services, 123
Pottery making, 179,180,181
Potts, Edmund, 237,238
Poydresses, 29,47
Poykes Mill, 52
Priory, 92,93,184,187
Prisoner of war camp, 36,117
Puffs Alley, 37

Quadruplets, 67
Quakers, 203

Quarry Lane, 161
Queen Mary, 274
Quoits team, 262

Railway, 222,223
Raikes, Lady, 267
Ralph, Doris, 255
Rates, 41,43,46
Red House, 123
Red Lion, 19
Relief of the poor, 137-142,150
Religion, 184
Religious riots, 200
Reservoirs, 111,114,117,156
Ribston Hall School, 28,261,263
Richardson, Dr,
     19,104,111,210,215
Roads, 217,218
Rogers family tree, 82
Rogers, William, 28,72,127
Roll of Honour, 228,229
Romans, 7-13,153
Ross Road, 4
Royal Oak, 19
Rudder, 43
Rudford, 5,12
Rupert, Prince, 90
Russo, Andy, 233,234,235

Sawmill, 164,165,264
Saxon Church, 184
Saxons, 13
Scarr, the, 3,29
Secondary School, 151,152
Severn Trent Water, 117,118
Sewage Works, 117
Sewerage, 117
Shaw, Phyllis, 242,243
Smallpox, 205
Solesbury, Anne, 235

Southend Lane, 3,29,165
Southerns, 29,41,158,165,205
Spa, 51,111
Spire collapse, 187
Square Field, 8
Stardens, 29,34,36,73,165,267
Stock prices, 47,48
Stocks, 16
Stone, 161
Stone Age, 1
St Mary's Church, 20
Street lamps, 121
Street names, 66
Subsidy roll, 58,59,60
Summers and Scott, 112,114
Survey of the Manor, 61,62,63
Surveyor of the Highways, 44
Sword, 87

Tan House, 24,26,53,66,203
Taylor, Edward, 187,188,206,214,215
Taynton, 12
Taynton Court, 4
Telephone, 119
Tennis Club, 279
Tewkesbury, battle of, 87
Thatched cottages, 33
Thrysma, 13,14
Thurston, 78
Tibberton, 12
Tithe assessments, 67,68
Tithings, 55,56
Tokens, 165
Toll-gates, 19,45,217
Tomlinson, Dr, 133
Town School, 126
Traders, 270,271
Tragedies, 69
Transportees, 106-109

Travellers Rest, 19
Tuckmill, 33,70
Turnpike Trusts, 45
Tysacs, 172

United Reformed Church, 20

Vaccination, 148
Vaughan, Thomas, 49
Vestry, 40,276
Vestry Minutes, 127,137,190
Veterinary Surgeon, 284

Walden Court, 68,77
War, 86,224
War memorials, 224,225,226,231
Warn, Thomas, 188,213
Waterdines, 47
Waters End, 29
Water supply, 111
Watery Lane, 23
Wesleyan Church, 23,197,198,199
Whipping post, 16
White, Frank James, 29,73,165
Whitehouse Lane, 159
Whittington, Dick, 61
Whittington, Sir Guy, 86
Wildsmith, 285
Wirdnam, Harold, 239
Wirdnam, Maud, 240
Women at war, 252
Womens Institute, 19,151
Woodward family, 206
Workhouse, 38,42,137,143,146,147,149
Workhouse school, 148
World War I, 224-226
World War II, 228,261

Yew Tree, the, 20

Local Heritage *initiative*

Heritage Lottery Fund

Nationwide

The Countryside Agency

LHI is a partnership between the Heritage Lottery Fund, Nationwide Building Society and the Countryside Agency

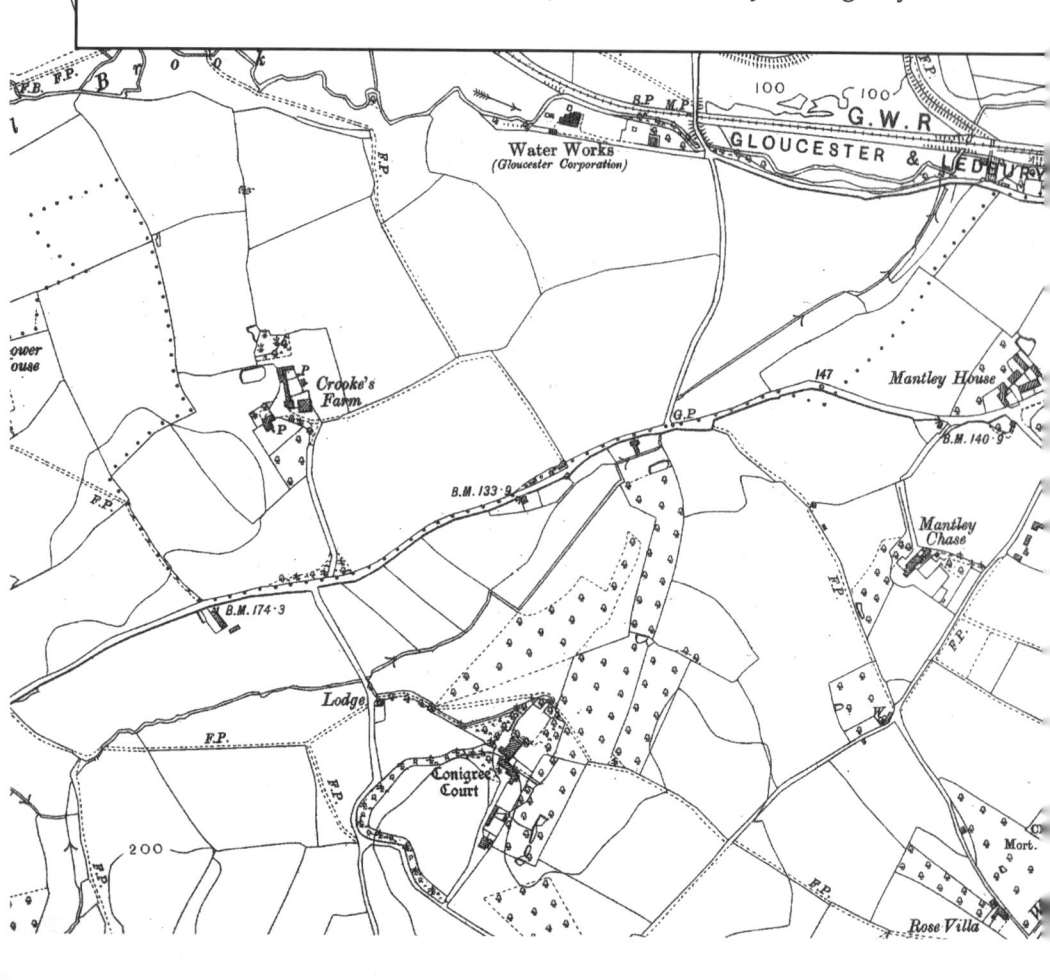